SMUGGLER'S COVE

EXOTIC COCKTAILS, RUM, AND THE CULT OF TIKI

MARTIN CATE

WITH REBECCA CATE

photography by Dylan + Jeni

TEN SPEED PRESS

Berkeley

Published in the United States by Ten Speed Press, an imprint of the
Crown Publishing Group, a division of Penguin Random House LLC, New York.
www.crownpublishing.com
www.tenspeed.com

Ten Speed Press and the Ten Speed Press colophon are registered
trademarks of Penguin Random House LLC.

Grateful acknowledgement is made to the following people for their contributions:

The Bruce Torrence Hollywood Photograph Collection: Photo, page 29
Central Press/Stringer/Getty Images: Photo, page 154
The Crazed Mugs: Lyrics, page 105
"Crazy Al" Evans: Kuhiko mug, cover, page 140
Dave Hansen: Carvings, pages 21, 99, 147, 213, 279
Dave Russell: Photo, page 153
Dave Stolte: Illustrations © 2016 by Dave Stolte
Dawn Frasier: Watercolor, page 6 © 2016 by Dawn Frasier
Ed Anderson: Photo, pages 130–31
Hanford Lemoore: Smuggler's Cove logo, artwork, and signature tapa
Martijn Veltman: Photos, pages 32, 53
Munktiki: Smuggler's Rum Barrel mug, page 138
Nat Farbman/Getty Images: Photo, page 254
Susannah Mosher: Recipe page corner illustrations © 2016 by Susannah Mosher
Sven Kirsten: Photo, page 57
Timothy "Sabu" Haack: Photos, pages 16, 24

Library of Congress Cataloging-in-Publication Data is on file with the publisher.

Hardcover ISBN: 978-1-60774-732-1
eBook ISBN: 978-1-60774-733-8

Printed in China

Design by Kara Plikaitis

10 9 8 7 6 5 4

First Edition

Dedicated to those merry souls who keep
the spirit of Polynesian Pop alive in their hearts
and homes, in their bars and basements,
and in their cocktails and character.

Contents

Recipe List

PREFACE

On the opposite page, you'll see the cover of the 1959 LP *Captivation*, by The Outriggers. Among my collection of colorfully designed albums of vintage exotica and Hawaiian music, no other image has ever struck me as so perfectly illustrating the magic and enchantment of Polynesian Pop culture and the exotic restaurant experience. It is a snapshot of a clear moment in time: The young couple enters their restaurant for the evening, a mysterious temple of dining where they are serenaded by the gentle, mingled sounds of soft music, running water, and distant cocktail shakers. It is a special night, perhaps a honeymoon or anniversary. He has presented her with a fragrant lei to celebrate, while he wears a tasteful boutonnière for the occasion. They are, of course, well dressed— jacket and tie were expected for gentlemen at such fine establishments. (Shorts and flip-flops have their place, but it is not here.) Our gentleman is a charmer, to be sure, but her face shows she is delighted by more than his attentions. Her eyes rise to the flotsam and jetsam dramatically suspended from the ceiling, having already taken in the lush flora and island tapa cloth that surrounds them. They are far removed from the world outside. Away from the noise and progress of 1950s America. Her eyes—and her smile—show that she is bewitched by her surroundings. To her, this is neither tacky nor kitsch, and the appeal is genuine, not ironic.

And silently in the background, nestled amid the tropical foliage, the ever-present tiki watches over the young lovers. That the tiki itself is a moai from Rapa Nui, an island thousands of miles southeast of Hawaii, is not an incongruity—it is the fairy tale of Polynesian Pop. That the restaurant they are photographed in is not hidden among the moon-kissed palms of a Honolulu night, but is in fact Trader Vic's in Beverly Hills, is the fairy tale of Polynesian Pop.

This is the world I fell in love with. This is the experience that stirs my soul. I was, and remain, *captivated*.

> *"If you can't get to paradise, I'll bring it to you."*
> —DON THE BEACHCOMBER

ACKNOWLEDGMENTS

To Donn Beach, Trader Vic Bergeron, and Steve Crane for their inspiration. Our heartfelt thank you to all Smuggler's Cove staff, past and present, who have not only kept our little spot open night after night, but have made it a world-class destination: John Arkelin, Bill Bain, Dane Barca, Jackie Brenner, Marcovaldo Dionysos, Joe Dixon, Matty Eggleston, Christine England, Reza Esmaili, Carie Fuller, Melissa Garcia, Charles Green, Ryan Hunt, Julian Lazalde, Steven Liles, Nick Melle, Justin Oliver, Patrick Ponikvar, Sudeep Rangi, Valerie Rico, Terry Shipman, Alex Smith, Dominic Venegas, Christopher Ward, Allison Webber, and Brent Wong, as well as the many door staff who have kept Smuggler's Cove and its patrons safe and sound. To the Buhen Family at the Tiki-Ti and to Kern Mattei, Pia Dahlquist, and everyone at the Mai Kai for keeping the torches burning on both coasts. To the many who have contributed to this endeavor, or to Smuggler's Cove in ways large and small, including: Jeni Afuso, Maria Allison, Shelby Allison, Ed Anderson, Roger Barnes, Johnny Bartlett, Daniel Nunez Bascunan, Jeff "Beachbum" Berry, Jeremy "Lucky Jackson" Brand, Ian Burrell, Barbara Cate, Charles Cate, Greg Clapp, Paul Clarke, Brother Cleve, Alejandro Covarrubias and his crew, Cheryl Crane, the Crawfordsville District Public Library, Dean Curtis, Wayne Curtis, Simon Difford, Dirty Donny, Johnny Drejer, Justin DuPre, Camper English, Adrian Eustaquio, "Crazy Al" Evans, Mickee Ferrell, Ron Ferrell, Dawn Frasier, Alexandre Gabriel, Armando Garay, Luca Gargano, Tim "Swanky" Glazner, Ignacio "Notch" Gonzalez, Chad "Woody" Greenwood, Heather Gregg, Melissa Gruenhagen, Timothy "Sabu" Haack, Ed Hamilton, Dave "Lake Surfer" Hansen, Kelley Hawks, Tom Hawks, Jim "Hurricane" Hayward, Craig Hermann, Lars Hildebrandt, Dylan Ho, Pauline Holland, Peter Holland, Bosko Hrnjak, Jane Jervis, Tatu Kaarlas, Annene Kaye, Sven Kirsten, Hanford Lemoore, Paul McGee, Greg Medow, the Miami Rum Renaissance Festival, Brian Miller, Rachael Miller, Falin "Tiki Kaimuki" Minoru, Susannah Mosher, Munktiki, Lindsay Nader, Jessica Najdek, Matty Najdek, Scott Noteboom, Oceanic Arts, Pablus, John Park, Lynn Peril, Kara Plikaitis, Mig Ponce, Puka,

Stephen Remsberg, Blair Reynolds, Sara Reynolds, Sonya Runkle, Dave Russell, the San Francisco chapter of the United States Bartenders Guild, my fellow San Francisco bar owners for their advice, sympathy, and hooch, Leroy Schmaltz, Richard Seale, Aaron Seymour, Jim Shoemake, Sandi Shorago, Kate Simmons, Marsha "Vintage Girl" Stevenson, Dave Stolte, Jonah Straus, Baby Doe von Stroheim, Otto von Stroheim, Super Sam Foods, Matt Talbert, Tales of the Cocktail, James Teitelbaum, tiki and rum bar owners worldwide, Tiki Central contributors past and present, Tiki Farm, Emily Timberlake, Humuhumu Trott, Bob Van Oosting, Martijn Veltman, Peter Vestinos, Charlotte Voisey, William Wade, Christie "Tiki Kiliki" White, Peggy Williams, Emily Winfrey, Terry "Trader Pup" Wolbert, Dave "Basement Kahuna" Wolfe, and David Wondrich. And, last but not least, to the Members of the Rumbustion Society, Voyagers of the Cove, and all of our wonderful regulars, thank you.

INTRODUCTION

Childhood memories have a uniquely powerful way of making a lasting impact. Certain sights and sounds, flavors and scents, can take you back instantly to strong emotions like joy, sadness, comfort, and excitement. For me, there is a magic word that triggers memories of delight and happiness, and fortunately, the word itself sounds like magic: ZANZIBAR! No, as a child, my family did not vacation in East Africa. We more often traveled to the slightly less exotic port of Santa Cruz, California, where my parents and I would stay to enjoy the sun and surf of the coast. And on those nights when we ate out, they would ask (with a look of sad resignation on their faces knowing my answer well in advance) where I would like to go for dinner. I would predictably scream, "ZANZIBAR!!" And if there was no talking me out of it, they would look at each other, shrug their shoulders, and with that combination of wanting to please your child mixed with equal parts exhaustion and defeat, acquiesce. So it was up to Mission Street to a somewhat dilapidated, tropical-themed restaurant. I have very little memory of what the place looked like inside. Nor do I really remember what I thought of the food. I suspect it was a little mediocre or my parents wouldn't have fought so much against it. But what I will never forget is what I ate there every time without fail: the fruit salad.

Now, I was a healthy, red-blooded American kid, and much preferred McDonald's to most things I should have been eating. But, oh the Zanzibar fruit salad. When it arrived from the kitchen, my eyes would light up at the sight of it. For the fruit salad came served spilling out from a giant conch shell like Neptune's own bounty. It was arranged on a little beach scene, with the fruit forming a winding river meeting the sea. At least that's how my brain has chosen to remember it—possibly even with a tiny deck chair on the plate with a little melon ball sunbather sitting in it. I have no idea if the fruit was just emptied out of a can in the back—I can remember only just picking at the fruit chunks, and probably asking to stop at a drive-thru on the way home. But what happened on those nights was my first introduction to the idea that food (and restaurants) could be an *experience*—more than just food on a plate. Dining as theater. That people did more than just eat the food—that the meal and the space could be sculpted and shaped to create a transformative effect. I was forever entranced. A seed had been planted.

Fast-forward to the fall of 1994. I was working at an embassy in Washington, D.C. A coworker was celebrating a birthday, and when asked where he wanted to go for drinks, he replied without hesitation, "Trader Vic's!" I had never heard of the place, so I asked him about it. His response was simply, "You're going to love it! They have drinks as big as your head!" So off we went to the Washington Hilton, home of Trader Vic's. Now, the sight of this imposing marble edifice certainly did not foreshadow wild times and giant drinks. As we descended into the depths of this gray, austere space, my eyes fell upon a striking sight: the entrance to Trader Vic's. The giant tiki carvings flanking the door, the bamboo, the flickering electric torches—you could not have imagined a sharper contrast to the surrounding hotel. As we entered,

Martin's first grass skirt

we found ourselves surrounded on all sides by woven mats, mysterious and dangerous-looking weapons, strange lanterns, and jade green tiles. I felt instantly removed from the noise and speed of modern Washington located far above our heads. The gentle sounds of traditional Hawaiian music whispered softly in the air, and the fragrant smell of citrus and gardenias filled the room. I silently absorbed the experience while my compatriots noisily ordered drinks for the table. Something in me changed on that frosty November night. What was this place? I didn't understand what any of it meant. What were these fearsome totems and enigmatic masks? What culture, what era did they come from? Why were dried spiny fish suspended above me? These questions receded (for now) into the distance as our group settled into our cocktails. For, as promised, the drinks *were* as big as my head.

What I had stumbled upon (and stumbled out of) was one of the last remnants of a decades-long fantasia that flourished in mid-century America. A creatively conceived celebration of the mysterious and "dangerous" world of the Polynesian and Caribbean islands that lay tantalizingly beyond our shores and out of reach at a time when the Great Depression curtailed travel. A world that sprung from the mind of one man in a vacated tailor's shop in Hollywood, in 1933. The totems, masks, and weapons? They came from everywhere and nowhere—from centuries of cultural traditions and from the fevered imaginations of artists and designers living in Southern California. The American obsession with all things Polynesian began to spread through restaurant chains, film, television, and theater. Soon homes, apartment buildings, hotels, and countless businesses began to adopt ersatz South Pacific design elements like A-frame roof lines, tropical landscaping, and tiki gods guarding the front doors.

But at the heart of this aesthetic fad were some of the most unique and interesting cocktails ever crafted. The exotic rum libations that fueled this engine of madness are now deemed worthy to sit alongside the punches, high-balls, sours, flips, and juleps in the pantheon of American cocktails. But these cocktails were more than just excellent and refreshing drinks. They brought a sense of adventure and escapism, promising a journey far from the mundane. Exotic cocktails, with their evocative names, elaborately layered flavors, and island-hopping blends of rums, were a vacation in a glass. Before color television and the Internet, before cruise ships were commonplace, and before Hawaii was a state, the journey to a far-off land began with just one sip . . .

Trader Vic's, Washington, D.C.

PARCHED?

In case you are anxious to whip up a tasty libation right away (as I hope you are!), here is a quick primer on how to make the featured drinks. Reading is thirsty work! No sense doing it without a cocktail in hand . . .

This book contains more than one hundred recipes—featuring exotic and traditional rum cocktails, both classic and modern—which appear at the end of each chapter. Many are originals from the Smuggler's Cove menu or that have been served at events or as specials at the bar over the years. We also include several historical recipes, but even these have nearly always been adapted by Smuggler's Cove to feature our preferred ingredients, proportions, or techniques. Most recipes are designed to serve one, but the Tiki Party chapter (page 295) has recipes specifically designed to be multiplied for punch (pages 311 to 313). At the end of the book (pages 324 to 333), you will find recipes for all the house-made ingredients used at Smuggler's Cove and referenced in the cocktail recipes. Most of these are straightforward to make yourself, but if you prefer to buy existing ingredients, check out Resources (pages 335 to 338).

PROVISIONING YOUR RUM BAR

You will notice straight away that the rums in our recipes are referenced by style rather than brand (with a few exceptions). The Understanding Rum chapter (page 183) features a thorough explanation of these various styles of rum—how they are made, and how they can be applied in cocktails. On pages 197 to 199, we provide a selected list of rums, organized according to style, to help guide your shopping.

By presenting a new way of looking at rum that is guided by production method, you'll note that there are a total of twenty-one categories in this style list, but never fear: With just eight rums, you can make most of the recipes in this book. To get mixing in a jiffy, we recommend you select a rum from each of the following eight categories:

Pot still lightly aged (page 197) ➊

Blended lightly aged (page 197) ➋

Blended aged (page 197) ➌

Column still aged (page 198) ➍

Black blended (page 198) ➎

Black blended overproof (page 198) ➏

Cane AOC Martinique rhum agricole blanc (page 199) ➐

Cane AOC Martinique rhum agricole vieux (page 199) ➑

You'll note that each of the categories above has a numbered icon next to it—here, in the rum list on pages 197–199, and in the recipes where it is referenced. We recommend that you similarly label your home bar rum bottles by writing the numbers on tape and affixing it to the neck of the bottle for quick visual reference. For example, you would put the number 1 on your pot still lightly aged rum(s). Then each time you see the icon ➊ in a recipe, you'll be able to quickly grab the bottle you need.

TIKI TECHNIQUES

There are a few drink-making techniques that are especially important for making exotic cocktails that you'll see referenced in our recipes, and which are described in more detail throughout the chapter The Theater of the Exotic Cocktail (page 215). For a quick reference, see below:

For tips on **how to use a drink mixer and flash blend**, see page 229.

To learn to **dry flash**, see page 229.

To learn to **open pour with a gated finish**, see page 232.

To learn to **double-strain**, see page 232.

For tips on **garnishes**, see page 238.

For an explanation of our preferred styles of **ice** and how to combine them, see page 226.

PART ONE

AN INVITATION TO ESCAPE

"With Prohibition officially repealed, and recognizing that people hadn't tasted a decent drink during the previous fourteen years of darkness, with the smell of Rhum always in my nostrils, I started to concoct some unusual, and at the time, exotic drinks."

—ERNEST GANTT

the Birth of Tiki

THE BEACHCOMBER CAFE   FAMOUS NIGHT SPOT   HOLLYWOOD, CAL. 49

Postcard from the original Don's Beachcomber Cafe

IN RETROSPECT, IT SEEMS AMERICA WAS DESTINED
TO BE THE BIRTHPLACE OF TIKI. AFTER ALL, AMERICANS
HAVE BEEN DRAWN TO THE ALLURE OF THE SOUTH
PACIFIC SINCE THE NINETEENTH CENTURY.

Paintings by Gauguin introduced the world to the beauty of Martinique
and Tahiti, and tales of adventure, both fictional and firsthand, from the likes
of Herman Melville and Robert Louis Stevenson became part of the popular
culture. Thanks to the Hawaiian music craze that swept America in the early
twentieth century, visions of graceful swaying palm trees now had a score to
accompany them. These island dreams manifested themselves in some of
the great nightclubs of the 1920s and 1930s, like the Cocoanut Grove at the
Ambassador Hotel in Los Angeles, and numerous "hurricane"-themed bars
across the country. These nightclubs offered a dazzling experience—often
with big band entertainment and dancing—under the towering fake palm
trees and thatched roofs.

These were glamorous destinations filled with elegantly dressed celebrities.
But despite their island pretenses, people still drank what they knew—like a
martini—while dancing under the coconuts. No one had yet thought to match
over-the-top drinks to the over-the-top décor. It took a globetrotter from Texas
to marry the drinks of the Caribbean with the look of the South Pacific under
one roof.

THE BEACHCOMBER

Ernest Raymond Beaumont Gantt was born in the small town of Mexia, Texas, in 1907. Or he was born in New Orleans—or in Jamaica. One of these is probably true; he was a little loose with the facts of his youth. Before Gantt was even a teenager, he found himself prowling the streets of New Orleans with his charismatic grandfather. Together they traveled to the Caribbean on Grandpappy's yacht as part of his, *ahem*, "import-export" business—a business that quickly turned to the import of some of Jamaica's finest strong waters when Prohibition arrived. Imagine this young and impressionable boy encountering a feast of sensory experiences: discovering the rich fragrant rums of Jamaica, the spices and flavors of Caribbean cuisine, the parade of French Creole foods, and the endlessly effervescent combinations of ingredients at the New Orleans pharmacy soda fountains.

By the time he was eighteen, having seen quite a bit of the Caribbean already, Ernest was offered a choice by his parents: head off to college or take his college money and use it as he saw fit. Ernest, not surprisingly (and I suspect at the urging of his Grandpappy), chose to take the money and run.

He spent the next several years roaming the seas in search of adventure. From the calm waters of the Caribbean to the distant South Pacific and beyond, Ernest visited dozens of islands and immersed himself in their various cultures and traditions. He drank in the people, he drank in their arts and crafts, and he drank in their drink. From the frosty, crisp daiquiris of pre-Castro Havana, to the long and refreshing rum punches of Barbados and Jamaica, to the bright juniper-filled elixir known as the Singapore Sling at the luxurious Raffles Hotel in Singapore, Ernest saw more of the world than had most people twice his age. It was fun while it lasted, but the funds eventually ran dry.

THE STYLE I: TROPICAL OR PRE-TIKI

The concept of organizing the tiki movement according to "styles" originated with Sven Kirsten in his *Book of Tiki* and *Tiki Pop*.

Tropical nightclubs, bamboo, and hurricane bars established and exemplified the lure of the tropics in the mind of the early twentieth-century American. Warm nights beneath the palms in a space filled with rattan and bamboo fixtures offered a highly idealized, but alluring, night on the town. Perhaps a macaw would make an appearance, but the carved idols were not to arrive until much later.

By 1931, Ernest was just twenty-four and back on American dry land, in Los Angeles, dragging a cargo of flotsam behind him: masks, carvings, and sundry Polynesian and nautical bric-a-brac. But he didn't have a penny to his name. He started taking odd jobs—dishwasher, bus boy, valet. It was while working as a valet that he began to meet celebrities, who entrusted him with their cars. He entranced them with tales of his South Pacific adventures, and soon found himself hired on as a "technical consultant" on low-budget films. Ernest's bits and pieces of Polynesian ephemera, scattered around a set, could make the beach in Santa Monica look vaguely like Tahiti for that thrilling new serial.

In late 1933, our hero saved enough pennies to hang his hat someplace. And that decision changed the course of American cocktail culture, dining, and design for the next forty years. It was a vacated tailor's shop on North McCadden Place in Hollywood. Not much to look at, just a 13 by 30-foot room. He built a bar with twenty-four seats, tossed in a few tables, and hung up all the crusty décor he'd been clinging to for the past several years. A window behind the bar was opened up and he hung a hot plate on the sill to whip up a little stir-fry for hungry guests. A ramshackle gate was erected out front to announce your arrival, and above it he hung a driftwood sign reading "Don's Beachcomber," so named for a pseudonym Ernest had once used while he was bootlegging. Don's Beachcomber Café was born.

Even in Hollywood, nothing quite like this had been seen before. Elegant, tropical-themed nightclubs like the Cocoanut Grove were well known and offered luxurious fantasy to the swells in black tie. But this was something else—a little coarse, a little rough around the edges. One man's vision of an island rum shack, from an island located somewhere between his left and right ears. The space was a secluded little oasis just a few steps from the hustle of Hollywood Boulevard, allowing patrons to feel they'd escaped time and place. But the décor was not what made the place. It was the drinks.

Ernest expanded upon all that he'd learned and imbibed during his travels, and in the process created an entirely new category of cocktail. He started with the centuries-old foundation of the Planter's Punch (page 258), a recipe immortalized across the Caribbean with the rhyme "one of sour, two of sweet, three of strong, four of weak." Building upon this, he created what he would later call his "Rhum Rhapsodies" using those four powerful components in new and innovative ways, moving beyond just lime, sugar, and a single rum. He devised a lifetime's worth of legendary cocktails from the harvest that was around him, and created a distinct taste that was rooted in the abundant citrus groves of Southern California.

Mixing and layering multiple spices and sweeteners provided a vast array of possibilities, and even small tweaks to a recipe could yield a much different result. And, of course, the blending of very dissimilar rums provided these drinks with a complex backbone that in some ways would even transcend the rest of the ingredients.

Mix three parts remarkable ingredients with one part evocative drink names (Missionary's Downfall, Cobra's Fang, and Vicious Virgin, just to mention a few) and you've got "The Exotic Cocktail." This was the mid-1930s, during the Depression, when international travel was out of reach for the average American—so exotic cocktails offered a vacation in a glass, a harpoon thrown at the ordinary. These drinks gave you the sensation of being somewhere else. Somewhere quite far away from your mundane home or your humdrum job. Somewhere . . . exotic. But it wasn't just the drink. It was how the ingredients came together, how the drinks were presented—in a coconut, in a cove of ice—and what they were called that set the stage. No one in Sumatra, Rangoon, or Tahiti really drank anything like this, but no one could afford to visit these places to find out the truth. Exotic cocktails were an immediate sensation.

A reporter from the *New York Tribune* described one of Ernest's creations, The Sumatra Kula, as "the finest [cocktail] he'd ever tasted." And the stars agreed: Chaplin, Dietrich, and more all came to pray at this temple of rum. By 1937, Ernest had to move to bigger digs across the street. He changed the name of the place to "Don the Beachcomber," and perhaps accepting fate, or simply being tired of everyone assuming his name was Don, changed his own name to Donn Beach.

Donn was a consummate showman with theatrical tendencies that did not go unnoticed in Hollywood. In an era of uniformity, his castaway cutoff pants and weathered linen suit gave the impression of a man whose carefree existence was spent beachcombing and quietly nursing a bottle of rum under a palm tree somewhere. This persona was just one calculated part of the experience, designed to keep the guest intrigued. As another example, when nights drew to a close at Don the Beachcomber, and guests would start making for the doors, Donn would turn on a hose that ran up to a tin roof over the bar, creating the effect of rain outside. Guests would then look at each other, shrug their shoulders, and figure, "Well, since it's raining out, we may as well stay for a nightcap."

In contrast to the nightclubs of the era, Don the Beachcomber never had an orchestra. The entertainment was the space itself. People came to be delighted by the space and were entertained by their food and drink and each other. Even though much of Donn's celebrity clientele at the time would have been supper club habitués, and likely to spend nights out in formalwear dancing to big bands at other Hollywood haunts, Don the Beachcomber's (slightly) more relaxed vibe presaged a shift in dining habits that would spread with the fall of the great nightclubs. People no longer felt the need to wear black tie to a nightclub, they simply wanted to eat dinner.

But, as we know, the star of the show continued to be the drinks. At the bar up front, a solitary bartender would quietly polish glasses, pour the occasional glass of wine, and perhaps stir a martini or two. But behind the bar wall, shielded from view, was a world of whirring drink mixers and flying ice cubes. It was here that the so-called "Four Boys" practiced their magic. The Four Boys were a team of Filipino bartenders trained in the art of shaping Donn's "Rhum Rhapsodies." From a small window adjacent to the bar, a perfectly

THE STYLE II: BEACHCOMBER STYLE

It's here that we see the formality of tropical style take a turn for the eccentric and ramshackle. Guests entering Don the Beachcomber would find a warren of small, dimly-lit rooms festooned with driftwood, flotsam and jetsam, nets, fish floats and traps, puffer fish lamps, shells, and more. As though an idle drifter who wandered the beach collecting detritus had simply hung it all up in a scrappy watering hole . . . because that's precisely what he did.

formed exotic cocktail would emerge from the chaos, its contents and construction a mystery. It was part of the show, but it was also a security measure.

From the moment his doors opened, rival bar owners attempted to crack the code of secrecy that surrounded Donn's drinks, even going so far as to poach Donn's bartenders to access their arcane recipe secrets. But ol' Donn was a wily one and always one step ahead. He had all of his ingredients poured into

Don the Beachcomber, Hollywood, California

unmarked bottles with a variety of codes. So when a rival tavern keeper would sidle up to one of Donn's bartenders at the service entrance, flashing a toothy grin and clutching a roll of dollars in his fist, and ask, "So what's in the Vicious Virgin?" the bartender would reply, "Oh sure, that's half an ounce of Spices #4, two of Dashes #8, one bar spoon . . ." He even took it so far as to play with the guests from time to time—menus sometimes referred to "munrelaf"—falernum (a spiced liqueur from Barbados) spelled backwards!

The drinks enchanted and bewildered his guests. This was (vicious) virgin territory for most of them. But they fell for Donn's Rhum Rhapsodies. And my how they ordered them. Thousands of cases of rum (often those personally selected by and blended for Donn in Jamaica and Guyana) would fly off Donn's shelves over the many years he was in business. And much of that rum landed in one drink: the Zombie. The Zombie was Donn's most infamous drink, a long and lavish cooler filled with an enticing blend of nearly five ounces of various rums. Tales of its origin vary widely, and Donn himself was likely responsible for many of the stories. The legend of the drink grew and grew—so much that Donn soon appended his menus to read "Limit of two." Too strong? Nah, too *dangerous!* He was basically saying, *"The last guy that tried to drink three of these went mad! We never saw him again!"* Brilliant marketing on the part of Donn, as usual. And a brilliant ploy to dare guest after guest to challenge the rule. It was not long before bars across America stole the Zombie name (if not the actual recipe) in an attempt to capitalize on its infamy.

Don the Beachcomber bridged Caribbean-inspired but wholly innovative drinks with the largely unknown and therefore "exotic" and "mysterious" imagery and décor drawn from the South Pacific, and this is the genesis of what became known as

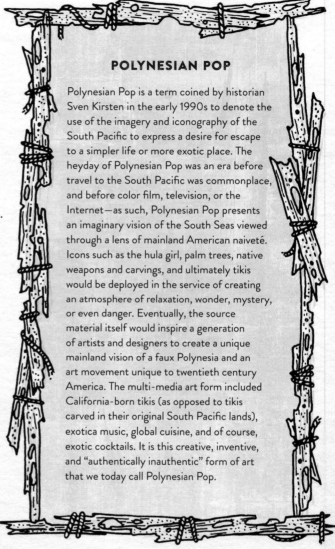

POLYNESIAN POP

Polynesian Pop is a term coined by historian Sven Kirsten in the early 1990s to denote the use of the imagery and iconography of the South Pacific to express a desire for escape to a simpler life or more exotic place. The heyday of Polynesian Pop was an era before travel to the South Pacific was commonplace, and before color film, television, or the Internet—as such, Polynesian Pop presents an imaginary vision of the South Seas viewed through a lens of mainland American naiveté. Icons such as the hula girl, palm trees, native weapons and carvings, and ultimately tikis would be deployed in the service of creating an atmosphere of relaxation, wonder, mystery, or even danger. Eventually, the source material itself would inspire a generation of artists and designers to create a unique mainland vision of a faux Polynesia and an art movement unique to twentieth century America. The multi-media art form included California-born tikis (as opposed to tikis carved in their original South Pacific lands), exotica music, global cuisine, and of course, exotic cocktails. It is this creative, inventive, and "authentically inauthentic" form of art that we today call Polynesian Pop.

Polynesian Pop. At a time when both fiction and non-fiction accounts of South Seas adventures were high on publishers' hit-parades, Donn brought together just the right combination of excitement, danger, and escape.

Donn proved to be an imaginative pioneer, and a revolutionary mixologist. He created the template for countless others to follow for decades. But whether it was love, lust, a serious dearth of business acumen, or as some reports would have it, the need for a legitimate name on the liquor license because of his bootlegging past, he made what some may consider in hindsight to be a misstep and sold his tender young empire to a former waitress from Minnesota named Cora "Sunny" Sund. Right on the cusp of a full-blown tiki craze, Sunny became first the president, then Donn's wife. With Sunny in charge, Donn found himself with little to do but tinker in the kitchen inventing new drinks, now just one of many on the payroll of the company that bore his *nom de rhum*. And even that was not to last long. Sunny divorced him in 1940, but remained at the helm.

Under Sunny's direction, the Don the Beachcomber empire expanded first to Chicago and Palm Springs, and later to several other cities. When the Chicago location opened, it paid itself off in just eight months. It is estimated that by 1948, the Hollywood Don the Beachcomber was doing $1.5 million in sales. The gift shop alone made twenty-five thousand dollars a year. The restaurant also began to serve Chinese food, cooked by a Chinese chef. The menu featured many ingredients imported from China, such as water chestnuts (deployed to great effect in Donn's own creation, rumaki), oyster sauce, and lychee nuts. Today, that hardly seems exotic, but in the 1930s and 40s, it certainly was. A photo caption beneath a picture of a satisfied diner in a 1948 issue of *Look* magazine tellingly reveals that, "Nine out of ten customers let their waiter order for them." An added touch was to keep a glass cabinet full of custom-labeled chopsticks for the celebrity guests.

Donn himself went off to World War II, and was charged with the wholly appropriate role of setting up rest-and-relaxation camps for officers in the Army Air Corps in such exotic locales as Capri, Nice, Cannes, and Venice. Upon his return to civilian life, barred by Sunny from opening any more restaurants in the United States, he took his skills to somewhere not yet part of the United States: Hawaii. When he arrived, he expected to find a Polynesian wonderland of tiki gods, thatched huts, and topless wahines. Instead, he found that the missionaries who preceded him had erected Victorian homes, destroyed the huts and tikis, and covered up the women. So Donn set out to remake Hawaii in his own idealized image of it; in effect, to make Polynesia more Polynesian. Beginning in 1947, he erected the first new thatched-roof buildings in decades along Kalakaua Avenue in Waikiki, and was the first to host commercial luaus for tourists, complete with local and Tahitian musicians, singers, and dancers, all providing the perfect backdrop to his exotic rum drinks. In Donn's own words, "We landscaped the property with water ponds, ferns, palms, and other assorted flowers and plant life to create a masterpiece. This is where my 'Don the Beachcomber' style of tourism really came to life in Waikiki." Within ten years, he would create the International Marketplace next door, which was filled with shops, restaurants, and island craftspeople, and he later created malls and resorts across the island chain.

Meanwhile, Sunny continued to expand the empire back on the mainland to ultimately include more than twenty locations before she sold the chain. And Donn eventually retired, dividing his time between a home in Hawaii, and a tiki-themed houseboat in Tahiti. Donn is buried today in the Punchbowl National Military Cemetery on Oahu, a fitting location for both his service to his country and the inspiration he drew from the swaying palms of the South Pacific.

THE TRADER

It was not what you'd characterize as an easy upbringing. Born Victor Jules Bergeron in San Francisco in 1902, he suffered from a string of childhood illnesses, culminating in tuberculosis of the bone at age four. He was in the hospital when the Great Quake of 1906 struck, and again two years later to have his leg amputated to stop the spread of TB. Raised by French parents who loved to hunt and cook, Vic's family settled in Oakland, California, when he was nine, and opened a small grocery store. As a young man, Victor moved through a series of jobs (and recurrent bouts of tuberculosis) before borrowing eight hundred dollars from his aunt and building a 22 by 26-foot, one-room restaurant across from the grocery store in 1934. It wasn't much to look at—room for thirty people inside if they felt like getting cozy; a potbellied stove to warm up the place and heat some meals on. But Victor knew how to entertain a guest—a little song, a little dance, maybe a card trick or two. Free lunches of salted herring or crab washed down with a couple of ten-cent beers kept the Depression-era crowds coming at all hours. Soon other rooms were added to the structure and the place took on the feel of a hunting lodge with snowshoes and animal heads gracing the walls. It was called Hinky Dinks, and despite being located on a dusty stretch of San Pablo Avenue and having cattle marched past the front door daily on their way to the slaughterhouse, it managed to become a sensation.

Although Vic had a rowdy and convivial hit on his hands, he knew better than to rest on his laurels. Vic served the kind of standard simple cocktails you'd find at a neighborhood saloon, but he took notice that one of his drinks, the creamy and rum-packed Banana Cow, was wildly popular. He started to wonder if maybe people might pay a few cents more

The Trader and his exotic wares

to drink something a bit more celebratory, a touch more . . . exotic. In an effort to improve his own knowledge of cocktails and hopefully make a few extra bucks upon his return, he and his wife took an extended trip to Louisiana and the Caribbean. His travels brought him to some of the most legendary bars in New Orleans and Havana, and he picked the brains of the bartenders he met there—the hows and whys, the tips and tricks. The menu was soon augmented with the drinks he'd seen on his travels, and a few creative spins of his own. It worked. His regulars were anxious to try his latest inventions, and first-time visitors became regulars soon enough.

But while Vic had seen the cradle of the daiquiri in Havana and tasted the cooling elixirs of New Orleans, there was a sound calling out to him from much closer to home. Word had traveled north of an unusual little watering hole in Hollywood that was drawing in both the stars and stargazers. Vic wanted to see it for himself. In 1937, he made his first pilgrimage to Don the Beachcomber. The first time Vic pushed open the rattan-and-jade tile doors left him a changed man. In fact, he never wanted to leave. While Vic would forever give credit to Donn in his menus, and freely admit that his visit offered inspiration, former Don the Beachcomber employees tell a tale of a man they called "The Rope Hanger." Between

> *"Vic didn't invent a better mousetrap. Rather, he evolved a delightful and welcoming mantrap, and the world beat a path to his swinging doors in no time flat."*
>
> —LUCIUS BEEBE, 1946, *TRADER VIC'S BOOK OF FOOD AND DRINK*

his constant questions about the food and drinks and his gawking at celebrities, Vic was eventually shown the door, but would stand outside against the velvet ropes all night just hoping for a chance to get back inside the palace.

Vic returned home inspired. Donn's rum and celebrity-filled boîte confirmed Vic's belief that tropical was the way forward. His wife agreed and they set about transforming the décor of the Hinky Dinks space. ("Lots of decoration causes lots of conversation, and lots of conversation sells lots of drinks," Vic would later recount in his autobiography.) Down came the snowshoes and deer heads and up went the fishnets and float lamps. He bought pieces from friends (and even Donn Beach), but it was his habit of offering his guests food and drink in exchange for decorative curios that earned both Victor and his joint a nickname that would be found above the doors of his restaurants for decades to come: Trader Vic.

At the same time, Vic had been traveling across the bay to San Francisco, dining at Chinese restaurants with an eye toward one day opening a Chinese place of his own. But he now realized that the Westernized version of Chinese food that had become popular around the West Coast during the Depression was the perfect foil to the kind of drinks he planned to serve. The food was filling and inexpensive, yet still maintained an air of the exotic, and the tastes were foreign to the uninitiated palates of the time. So Victor sniffed around Chinatown and came back with a few ideas of his own. He had Chinese ovens built, which were capable of quickly cooking and smoking meats with an indirect flame, and these would become a signature of all of his future restaurants.

As Vic himself wrote, "There was no fanfare about the opening. Just closed one day as Hinky Dinks selling sandwiches and opened the next day as Trader Vic's selling tropical drinks and Chinese food." What that uncharacteristically modest statement does not reveal was that, at the heart of both ventures, there was a man whose outsize personality became one of the restaurant's most featured attractions. His bellowing laugh and warm but gruff demeanor became well known throughout the San Francisco Bay Area. Vic's tales of South Seas adventure and of his own birth on a distant atoll were purely imaginary—he wouldn't travel there until years later. His wooden leg, a legacy of childhood tuberculosis, now became the memento of a shark attack, and guests were shocked and delighted as he drove a knife into it for their amusement. By 1941, Pulitzer-Prize–winning San Francisco columnist Herb Caen declared, to the everlasting delight of Vic, "The best restaurant in San Francisco is in Oakland," a statement that ruffled the feathers of San Franciscans then just as it would now.

For guests seated among the engaging artifacts of South Seas commerce, both real and imagined, it wasn't just the décor on the walls that had them talking; it was the décor in their hands as well. Drinks came in elaborate bowls and vases depicting island scenes, topped with fragrant flowers and souvenir swizzle sticks, all of which added to the experience and fueled repeat sales. Vic's foray into exotic cocktails was a unique hybrid of his travels and observations, with a few genuine inventions of his own. In 1944, it all coalesced into his ultimate creation—the Mai Tai, the drink that would cement his place in history (discussed in excruciating length on pages 261 to 264).

Expansion beckoned. Seattle would be first, with a small cocktail lounge called The Outrigger. Then to Beverly Hills, and ultimately, in 1951, the grand prize: San Francisco. Located in a quiet lot in the back of an alley with just a small garage on it—it was an unlikely spot for a destination that would remain a landmark of San Francisco dining for four decades.

It was at the San Francisco location that Vic's food program really blossomed and would ultimately make it a culinary landmark. Of course, for most readers the expression "culinary landmark" referencing a tiki bar would give one pause. After all, if there's anything tiki bars are (in)famous for, it's (let us charitably call it) less-than-stellar dining. But that wasn't always the case. Vic was already serving a unique hybrid cuisine at the Oakland location. His "refinement" of Chinese cooking was in reality a refinement of Americanized Chinese cooking, already well removed from regional Chinese authenticity. He further developed this idea at his San Francisco location by continuing to seek inspiration from other countries—discovering new dishes and adapting them to the American palate. He called it "Imaginative American Food." Trader Vic's became the first restaurant in the United States to serve Indonesian curry, albeit blended with French and American cooking techniques. A unique mid-century amalgamation of styles—fusion cooking before there was fusion cooking. "International cuisine," as it came to be known, and perhaps best exemplified by Vic's own creation, Crab Rangoon. It was a hit. Dining awards followed, and Vic's reputation for fine dining spread. (Fun fact: Though not until decades later [1983], Queen Elizabeth II ate the first meal of her life not prepared by a palace chef at Vic's San Francisco outpost.) Vic was also an early and vocal supporter of the California wine industry, always insisting that the Golden State was producing some of the world's finest wines, and hosting winemaker dinners long before the 1976 Judgment of Paris. Make no mistake: a night out at Donn's or Vic's places was considered fine dining, and for many people, reserved for a special occasion.

Trader Vic's San Francisco was a vast, multistory affair with multiple bars and dining rooms. It did more than duplicate the success in Oakland;

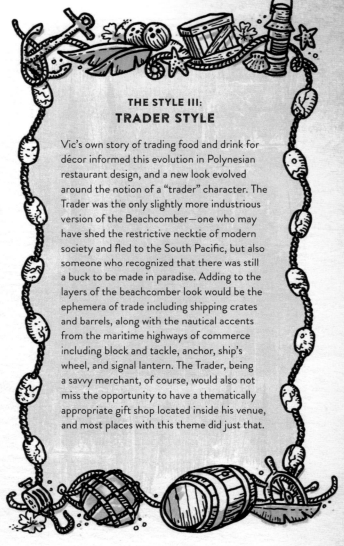

THE STYLE III:
TRADER STYLE

Vic's own story of trading food and drink for décor informed this evolution in Polynesian restaurant design, and a new look evolved around the notion of a "trader" character. The Trader was the only slightly more industrious version of the Beachcomber—one who may have shed the restrictive necktie of modern society and fled to the South Pacific, but also someone who recognized that there was still a buck to be made in paradise. Adding to the layers of the beachcomber look would be the ephemera of trade including shipping crates and barrels, along with the nautical accents from the maritime highways of commerce including block and tackle, anchor, ship's wheel, and signal lantern. The Trader, being a savvy merchant, of course, would also not miss the opportunity to have a thematically appropriate gift shop located inside his venue, and most places with this theme did just that.

it expanded upon the theme and refined it. It was in San Francisco that you saw the ramshackle look of Oakland's informal Trader style coalesce into a sense of order. Masks, weapons, and giant clamshells were neatly arranged on tapa and lauhala-covered walls. Some of the old formality of the tropical bars of the 1920s and 1930s would return, augmented with more "authentic" island artifacts, plenty of trader-style

THE TIKI

The word *tiki* originated in New Zealand and the Marquesas Islands, where it can refer to a carving of a first man, a god, or a symbol of procreation depending on which culture it originated from. But eventually, mainland Americans appropriated the word to describe any Polynesian carving with a largely human form, exaggerated features, and a menacing visage. What's more, mainlanders started carving the tikis themselves, occasionally with an eye to their South Pacific origins, but more often with a "whimsical and naïve attitude toward another people's extinct religion," as historian Sven Kirsten puts it. These artists were inspired to add their own flair and style to the carvings. Thus was born a new kind of tiki whose provenance lay in many lands and imaginations, and would later become a tenet of Polynesian Pop.

These figures guarded the entrances to countless restaurants, bars, hotels, and apartments, and inside each of those places, more were to be found watching over patrons and residents. Some were for good luck, other repurposed by canny restauranteurs into an imagined "god of drink" of "god of fine food and good cheer." The tiki was a useful vessel to imbue with your own sales goals. The take-home souvenir tikis in the gift shops of the era were also given imaginary attributes by these mid-century marketers of merriment, referring to individual designs as the "god of romance" or "god of adventure," ignoring their respective cultural significance (if the designs themselves had any to begin with).

What might be perceived now as culturally insensitive were then simply enjoyed for their uncommon appearance and "dangerous" appeal. Their ubiquitous presence on buildings, artwork, matchbooks, and more made them one of the most identifiable images in the American subconscious for decades.

nautical pieces . . . and the arrival of a new feature into the landscape: the tiki.

By the early 1960s, there were twenty-five Trader Vic's locations around the world. The expansion itself furthered the craze for all things exotic, particularly in American cities far from the California sun: Chicago, Denver, Kansas City, Atlanta, Houston, Boston, Detroit, and more. Back home, the "mother church" in Oakland could no longer resist the crumbling of both its infrastructure and neighborhood. In the early 70s, it moved up to nearby Emeryville where it remains to this day. During his forty-plus years in hospitality, Vic became a prolific writer and authored several cookbooks, bartender's guides, and ultimately an autobiography in 1973. Vic's salty character is neatly illustrated by his 1947 *Bartender's Guide*, which opens with "Phonies, Check-Dodgers or The Perils of Bartending" as its first chapter, only to be followed immediately by "People that Bartenders Have Learned Not to Like" as the second.

While Donn's affinity for the lure of paradise would remain with him until his final days aboard his tiki-themed houseboat, Vic was more likely to be found with a glass of Scotch and painting ice-skating nuns in his golden years. But in many ways, that was the perfect contrast for these two titans of the tropics. Donn, the inspired dreamer whose travels would become the foundation of both a cultural and cocktail movement, was always drawn first to the experience and the desire to share his fantasy with the world. Vic, whose salt-of-the-earth pragmatism and business savvy served him well, saw an opportunity and ran with it—and made huge contributions to the design, cuisine, and libations of the era. With over fifty locations around the world having come and gone over the seventy-five-plus-year history of the company, Trader Vic's was certainly the most successful of the era and is the only one to survive today in its original form.

Aku Aku

AKU AKU

This inspired use of fresh mint and pineapple seems wholly contemporary, but has its roots in the 1930s when it was originally served at Don the Beachcomber and named the Missionary's Downfall.

ORIGIN *Based on Don the Beachcomber's Missionary's Downfall*
SOURCE *Trader Vic's Bartender's Guide, Revised*
GLASSWARE *Chilled coupe*

> 5 (1-inch-square) chunks fresh pineapple
>
> 8 mint leaves
>
> 1 ounce fresh lime juice
>
> Scant ½ ounce SC Demerara Syrup (page 324)
>
> ½ ounce natural peach liqueur (such as Mathilde, Combier, or Giffard)
>
> 1½ ounces blended lightly aged rum ❷

GARNISH *Large mint leaf or a small cluster of mint sprigs*

Muddle the pineapple chunks in a drink mixer tin. Add the remaining ingredients and 12 ounces of crushed ice and flash blend for 10 seconds. Double-strain into a chilled coupe glass. Float a large mint leaf on the surface of the drink or rest a small cluster of mint sprigs against the side of the glass to garnish.

PUPULE

ORIGIN *Don the Beachcomber, mid-1930s*
SOURCE *Beachbum Berry's Sippin' Safari adapted by Smuggler's Cove*
GLASSWARE *Footed pilsner*

> Spiral-cut orange peel
>
> ¾ ounce fresh lime juice
>
> ¾ ounce fresh orange juice
>
> ¼ ounce SC Cinnamon Syrup (page 327)
>
> ¼ ounce SC Vanilla Syrup (page 326)
>
> ¼ ounce St. Elizabeth Allspice Dram
>
> 2 ounces column still aged rum ❹
>
> 1 dash Angostura bitters

GARNISH *Swizzle stick and mint sprig*

Line a footed pilsner glass with the orange peel with one end hanging over the rim of the glass. Add the remaining ingredients to a drink mixer tin. Fill with 12 ounces of crushed ice and 4 to 6 small "agitator" cubes. Flash blend and open pour with gated finish into the glass. Add garnish.

NOTE This well-spiced delight was later renamed "The Nui Nui."

DON'S OWN GROG

ORIGIN *Don the Beachcomber, circa 1937*
SOURCE Beachbum Berry's Sippin' Safari,
adapted by Smuggler's Cove
GLASSWARE *Double old-fashioned*

¾ ounce fresh lime juice

¼ ounce SC Demerara Syrup (page 324)

1 dash SC Grenadine (page 328)

½ ounce Leopold Brothers Rocky
Mountain Blackberry Liqueur

1 ounce blended aged rum ❸

½ ounce blended lightly aged rum ❷

½ ounce black blended rum ❺

1 dash Angosutra bitters

GARNISH *Freshly grated nutmeg*

Add all the ingredients to a drink mixer tin. Fill with
12 ounces of crushed ice and 4 to 6 small "agitator"
cubes. Flash blend and open pour with gated finish
into a double old-fashioned glass. Top with freshly
grated nutmeg.

PORT AU PRINCE

ORIGIN *Don the Beachcomber, circa late 1930s*
SOURCE Beachbum Berry's Sippin' Safari,
adapted by Smuggler's Cove
GLASSWARE *Footed pilsner*

½ ounce fresh lime juice

½ ounce pineapple juice

¼ ounce SC Demerara Syrup (page 324)

1 dash SC Grenadine (page 328)

½ ounce John D. Taylor's Velvet Falernum

1½ ounces cane coffey still aged rum (see page 199)

1 dash Angostura bitters

GARNISH *Lime wedge speared with a cocktail umbrella*

Add all the ingredients to a drink mixer tin. Fill with
12 ounces of crushed ice and 4 to 6 small "agitator"
cubes. Flash blend and open pour with gated finish
into a footed pilsner glass. Add garnish.

Clockwise from top right: Port Au Prince, Don's Own Grog, Pupule (page 39)

Three Dots and a Dash

THREE DOTS AND A DASH

Created during World War II by Donn Beach, the name is Morse code for "Victory."

ORIGIN *Don the Beachcomber*
SOURCE *Beachbum Berry's Sippin' Safari, adapted by Smuggler's Cove*
GLASSWARE *Footed pilsner*

½ ounce fresh lime juice

½ ounce fresh orange juice

½ ounce SC Honey Syrup (page 325)

¼ ounce John D. Taylor's Velvet Falernum

¼ ounce St. Elizabeth Allspice Dram

1½ ounces cane AOC Martinique rhum agricole vieux ⑧

½ ounce blended aged rum ③

1 dash Angostura bitters

GARNISH *Three maraschino cherries and a pineapple chunk speared on a cocktail pick, or three maraschino cherries on a cocktail pick plus a pineapple frond*

Add all the ingredients to a drink mixer tin. Fill with 12 ounces of crushed ice and 4 to 6 small "agitator" cubes. Flash blend and open pour with gated finish into a footed pilsner glass. Add garnish.

NOTE The garnish cleverly represents the Morse code. The three cherries are the "dots," and the "dash" was, traditionally, at Don the Beachcomber, a rectangular chunk of pineapple. At Smuggler's Cove we choose to use a pineapple frond as our dash.

MEXICAN EL DIABLO

As Vic said of his 1946 invention, "I hate like hell to bring up unpleasant things at a time like this, but go easy on this one because it's tough on your running board."

SOURCE *Trader Vic's Book of Food and Drink, adapted by Smuggler's Cove*
GLASSWARE *Collins or highball*

1 lime wedge

½ ounce fresh lime juice

½ ounce natural crème de cassis

1½ ounces blanco tequila

4 ounces real ginger ale

GARNISH *Swizzle stick*

Squeeze and the drop lime wedge into a Collins or highball glass. Fill glass with cracked ice. Build the drink by adding the remaining ingredients; stir. Garnish with a swizzle stick.

PORT LIGHT

This Trader Vic original will guide you out to sea!

SOURCE Trader Vic's Bartender's Guide, Revised, *adapted by Smuggler's Cove*
GLASSWARE *Footed pilsner*

- 1 ounce egg white
- 2 ounces bourbon
- 1 ounce fresh lemon juice
- ¾ ounce SC Honey Syrup (page 325)
- ½ ounce SC Passion Fruit Syrup (page 325)

GARNISH *Swizzle stick*

Combine the egg white and bourbon in a drink mixer tin and dry flash without ice for 10 seconds (see page 229). Then add the remaining ingredients. Fill with 12 ounces of crushed ice and 4 to 6 small "agitator" cubes. Flash blend and open pour with gated finish into a footed pilsner glass and garnish.

DEMERARA DRY FLOAT

Served with a side of danger!

ORIGIN *Don the Beachcomber*
SOURCE Beachbum Berry's Intoxica!, *adapted by Smuggler's Cove*
GLASSWARE *Double old-fashioned glass and an old-fashioned or small shot glass*

- ¾ ounce black blended overproof rum ⑥
- 2 ounces fresh lime juice
- 1 teaspoon fresh lemon juice
- 1½ ounces SC Passion Fruit Syrup (page 325)
- ¼ ounce SC Demerara Syrup (page 324)
- ¼ ounce Luxardo Maraschino liqueur
- 1½ ounces blended aged rum ③

GARNISH *None*

Pour the overproof rum into a separate old-fashioned or shot glass and set aside. Add the remaining ingredients to a drink mixer tin. Fill with 12 ounces of crushed ice and 4 to 6 small "agitator" cubes. Flash blend and open pour with gated finish into a double old-fashioned glass, and serve with the side of over-proof rum (the side of danger!). Encourage guests to pour as much or as little of the overproof rum into their drink as they like, and experience how the drink flavor changes.

From left: Port Light, side of danger, Demerara Dry Float

"America's love affair with Polynesian Pop style was the Mauna Loa of cultural fads, a volcanic eruption that lasted forty years."

—JEFF BERRY, *BEACHBUM BERRY REMIXED*

the Golden Era

Mai Kai, Fort Lauderdale, Florida

DONN AND VIC REPRESENTED THE START OF A
POPULAR NEW MOVEMENT IN AMERICAN FOOD AND
DRINK. BUT JUST AS IT WAS GAINING MOMENTUM,
THE COUNTRY WAS PLUNGED INTO WORLD WAR II.

The Polynesian fad was put on the back burner while more pressing
matters gripped the nation and world, but there was one group for whom the
experience took on a much more profound meaning—the GIs actually serving
in Polynesia during the Pacific Campaign. Inundated with brutal hardships
and daily horrors, they took solace where and when they could on the white
sands of those rarely peaceful islands. One of them, a sailor in the US Navy
who'd seen action throughout the South Pacific, returned home and chronicled
his experiences in a semiautobiographical new work. The book was called
Tales of the South Pacific, and it not only won its author, James Michener,
the Pulitzer Prize in 1948, it (along with its subsequent musical adaptation)
sparked a huge wave of nostalgia among the thousands of returning servicemen for the warm beaches, swaying palm trees, and island wahines that filled
their hours between the brutal firefights. Their experiences added to the newly
sprouted Polynesian fad, and the next two decades would see this American
culinary and design phenomenon thrive far beyond California.

THE TIKI CRAZE

The style and fad became known at the time to many simply as "tiki"—named for the most recognizable icons of the movement. These totemic figures from islands across the South Pacific represented different legends and tales to many Polynesian cultures. But to mid-century Americans, the angry humanoid figures simply represented escape—from the ordinary, from the Protestant work ethic and other stresses of the Eisenhower era, or simply from sobriety. Restaurants and bars, big and small, embraced the tiki theme across the country, in places as untropical as Columbus, Chicago, and Detroit. In fact, during the tiki heyday, Chicago had as many as ten tiki bars, including one of each of the larger chains: a Don the Beachcomber, a Trader Vic's, a Kon-Tiki Ports, and a Kona Kai.

Walt Disney, too, saw how American leisure was embracing the South Pacific and in 1962 opened the Tahitian Terrace within Disneyland, a Polynesian restaurant with full floor show complete with dancers emerging from behind a waterfall, and tropical drinks (minus the rum), all situated under a dramatic thirty-five-foot artificial tree. This was followed in 1963 with the Enchanted Tiki Room—taking an already over-the-top concept and adding the then cutting-edge invention of Audio-Animatronics. Originally also designed as a full restaurant with dinner show, the spectacular theatrics instead took center stage and it opened as a smaller, but magically impressive show, complete with talking and singing birds, flowers, and tikis that continues to entertain people of all ages today. In 1960, just north of Disneyland, was the fantastical attraction known as "The Tikis." A creation of Danny Balsz and his wife, Doris Sampson, The Tikis sat on three acres in Monterey Park, California, and included an erupting volcano, waterfalls, and party and banquet facilities for up to fifteen hundred people.

> *"An alternative world had to be created where one could assume a less restrained persona. The seemingly carefree culture of Polynesia became the escapist counter-reality of choice. Wherever fun could be had, Tiki ruled."*
>
> —SVEN KIRSTEN, *THE BOOK OF TIKI*

There were a few forces that converged to feed the tiki craze that gripped America throughout the 1950s and 1960s. In addition to James Michner's *South Pacific*, the book and Academy-award winning documentary *Kon-Tiki*, about Norwegian Thor Heyerdahl's expedition from Peru to Polynesia on a log raft named Kon-Tiki, was released in 1950, followed a few years later by his book *Aku Aku* about his travels to Easter Island. All of these added to a growing interest in Polynesian culture, creating a kind of "Kon-Tiki fever," and spawning businesses that used the names and imagery—so much so that people referred to Polynesian-inspired architecture as "Kon-Tiki style." It was a style that grew ever more popular as apartments, bowling alleys, and shopping centers all began to appear, strewn with towering A-frame rooflines, lava rock water features, and flickering gas torches. And nestled inside homes, "primitive" arts became a décor trend while the backyard luau became the party theme of choice.

And then there was Hawaii. While certainly both Donn and Vic had been inspired by travels to Hawaii for their restaurants, it is a perfect example of Polynesian Pop that both Don the Beachcomber and Trader Vic's opened in California before Hawaii. Tiki spread to Hawaii because, after exposure to tiki on the mainland, tourists *expected* tiki to be in

Hawaii when they arrived. This is an example where, as Kirsten puts it, "fiction had conquered fact, as so often in Polynesian Pop." In 1953, Matson Lines, now offering cruises from San Francisco to Hawaii for newly flush Americans enjoying the postwar economic boom, commissioned Trader Vic to create the cocktail menus for their cruise ships and the Royal Hawaiian Hotel, and this would forever cement the Mai Tai as synonymous with Hawaii. Travel became more affordable, and Americans began heading to Hawaii in droves by sea and by air. Much as the mainland tiki bar was a "safe" and easy way to experience the exotic and tropical, so now was Hawaii, where people spoke English and the greenback was the currency of choice. Donn's luaus became famous and were copied across the island chain. And the mainland's draw to Hawaii was further solidified in 1959 when Hawaii became the fiftieth State. That same year, *Hawaiian Eye* and *Adventures in Paradise* both premiered on TV, exposing viewers to the paradise that was now part of their country. The Polynesian Pop fantasy had become American reality.

Tiki apartments, Redondo Beach, California

MUSIC

Donn Beach understood the importance of the soundtrack to his Waikiki luaus, and brought Tahitian dancers, singers, and other musicians over to Hawaii as part of the entertainment, alongside local musicians like Alfred Apaka. But it was a few years later, across the street from Donn's luaus in the Shell Bar of the Hawaiian Village Hotel, that another type of music could be found that perfectly epitomized the tiki movement: the Polynesian Pop sounds of "Exotica." Exotica was the seemingly inevitable emergence of an imagined soundtrack evoked by the tiki craze, in which non-Western rhythms, percussion, and "other-worldly" vocals create a sense of the "exotic." Albums such as Yma Sumac's *Voice of the Xtabay* (1950) and Les Baxter's *Ritual of the Savage* (1951) are early examples of this musical style. In the mid-1950s while playing at the Shell Bar, bandleader Martin Denny's quartet, featuring Arthur Lyman on the vibraphone (who would go on to have a huge career of his own), one night jokingly made birdcalls in response to the loud frogs that could be heard.

What started as a joke became a sensation. To quote archivist Dan Shiman, "Exotica was an indiscriminate potpourri of influences, themes, and motifs, and none of it ultimately diverged much from Western popular forms. In most cases—Sumac perhaps being the exception—the artists' connections to the faraway lands they paid homage to were marginal. In summoning its desert oases or tiki-besotted, bare-breasted paradises, exotica was nothing if not imaginative, though. Set against tableaux of lush strings, punctuated by bird calls, made to shimmer and dance with Afro-Cuban percussion, vibraphones and mad jungle flutes, it was music manufactured to take the suburban classes to five o'clock dreamland."

THE THIRD MAN

The tales of Donn and Vic and their humble beginnings are dramatic, but nobody brought drama to tiki quite like Joseph Stephen Crane. Born in 1917 in the small town of Crawfordsville, Indiana, this middle-class Hoosier kid seemed destined for a small town life. Yet, here was a man who would take the theater of tiki to new heights and further feed the tiki craze.

Growing up, Joseph's father owned a cigar and ice cream shop that was a front for a pool hall and gambling den in the back. Joseph was a good kid and did well at school, but he figured out pretty quickly what he really liked: money and girls. He was already dreaming of a life outside of Crawfordsville, but the sudden death of his father kept him at home running the pool hall, going to college, and marrying a pretty co-ed named Carol Ann Kurtz. But Joseph's ambition, even then, couldn't be contained. Attempts at his own line of cigars, running a theater in Chicago, driving a taxi in New York, and betting on the stock market went nowhere and led to a separation from Carol Ann. By the end of 1939, he took what cash he'd scraped together, hopped in a yellow Buick convertible, and drove west to Hollywood to reinvent himself.

He started with his name: Joseph Crane belonged in Indiana; "Steve Crane" belonged in Hollywood. He set himself up in an apartment just off Sunset near the clubs and quickly made a name for himself as a man about town. He had some scratch, nice clothes, and was a smooth talker with some class . . . and he earned the respect of the club operators.

He began to build up the lifestyle to match the new name and persona. Steve Crane wouldn't be seen in a Buick, so he stepped up to a Lincoln Continental. A regular at many of the Golden Age–era Hollywood nightclubs, he began to be seen on the arm of starlets like Simone Simon and Sonja Henie.

In 1942, at his favorite spot, the Mocambo, Steve approaches an attractive young blonde and asks for a dance. The blonde in question happens to be the biggest young starlet in Hollywood—Lana Turner. Lana later described it as love at first sight. Within three weeks, they had eloped to Las Vegas. It was Lana's second marriage and she was only twenty-two. The gossip columns were set ablaze: Who was this nobody who swept in and married Lana Turner? It was reported in the Hollywood press at the time that he was in fact J. Stephen Crane III, playboy heir to big Indiana tobacco money who lived with fellow bachelor (and department store heir) Alfred Bloomingdale in a Malibu beach house. This was all far from the truth, of course.

Within months of the marriage, Steve and Lana were miserable. But they were the talk of the town, and Steve craved the attention and loved being featured in the gossip columns. Not only were they miserable, they weren't even married—a technicality meant that he was still married to Carol Ann in Indiana. So they stayed together, enduring each other and a hasty remarriage in Tijuana, and Lana was soon pregnant.

In July of 1943, their daughter, Cheryl, was born, and the whole family went to Crawfordsville for a triumphant hometown tour. Steve was proud to be the local boy who made good, and the town made a big affair of it. It was there that Lana quickly realized that all the tales of the tobacco fortune and family wealth were just part of the "Steve Crane" story. The moment she set eyes on the pool hall and the modest family home, she knew it was over, and they agreed to divorce in November 1943. Steve tried his hand at the movies, making the most of his Hollywood connections to land bit parts in cinematic classics like "Cry of the Werewolf." Though he was soon back out on the town, and seen on the arms of Rita Hayworth and Ava Gardner, he was adrift professionally.

In the spring of 1946, Steve made a fateful decision that would shape the rest of his life. He bought a share in Lucey's, a popular steakhouse and star hangout located next to the main gate at Paramount Studios. Regulars included Humphrey Bogart, John Garfield, Ava Gardner, and Robert Mitchum. This turned out to be the perfect role for Steve—he could be host, impresario, and full-time charmer. Steve had finally come into his own.

A scandalous relationship sent Crane fleeing to France in 1948, where he married French film star Martine Carol, and lived like a king for a time, until a serious car accident and the end of his marriage conspired to return him, once again, to Southern California. He arrived with a mysterious stack of cash: was it from gambling wins in Monte Carlo as was rumored? (As ever, Crane's relationship with the truth was a mercurial one.) He sold his stake in Lucey's, and he then put into action a plan he had been forming the last three years: to open the biggest and most extravagant Polynesian palace Hollywood had ever seen.

The first step was location. Increasingly, Hollywood was no longer the place to go for nightlife.

The great post-Prohibition clubs were in decline, their top entertainment acts lured away by Las Vegas and television. People no longer wanted to put on black tie to go out; they just wanted to eat a fine meal. Though Beverly Hills was still a sleepy suburb in the early 1950s, Steve set his sights on Sugie's Tropics, a small but popular nightspot at 421 Rodeo Drive that even had a cocktail on their menu named for Lana Turner. He rebuilt it from the ground up, using plenty of design inspiration from Donn and Vic, but building upon their success with a number of innovative ideas of his own. The Luau opened July 25, 1953, and would become a landmark for more than two decades.

Like the other great temples of tiki in that era, much time and effort was lavished upon the exotic cocktails. Before opening, Steve traveled to Hawaii to meet with Donn, an old friend from his Lucey's days. Donn had certainly always played his cards close to his chest when it came to recipes, so either he'd grown soft in his old age, or Steve really was a world-class snake charmer after all, because through either Donn or his staff, Steve was able to acquire some of the most iconic recipes of the era. Steve returned to Beverly Hills and brought with him the mysterious mixologist Dr. Fong Foo. Dr. Fong Foo was an expert with exotic cocktails who had worked with both Vic and Donn and personally created The Luau menu. Dr. Foo filled the back page with florid prose about his skills, experience, and extensive travel to many exotic ports of call. Of course, no one drinking at The Luau ever met the good doctor . . . because he wasn't real. Dr. Fong Foo existed only in the imagination of Steve Crane.

Steve knew another secret to a successful nightspot: Women. Lots of 'em. Before The Luau even opened, the first party was an all-female sneak preview with two hundred of Hollywood's most powerful women. The Luau had flattering lighting to keep the ladies looking pretty. The drinks were romantic. The "Captain Steve's Pearl" cocktail (originally the Pearl Diver at Donn's place) was served with a real pearl in it that would be set into a necklace or earring on your way out.

For the guys, the charms lay not just in the ladies, but in the dark and mysterious atmosphere, and the faux sense of danger. The urinals in the men's room were made from "man-eating" giant clamshells. The ashtrays on the table were of the same species of clam, and the menu noted that "Presumably the smaller ones eat smaller men." There was also appeal in the high-priced escorts who were scattered liberally around the bar. Sophisticated enough in appearance to attract the well-heeled guy, but discreet enough not to upset Steve's female guests.

Customers loved it. Stars loved it. Clark Gable, Jack Benny, Lena Horne, and many more. Celebrity gossip columnists came nightly. The discreet entrance kept secret the wonders that lay behind the hostess stand . . . and it also hid the stars who lurked among The Luau's jungles. In an era when there were so few paparazzi in Hollywood that they were all known by first name, The Luau could do an excellent job of keeping them out, creating a safe haven for celebrities within.

And Steve loved it all. He greeted guests nightly in a safari suit, ascot, panama hat, leis—the works. He took to calling himself "High-Talking Chief Stefooma." It was the role of a lifetime.

And it all threatened to come crashing down on April 4, 1958.

Nominated for a Best Actress Oscar for *Peyton Place*, Lana Turner was back on top of Hollywood. She was dating small-time mobster Johnny Stompanato at the time, a man notorious for his quick temper and jealous outbursts. He and Lana fought frequently and with ever-increasing intensity and violence. On the night of April 4, Lana told Johnny she'd had enough

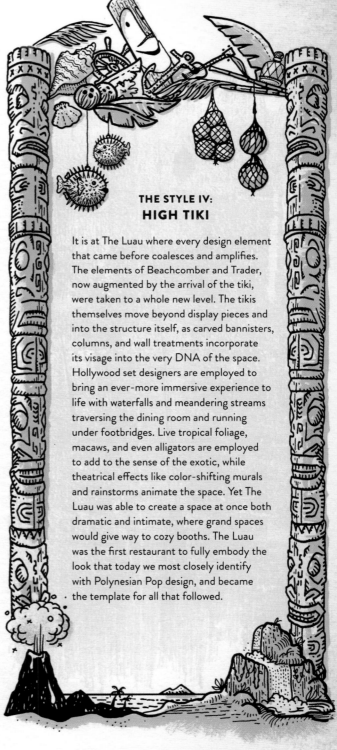

THE STYLE IV:
HIGH TIKI

It is at The Luau where every design element that came before coalesces and amplifies. The elements of Beachcomber and Trader, now augmented by the arrival of the tiki, were taken to a whole new level. The tikis themselves move beyond display pieces and into the structure itself, as carved bannisters, columns, and wall treatments incorporate its visage into the very DNA of the space. Hollywood set designers are employed to bring an ever-more immersive experience to life with waterfalls and meandering streams traversing the dining room and running under footbridges. Live tropical foliage, macaws, and even alligators are employed to add to the sense of the exotic, while theatrical effects like color-shifting murals and rainstorms animate the space. Yet The Luau was able to create a space at once both dramatic and intimate, where grand spaces would give way to cozy booths. The Luau was the first restaurant to fully embody the look that today we most closely identify with Polynesian Pop design, and became the template for all that followed.

and wanted him out of the house. He erupted in anger, hitting Lana and threatening to slash her face to make her unemployable. Lana and Steve's sixteen-year-old daughter, Cheryl, rushed into her mother's room with a knife from the kitchen and stabbed Johnny in the stomach. Lana and Cheryl stared in horror as Johnny died on the bedroom floor. Cheryl's first call was to Steve at The Luau.

The trial became a nationwide media sensation. Days of emotional testimony from Lana ("the performance of her career," noted one wag) ended with a ruling of justifiable homicide. The Luau profited from the notoriety and continued to be a top destination and attract the rich and famous from around the world. One of its biggest fans and regulars was Ernie Henderson, founder of the Sheraton Hotel chain. Both Don the Beachcomber and Trader Vic's had signed arrangements with major hotel chains like Hilton to duplicate their success with franchised outposts, and Ernie wanted the same for Sheraton. The first opened in the Sheraton Mt. Royal Hotel in Montreal in 1959, and was christened the Kon-Tiki, named with permission from Thor Heyerdahl. More Kon-Tiki locations across the United States followed through the 1960s, in addition to Steve's other, even more elaborate concept called Kon-Tiki Ports, whose menu intoned, "Nature has been tamed for this tropic hideaway . . . But spears and pelts remind the diner that the simple life does have its excitements."

While there was continued success into the early 1970s, the tiki fad had begun to slowly fade. In 1978, a business consortium offered Steve $4.1 million for The Luau. Rodeo Drive was no longer the sleepy side street it once was and the value of the land was now tremendous. The entire raison d'être of the Kon-Tiki chain had been to spread the Hollywood glamour of The Luau to the rest of the nation, and Sheraton had a contractual clause that the Kon-Tiki chain would only exist as long as The Luau was in business.

The Kon-Tikis reverted to Sheraton control and quickly began to fade, closing one by one in the exact opposite order they were opened.

Steve was a born host, charmer, and entertainer, and his stage was now gone. The wind left his sails. He moved alone into a hotel suite in Westwood, grabbed a bottle of Scotch, and proceeded to spend the next six years quietly drinking himself to death. He told Cheryl simply, "I never wanted to be an old man." And he got his wish. Steve Crane died on February 6, 1985, one day shy of his sixty-ninth birthday. The hero of Crawfordsville was returned home and buried per his wishes in his hometown. Only seven people attended the service: no one in Crawfordsville remembered the man who had once returned home to a main street parade with a glamorous Hollywood movie star on his arm.

Nothing remains of The Luau or the Kon-Tiki chain, save for a few old menus and pieces of décor that have turned up in estate sales or in new tiki bars. When The Luau was on top of the world, the first table in the bar, "Bar One," was the center of that world—the most sought after table in the film industry, reserved for entertainment writers, Steve himself, and only the biggest stars. Cheryl Crane, today a successful real estate agent and mystery novelist, keeps Bar One in her garage at home, a reminder of when her father and his stunningly realized tiki bars were at the heart of a nationwide sensation.

The Luau, Beverly Hills, California

TIKI'S DECLINE

The fate of The Luau mirrored the fate of most of the tiki palaces, which began to fall by the end of the 1960s. By that time, the boomers had arrived on the scene. What once seemed like charming naiveté about island peoples and cultures, now seemed, to a generation raised in a more globally aware world, to be at best patronizing or inauthentic, and at worst simply racist. Tiki bars, enjoyed by the likes of Richard Nixon, became symbolic of the establishment that the new generation was protesting against. Where at one time the understanding of island cultures was limited by a lack of travel, media exposure, and economic hardship, and was informed instead by Hollywood set designers and saloonkeepers who had never set foot in the South Pacific, the boomer generation knew all too well the realities through the wars raging across Southeast Asia. And besides, it's generational tradition to distance yourself from your parents' interests. To spend a meal being served by a desultory white waiter in a coolie hat in the Saigon Room of Kon-Tiki Ports, and find yourself shipped out the next day to kill people in coolie hats . . . needless to say, the allure was lost.

Where once the mainland tiki bar inspired guests as a dark and mysterious place, resolutely adults only, and a tantalizing glimpse of the exotic dangers of the islands . . . now Hawaii, America's own paradise, had become a sunny destination for the whole family, full of wholesome entertainment and diversions. Somehow, the tiki bar didn't feel special anymore, and certainly not mysterious. The tikis themselves faced a terrible fate. Derided by the beginning of the 1970s as tacky or kitsch, these proud guardians who once watched over the fine dining of their guests found their way to the trash heap, wood chipper, or fire pit—a fate that sadly mirrored that of the Hawaiian people's arts and gods in the hands of the Western missionaries of the previous century. One by one the tikis fell, in the name of progress and "good taste." By the end of the 1970s, the destruction was so thorough, it was almost as if none of it had ever happened—like some kind of mass tropical fever dream had overtaken the populace, and everyone had now awakened.

As the 1970s marched into the 1980s, even the legendary venues began to fall. Don the Beachcomber locations, long since sold by Sunny Sund and subsequently purchased by the Getty Corporation, shuttered, and Vic's empire of outposts began to slowly contract. As a sign of the times, in 1989, Donald Trump, who had recently bought the Plaza Hotel in New York, decided to close the beloved Trader Vic's that had been there since 1965, declaring it "tacky," and that it didn't "fit in with the image of the hotel that I want to achieve." While, tragically, some of the grand palaces of the era were razed, perhaps they were saved the greater indignity that befell many of their colleagues: the remodel. Stripped of their noble bamboo and lauhala matting, and tarted up with white stucco and pink neon, these hollow shells were a special cruelty—a 1980s "Miami"-style version of the tropics. They would be remodeled again and again until there was no one left who remembered what had once stood.

And, beyond the destruction of the look of tiki, there was the equally horrific destruction of the *flavor* of tiki. While the classic cocktail lover could seek solace in a hotel bar program and find a quality drink during the cocktail nadir of the 1970s, for the exotic cocktail lover of the same era, there was nowhere to hide. As the tiki venues shuffled off into the sunset, so too did the great tiki bartenders, often taking their recipes with them. Beyond that, these recipes were written in codes undecipherable to anyone else. It became harder and harder to find new bartenders willing to make a cocktail with eleven carefully measured ingredients. Concurrently, we saw the rise of labor-saving cocktail ingredients like powdered instant sour mix, coconut "snow," synthetic passion fruit, and ever cheaper, flavorless rums. From the standpoint of the operators of the era, there was much money to be saved using these cost cutting ingredients, and there was little call for a Navy Grog outside of a tiki restaurant anyway. So as the grand exotic cocktails faded from the collective memory, and synthetic ingredients began their ascent, the fall was fast and far. Soon, most people's impression of an exotic cocktail was a brightly colored syrupy concoction that was handed to you as you stepped off the plane in Honolulu.

During this time, tiki was subsumed beneath a more blanket tropical aesthetic. Beach bars, margaritas, surf and sand—anything to do with vacation and relaxation came to be the dominant vision of the tropics for most, be it Hawaii, Mexico, or the Caribbean. Simplified boat drinks, the music of Jimmy Buffett, and bare feet on warm beaches emphasized a far more casual approach to island escapism. It certainly had a strong appeal, and its even deeper rejection of the conservative restrictions of the previous generation seemed a potent response to the horrors of Vietnam and fed into the sense that relaxation was a right that had been more than earned. Yet this new tropical vision was (and often continues to be) mislabeled as tiki—whether it be a Gulf Coast "tiki" beach bar with a thatched roof and no tikis, or a "tiki" party with Caribbean food and a salsa band.

The quest for relaxation can take many forms. Some may find paradise in a mountain cabin, some on the open sea. Whatever your pleasure, its lure is powerful. And when paradise is denied, the quest to reclaim it begins. For those of us who long for the very specific mysterious escapism of the Polynesian Pop palaces of days long past, the hunt to uncover its golden age began in earnest a few decades ago, and the resurrection of its "authentically inauthentic" aesthetic began and grew with a passionate fervor.

Outside Tiki Bob's, San Francisco

Jet Pilot

JET PILOT

With the growth of aviation and the space race, tiki bars went from serving Test Pilots to Jet Pilots to Space Pilots to celebrate their daring feats. This 1950s version from The Luau in Beverly Hills will fuel your tanks with citrus, spices, nerves of steel, and a blend of rums. This is basically a reproportioned and tweaked Zombie, but a little roll, pitch, and yaw make this an interesting variation.

ORIGIN *The Luau, 1950s*
SOURCE Beachbum Berry's Sippin' Safari, *adapted by Smuggler's Cove*
GLASSWARE *Double old-fashioned*

- ½ ounce fresh lime juice
- ½ ounce fresh grapefruit juice
- ½ ounce SC Cinnamon Syrup (page 327)
- ½ ounce John D. Taylor's Velvet Falernum
- 1 ounce black blended rum ❺
- ¾ ounce blended aged rum ❸
- ¾ ounce black blended overproof rum ❻
- 1 dash Herbstura (page 228)

GARNISH *None*
Add all the ingredients to a drink mixer tin. Fill with 12 ounces of crushed ice and 4 to 6 small "agitator" cubes. Flash blend and open pour with gated finish into a double old-fashioned glass.

HALEKULANI COCKTAIL

Open the door to paradise with this 1930s treat from the famous House Without a Key on Waikiki Beach.

ORIGIN *House Without a Key lounge, Halekulani Hotel, Waikiki Beach, circa 1930s*
SOURCE Beachbum Berry's Sippin' Safari, *adapted by Smuggler's Cove*
GLASSWARE *Chilled coupe*

- ½ ounce fresh lemon juice
- ½ ounce fresh orange juice
- ½ ounce pineapple juice
- ¼ ounce SC Demerara Syrup (page 324)
- ½ teaspoon SC Grenadine (page 328)
- 1½ ounces bourbon
- 1 dash Angostura bitters

GARNISH *Edible orchid*
Combine all the ingredients in a cocktail shaker with cracked or cubed ice. Shake and double-strain into a chilled coupe and garnish with an edible orchid on the edge of the glass.

SIDEWINDER'S FANG

As it used to be at the legendary Lanai restaurant in San Mateo, California. Beware this serpent's bite!

ORIGIN *Lanai, San Mateo, California, circa 1960s*
SOURCE Beachbum Berry Remixed
GLASSWARE *Large (22-ounce) brandy snifter*

Sidewinder's Fang peel (see page 242)

1½ ounces fresh lime juice

1½ ounces fresh orange juice

1½ ounces SC Passion Fruit Syrup (page 325)

3 ounces seltzer

1 ounce blended aged rum ❸

1 ounce black blended rum ❺

GARNISH *Mint sprig*

Line a snifter with the Sidewinder's Fang peel, with one end hanging over the rim of the glass. Fill glass with cracked or cubed ice to hold the peel in place. Put the remaining ingredients in a drink mixer tin with 12 ounces of crushed ice and 4 to 6 small "agitator" cubes. Flash blend then strain into the snifter. Garnish with a mint sprig.

HAWAIIAN SUNSET

A lost gem from the Aku Aku Polynesian Restaurant, once part of the now-also-lost Stardust Casino in beautiful Las Vegas, featuring a little vodka and a lot of lady luck!

ORIGIN *Aku Aku, circa 1960s*
SOURCE Beachbum Berry's Sippin' Safari, *adapted by Smuggler's Cove*
GLASSWARE *Chilled coupe*

½ ounce fresh lime juice

½ ounce fresh lemon juice

½ ounce SC Orgeat (page 330)

1 teaspoon SC Grenadine (page 328)

1½ ounces vodka

GARNISH *Lime peel*

Add all the ingredients to a cocktail shaker and shake with cracked or cubed ice. Double-strain into a chilled coupe. Garnish with a lime peel.

Sidewinder's Fang

Captain's Grog

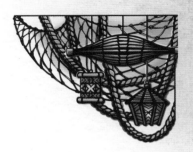

CAPTAIN'S GROG

From the Captain's Inn, Long Beach, California, this hearty blend will help keep you on an even keel.

ORIGIN *Captain's Inn, Long Beach, California, circa 1962*
SOURCE Beachbum Berry Remixed,
adapted by Smuggler's Cove
GLASSWARE *Double old-fashioned*

> ½ ounce fresh lime juice
>
> ½ ounce fresh grapefruit juice
>
> ½ ounce grade A maple syrup
>
> 3 drops pure vanilla extract
>
> 3 drops pure almond extract
>
> 1 ounce seltzer
>
> ½ ounce John D. Taylor's Velvet Falernum
>
> ½ ounce Pierre Ferrand Dry Curaçao
>
> ¾ ounce black blended rum **❺**
>
> ¾ ounce blended lightly aged rum **❷**
>
> ¾ ounce blended aged rum **❸**

GARNISH *Mint sprig*

Add all the ingredients to a drink mixer tin. Fill with 12 ounces of crushed ice and 4 to 6 small "agitator" cubes. Flash blend and open pour with gated finish into a double old-fashioned glass. Add garnish.

NOTE It's easy to batch up a Captain's Mix like we do at Smuggler's Cove: multiply the ingredient quantities of the falernum, curaçao, maple syrup, and vanilla and almond extracts by the number of grogs you plan to serve and combine in a sealable container. Then, substitute 1½ ounces of this Captain's Mix for those ingredients in the recipe.

SUFFERING BASTARD

Created at the Shepheard Hotel in Cairo by legendary globetrotting barman Joe Scialom, this was the drink that fortified Montgomery's boys during the Second World War as they pushed back against Rommel in North Africa.

ORIGIN *Shepheard's Hotel, Cairo, 1942*
SOURCE Beachbum Berry Remixed,
adapted by Smuggler's Cove
GLASSWARE *Collins or highball*

> 4 ounces ginger beer
>
> ½ ounce fresh lime juice
>
> ¼ ounce SC Demerara Syrup (page 324)
>
> 1 ounce London dry gin
>
> 1 ounce brandy
>
> 2 dashes Angostura bitters

GARNISH *Mint sprig and swizzle stick*

Add the ginger beer to a Collins or highball glass, then add the remaining ingredients to a cocktail shaker. Fill with cracked or cubed ice. Shake and strain the contents into the glass and gently fill with cubed or cracked ice and then garnish.

Merciless Virgin

MERCILESS VIRGIN

Frank "Skipper" Kent, owner of San Francisco's Skipper Kent's, quoted *The Rubáiyát of Omar Khayyám* in his description of this drink in an unpublished book of his recipes: "She must be merciless. Ah! Moon of my delight—that knows no wane—The moon of Heaven has risen once again. How oft hereafter rising—shall she look—through this same garden—after me—in vain!"

ORIGIN *Skipper Kent's*
SOURCE *Previously unpublished recipe from the collection of Jacqueline Zumwalt, adapted by Smuggler's Cove*
GLASSWARE *Footed pilsner*

¾ ounce fresh lemon juice

½ ounce seltzer

½ ounce Cherry Heering liqueur

½ ounce John D. Taylor's Velvet Falernum

¼ ounce Pierre Ferrand Dry Curaçao

1 ½ ounces blended lightly aged rum ❷

GARNISH *Maraschino cherries on a cocktail pick*
Add all the ingredients to a drink mixer tin. Fill with 12 ounces of crushed ice and 4 to 6 small "agitator" cubes. Flash blend and open pour with gated finish into a footed pilsner glass. Add garnish.

SATURN

This is a winning combination of gin, lemon, passion fruit, falernum, and orgeat. And don't just take our word for it: J. "Popo" Galsini, as part of the California Bartenders' Guild, won the International Bartender's Association World Championship in 1967 with this beauty. We chose a garnish that represents the rings of Saturn (see photo on page 243).

ORIGIN *Created by J. "Popo" Galsini*
SOURCE Beachbum Berry Remixed, *adapted by Smuggler's Cove*
GLASSWARE *Chilled coupe*

¾ ounce fresh lemon juice

½ ounce SC Passion Fruit Syrup (page 325)

¼ ounce SC Orgeat (page 330)

¼ ounce John D. Taylor's Velvet Falernum

1 ¼ ounce London dry gin

GARNISH *Long spiral-cut lemon peel wrapped into rings*
Add all the ingredients to a cocktail shaker. Fill with cracked ice. Shake and strain into a chilled coupe. Rest garnish on top of the drink.

TIKI BOWL

A Kon-Tiki original, but still very closely related
to any number of drinks in Donn's style. Donn's
signature "secret weapon" was a combination of
honey, Angostura bitters, and Pernod, which features
in many of his cocktails. The "diaspora" of Donn-
style exotic cocktails was spread both by his acolytes
and imitators to venues around the world.

ORIGIN *Kon-Tiki, Portland, Oregon, 1960*
SOURCE Beachbum Berry's Sippin' Safari,
adapted by Smuggler's Cove
GLASSWARE *Small (16- to 20-ounce) scorpion bowl
or other decorative bowl*
SERVES 2

  1½ ounces fresh orange juice

  ¾ ounce fresh lime juice

  1 ounce SC Honey Syrup (page 325)

  1¼ ounce black blended rum ⑤

  1 ounce black blended overproof rum ⑥

  1 ounce column still aged rum ④

  2 dashes Herbstura (page 228)

GARNISH *Edible orchid*

Combine all ingredients in a drink mixer tin. Fill
with 18 ounces crushed ice and 4 to 6 small "agitator"
cubes. Flash blend and open pour with gated finish
into a tiki bowl for two and float garnish in bowl.

HURRICANE

A perfect three-ingredient drink that captures exotic
flavor in the simplest way. Even though Pat O'Brien's
is an Irish-themed bar, this drink became a tiki bar
staple around the world. Much like the Mai Tai, the
Hurricane you will be served today is often bright
red, a far cry from the original.

ORIGIN *Pat O'Briens, New Orleans, circa 1940s*
SOURCE Beachbum Berry Remixed
GLASSWARE *Small (15-ounce) hurricane ("squall") glass*

  2 ounces fresh lemon juice

  2 ounces SC Passion Fruit Syrup (page 325)

  4 ounces black blended rum ⑤

GARNISH *Wind-ravaged cocktail umbrella speared into
a lemon wedge*

Combine all the ingredients in a drink mixer tin.
Fill with 12 ounces of crushed ice and 4 to 6 small
"agitator" cubes. Flash blend and open pour with
gated finish into a hurricane glass. Add garnish.

Hurricane

the Tiki Revival

Ron and Mickee Ferrell's home bar, the Rincon Room

**TRAFFIC MOVES SWIFTLY AT THE BUSY INTERSECTION
OF SIXTY-FIFTH STREET AND SAN PABLO AVENUE IN
OAKLAND, CALIFORNIA.**

Modern apartment buildings look down upon a small dirt lot that sits on
one corner, flanked by an empty, graffiti-covered building. The lot, surrounded
by a cyclone fence, is nondescript and unnoticed by both driver and pedestrian.
Only two palm trees in the sidewalk offer any clue that they once welcomed
guests stepping from their cars into the exotic confines of Trader Vic's original
location.

    Multiply this image hundreds of times over across the United States,
and you start to have a feeling for what little of the once-ubiquitous tiki bars,
restaurants, and other buildings remained after the downfall. When the
champions of good taste declared that Polynesian Pop was déclassé, the purge
was broad and merciless. It seemed so far removed from the shared cultural
memory that even on San Diego's Shelter Island, whose restaurants, hotels,
and shops were designed with Polynesian Pop influence and still stand today,
a signpost on a walking trail has to explain to the passerby why the island looks
as it does. It explains that it was a popular architectural style in the 1950s—as
though you were looking at a museum exhibit of a culture long past.

    Polynesian Pop might have been buried forever—destined only for a
handful of home tiki bars hidden in basements, garages, and rumpus rooms
throughout the country, were it not for a few intrepid souls who began to
uncover the past and begin to rebuild. These "Tiki Revivalists" were mostly
amateur enthusiasts who in the 1980s and 1990s devoted themselves to
researching, diligently documenting, and openly sharing everything they could

Some of Sven Kirsten's exotic ephemera

learn about the bygone era. Through books, zines, and online forums, the Tiki Revivalists helped open the eyes of many in the public and media to the look and feel of Polynesian Pop, and went a long way toward dispelling the notion that it was kitsch. It was because of them that I was able to understand what it was that I had stumbled into on my fateful visit to Trader Vic's in Washington, D.C. It was because of them that I ever tried my hand at making some of the epic libations "as big as my head" in my home bar, or began to attend events and meet other tiki aficionados. Had I not discovered this like-minded band of tiki misfits, you would not be reading these words today.

Explorers around the country would wander into a Goodwill and discover a small angry ceramic face staring back at them from a forlorn and dusty shelf. These were tiki mugs, some of the sole surviving artifacts of the great purge. A popular souvenir from your exotic dining experience, untold thousands of these ceramic idols were sent into the wild, most ending up holding pens on a desk, forgotten in a kitchen, or ultimately set adrift at thrift shops and garage sales. Inspection of the idol would reveal a price tag of twenty-five cents and most intriguingly, a name stamped on the bottom or the back: The Islander. The Luau. Tradewinds. Leilani. Where were these places? In an era before the Internet, trips to the library and old phone books were often the only way to decipher the puzzle. Maybe an old menu or matchbook would turn up in the shuffle, and once a location was pinpointed, a visit might reveal bits and pieces of the desiccated, termite-filled ruins of a former tiki palace hiding behind overgrown landscaping. One of these Tiki Revivalists, Sven Kirsten, would dub these efforts "urban archeology," and encouraged others to join the quest.

And join the quest they did—and continue to do. At first, in the pre-Internet and early Internet days, a lot of it was done in person—at "Tiki Symposiums" held by Kirsten, or tiki art events. Since then, the Internet has allowed the collective knowledge of tiki's past to grow and to be documented. Even today, someone will find an old matchbook and can post a picture online and try to gather information about bars long forgotten. We are able to crowdsource answers to tiki mysteries that otherwise might never have been solved—where was the tiki bar on that matchbook cover? Why was it named that? Does anyone have a menu or a picture of it or know anyone who ever went there? As Kirsten put it to me, he and others start with individual objects and artifacts and, very much like archaeology, piece these individual décor items together to eventually "form a mosaic of the whole place."

For a handful of these explorers, the tiki quest became more than a passing interest. Decoding the secret formulas behind the exotic cocktails became the passion of some, while others studied the art, architecture, and aesthetic. Some discovered the music of the era, or started to curate art shows. These Tiki Revivalists all brought their own pieces to the tiki puzzle, but their most important contribution may have been to bring us all together. The Hawaiian word *ohana* refers to the bond between family or other community, and has come to be an important theme. It was in the truest spirit of ohana that the Tiki Revivalists shared their love and knowledge of Polynesian Pop and encouraged us all to share our stories and pictures and discoveries. The community grew, and the appreciation grew. New exotica bands were formed, and new artists emerged in a variety of media. Others, like myself, were compelled to erect

"People inevitably use the word kitsch or tacky to describe tiki. Still, to this day. It pisses me off. Right away from the first article written about me in 1995 the headline had "tiki tacky" in it. Tiki didn't become kitsch until the 1970s or 1980s, until it was over, then it was looked upon as kitsch in the past, as a retrospective sort of thing. It wasn't kitsch in the 1940s, 50s, 60s. The tiki bar was serious fantasy."

—OTTO VON STROHEIM

new temples dedicated to the iconic drinks from the heyday of tiki, where the drinks could be tasted exactly as intended, and the ethos of the flourishing craft cocktail movement meant new exotic cocktails could be created.

More than just exotic cocktails or a thatched roof, tiki is a lifestyle. No other cocktail craze is surrounded by an entire pop culture movement encompassing art, music, ceramics, carving, fashion, and more. The drinks, while valid and vital on their own, do not exist in a vacuum. Today, the tiki revival in the United States is in full swing, and interest continues to grow at an astounding rate and to draw people from wildly different backgrounds and subcultures. And the reason is simple—it is the same as what drew people to tiki in the first place: a sense of escape, of wonder, of mystery. An affordable journey to a far off place. Because sometimes paradise is much closer than you think.

These are the stories of just some of the people for whom tiki became an all-consuming passion and led them to help further the understanding and appreciation of Polynesian Pop. Through their efforts, and the efforts of many others who played a part in the movement, it will never be lost again.

THE REVIVALISTS

There was an early prereval wave of renewed interest in tiki in the late 1970s and early 1980s among a small group of artists and musicians, including Jeffrey Vallance, Boyd Rice, Michael Uhlenkott, Steve Thomsen, and members of the band Throbbing Gristle, all of whom had grown up during tiki's golden era and been influenced by its imagery and magic. Some traveled to the South Pacific, others only as far as their local thrift stores, but these early tiki-philes certainly paved the way for the larger revival to come. One possible reason this early wave didn't take off in the same way it would later may be that it was simply too soon for a cultural reappraisal—though the tiki heyday was certainly over, and the decline rapidly occurring, a few of the chains and larger temples were still around, and by then people were either derisive or indifferent to the carved idols of the previous generation.

While tiki was starting to bubble up and reemerge in pockets here and there around the country, there were a few events and occurrences that, in hindsight, were watershed moments in the tiki revival, as seen in the tales of three key revivalists: Sven Kirsten, Otto von Stroheim, and Jeff "Beachbum" Berry.

Sven Kirsten

Growing up in Hamburg, Germany, Sven Kirsten had always been an Americanophile, with an interest in American movies and mid-century pop culture. Having studied film in Germany, it was filmmaking that brought Sven ultimately to Los Angeles to further his career, first attending the American Film Institute, and then by finding work as a director and cinematographer on projects here and back in Germany. In the early 1980s, he discovered Sea and Jungle, a patio store that still stocked tiki décor and

where he bought some early tiki artifacts. But on his third visit, he was shocked to discover . . . that the store was gone. It was this first experience of tiki loss that spurred him to dig deeper and learn more, and ultimately led him to the doors of another tropical décor supplier, the legendary Oceanic Arts.

It was there Sven would have his epiphany. Entering the then sleepy store in 1989, co-owner and carver Leroy Schmaltz was excited that someone was so enthusiastic, and showed him around. But for Sven, the key experience was when Leroy brought out a stack of menus from underneath the counter. "The graphic art on these menus just blew me away. The menus are like the album cover art of tiki to me. They are the ultimate canvas for the graphic tiki artist to practice the art and language . . . . I said to myself, someone should do a book about this." And a seed was planted.

Inspired, Sven began to explore LA in search of tiki places, like tiki-themed apartments or "villages," and photographing what he found. It was through his late friend Bruce Elliot, a member of the Cacophony Society, that he met with others who shared his interest to discuss what they thought tiki was, and it was then that Sven realized the wealth of material and knowledge he had already accumulated. But a 1992 proposal for what would become *The Book of Tiki* drew little interest from publishers.

It would ultimately take eight years for *The Book of Tiki* to find a home. However, that ended up being a blessing in disguise because Sven never stopped collecting ephemera or photographing now-lost locations. Sven began to give slide-show lectures on his tiki discoveries, first in 1992 at the LA Forum for Architecture and Urban Design, and then at monthly symposiums he hosted around town. In the early

Sven Kirsten and Sadie

nineties, Sven continued to meet other like-minded enthusiasts, including Jeff Berry, Otto von Stroheim, and tiki-inspired artists Bosko Hrnjak and Mark Ryden, both of whom had been collecting tiki and creating tiki art since the mid-1980s—Bosko who had resuscitated the nearly dead art form of carving tikis and masks, and Mark Ryden through his striking paintings, including the now-famous "Exotica."

In 1994, Sven wrote his first article for an art magazine in which he coined a phrase that beautifully captured a culture and an era: "Polynesian Pop." In 1995, he began to collaborate on Otto von Stroheim's tiki zine, *Tiki News*, writing articles that would become some of the content of *The Book of Tiki*. As Otto began to throw tiki events and art shows, Sven would be the resident historian, providing cultural context alongside the music, art, and cocktails.

In 1996, Sven contributed pieces to an exhibit for the Anaheim Museum titled "Tiki: Native Drums in the Orange Grove." Cocurated by Disney designers Kevin Kidney and Jody Daily, the exhibit is considered one of the watershed moments in the tiki revival, as it was the first museum exhibit about tiki culture from a historical perspective. The show focused on Southern California tiki, but had other general tiki artifacts for context and, of course, being centered in Anaheim, also included an entire display of rare Disney tiki ephemera. A new 1996 BBC tiki documentary, *Air Conditioned Eden*, played on a loop at the exhibit, featuring interviews with Sven, James Michener, and Martin Denny, among others.

The importance of Sven's work cannot be overstated. *The Book of Tiki* is not just a collection of photographs and artifacts. It draws from history, archaeology, and cultural anthropology to create for the first time an understanding of what this movement was, how it came to be, and what was so unique about it: "To me, what is so interesting about the whole subject is the use of the tiki. Everything else

is in addition to it, and necessary, and is great fun, but what is unique about it is that Americans used this pagan figure in all sorts of forms at home or for leisure. That an idol was picked from another country and recreated and used as a symbol here aesthetically and from an art perspective, that had never been done." The culmination of Sven's work came in 2014 when the largest ethnographic museum in Europe, the Musée du quai Branly in Paris, invited him to curate an exhibit of the history of Polynesian Pop called "Tiki Pop." Over one hundred thousand people visited the show, making it one of the most successful in the museum's history.

Otto von Stroheim

Like many others, graphic artist Otto von Stroheim came to tiki by way of the LA punk scene. This may seem like a strange path, but for Otto, it made perfect sense. First, many punk rockers were into industrial music, and so bands like Throbbing Gristle who incorporated elements of exotica at performances offered them their first exposure to the genre. Then, as Otto explains, in the mid-to-late 1980s, punk was becoming very mainstream and generic, and those who had been drawn to it when it was counterculture had now lost interest. LA area punks were looking for something new that could fit their need for counterculture. As Otto put it, "What was the antithesis to punk? Wearing a suit."

Alongside the renewed interest in cocktail bars and cocktail culture in the late 1980s and 1990s was a renewed interest in the sounds that accompanied those cocktails (now generally referred to as "lounge" music), including singers of pop standards like Frank Sinatra and Bobby Darin, space age pop like Esquivel, and the exotica sounds of Denny, Lyman, and others. And so, many ex-punks, including Otto, started to gravitate to the lounge renaissance that

Baby Doe and Otto von Stroheim

was happening in Los Angeles. DJs, record collectors, and new bands, such as Combustible Edison, brought renewed recognition to the exotica and wider lounge genre. Long out-of-print albums were reissued and once again enjoyed, fueled by radio shows like the Molotov Cocktail Hour on KXLU, Joey Cheezhee's performances at Kelbo's, and Stuart Swezey's release of Rhino's *The Best of Martin Denny* in 1990. Punk had also brought its followers into thrift stores for used clothes and obscure records, which brought them in contact with lounge and exotica albums and ultimately tiki ephemera.

In 1987, Otto's roommate Ivan had suggested they throw a backyard tiki party, and so Otto went out and found bamboo bowls, trays, and Hawaiian records at thrift stores, and his tiki-collecting days began. The parties became annual shindigs that grew in popularity, and attracted other like-minded souls, and through these parties and other gatherings, Otto met author and preservationist Pete Moruzzi, Sven Kirsten, Mark Ryden, and Bosko Hrnjak. Otto was also developing a growing obsession with vintage tiki mugs, and looked to connect with other collectors. Having been heavily involved in the bootleg tape scene in punk, he had already developed a newsletter and mailing list for tape trading with people all over the world. Through this experience, he had the idea to build a similar community for tiki, realizing that,

> *"OK, so it's not a cure for cancer, an economically feasible form of alternative energy, or a diplomatic solution to political tensions between emerging nuclear powers—but if we can get you pleasantly potted enough to stop worrying about all those things for a moment or an hour or an evening, then we have made some small contribution to the betterment (or at least refreshment) of society."*
>
> —JEFF BERRY, *BEACHBUM BERRY'S INTOXICA!*

"in all these cities where there've been big tiki bars, there must be at least one guy like me, and I gotta figure out how to connect the dots with these people."

And so, in January of 1995, the *Tiki News* zine was born. The first issue included a tiki manifesto, containing several edicts, including "It is our mission to preserve any and all remaining elements from the Polynesian Pop era of the mid-1930s to the mid-1970s," and "We intend to create a forum for sharing current and past information regarding any sort of tiki culture. All information will be dispersed in an effort to promote growth of current tiki culture." From day one, Otto made *Tiki News* an inclusive and collaborative effort. As he met tiki artists, he solicited their work. He asked Sven to contribute articles on tiki history. Others would write bar reviews or music reviews. The subscriber list quickly grew to hundreds of people, and became a natural forum to organize people around causes and plan events.

And it was in planning tiki events that Otto really found his niche. In 1994, he threw his first tiki mug party, aimed at beginning to document mugs for a hoped-for book project. He also began to hold release parties for *Tiki News*, featuring the works of artists appearing on the covers of the issues, one of which was SHAG's first one-man show. In 1995, Otto and two partners also threw a sold-out LA lounge culture event at the Park Plaza Hotel, called Exoticon, featuring performances by Combustible Edison and the Phantom Surfers. The next year, Otto cocurated the first contemporary tiki art show, "20th Century Tiki," at La Luz de Jesus Gallery in Los Angeles that featured Mark Ryden, SHAG, Bosko, and others.

Otto met his future wife and coconspirator, Baby Doe, in San Francisco in 1995, and moved there in 1996, where they began producing tiki events. In 2000, Otto had the honor of planning the farewell party for the beloved Kahiki Supper Club in Columbus, Ohio, one of the last remaining large-scale tiki temples, destined ultimately to be turned into a drug store. In 2001, a rumor grew of a similar impending demise of the tiki-themed Caliente Tropics motor lodge in Palm Springs, and Otto, with his event-planning experience and growing *Tiki News* mailing list, was recruited by Pete Moruzzi to help organize an event to raise awareness about the hotel, and fill their otherwise vacant rooms during their offseason. The "Save the Tropics" event not only saved the hotel, but became such a hit that it is now produced annually by Otto and Baby Doe as Tiki Oasis, and has grown to be the largest tiki event in the country.

Jeff "Beachbum" Berry

Before the release of Jeff's books, I would sip on my Mai Tai at Trader Vic's and pour over the flowery prose on the back of the menu. It details the rum and cocktail exploits of Vic as he travels around the world meeting bartenders who he would liberally borrow from. Among the small illustrations is one of a man sitting on a beach in cutoff pants labeled "Don the Beachcomber." For years, my understanding of Donn remained limited to this sketch. I thought, "Why is Vic thanking this hobo? Who was this guy?" While Jeff "Beachbum" Berry is credited with unearthing many lost libations, it is perhaps his greatest legacy that he brought Donn out of the shadows and into not just the tiki spotlight, but into the cocktail spotlight, restoring Donn to his rightful place as the father of exotic cocktails.

A child of 1960s Los Angeles, Jeff was enchanted by tiki at a young age when his parents took him to Ah Fong's on Ventura Boulevard. It had started life as the Bora Bora Room, and was still decorated with a canoe, waterfall, lagoon, dawn-to-dusk lighting, and a miniature island. As Jeff says, "That's what did it. I was into it ever since." Later, as a film student and young copywriter, he couldn't afford much, but did discover the small but legendary neighborhood bar Tiki-Ti, run by an ex-Don the Beachcomber bartender and had his first "real, true tiki drink" there—probably a Ray's Mistake. Much to his regret, he only ever ate lunch at the Don the Beachcomber, despite being able to literally see it from his apartment window, and could only afford the occasional drink at Trader Vic's.

As his film and advertising career grew, Jeff began to have more disposable income and could finally afford to travel, first to Hawaii, then Easter Island and Tahiti. While in Easter Island, he filmed part of his hilarious short film, *The Secret of Easter Island*. He became a Tiki-Ti habitué, went to Trader Vic's more often, and began the habit of opening a phone book in any new town he ventured to looking for Polynesian or tiki restaurants. In 1991,

Jeff "Beachbum" Berry

he began dating his now wife and partner-in-crime, Annene Kaye, and through a friend of hers was introduced to Sven Kirsten. Even though they were both in the film industry, according to Jeff, "Sven never wanted to talk about films. He was completely overtaken by tiki. As I recall, to my eye, he was obsessed in a way that even I wasn't obsessed. And I had already gone to Easter Island to make a movie about it! But it rubbed off on me. If I wasn't as obsessed as he was then, I certainly got that way after hanging out with him for a while."

At this point, Jeff was into all aspects of tiki. The drinks didn't stand out as a special focus, and it never occurred to him to try to make them himself. For him, "more than the drinks, I sought out the places to drink them in. Because nine times out of ten you were going to have a shitty drink. But, if you got lucky, you were in an atmosphere that you liked so much that it just didn't matter. You just ordered a drink. You were basically buying a seat at the table— you were renting a space for a while."

Visiting the magnificent Mai Kai in Fort Lauderdale, Florida, for the first time changed all that. As he says, it was "the ultimate Holy Shit moment." Not only did the place look amazing, but the drinks tasted great, and were still being served in the old glassware from the menu illustrations, garnished with ice cones and shells. Jeff took notes about the flavors he experienced, especially those he had never tasted in a tropical drink, such as coffee in the Black Magic and the Mutiny. He returned to Los Angeles and found a few of the old golden era bartenders, like Dennis Kwan, still making Navy Grogs at the Sampan, and Tony Ramos who "was making straight down the line, unaltered Don the Beachcomber drinks" at Madame Wu's. According to Jeff, "I just started to wonder whether I could experience those tastes from the Mai Kai without traveling three thousand miles to Florida, or chasing down all

these places that were all starting to go out of business." It was his wife, Annene, a former bartender, who was able to parse flavors and reverse engineer what they'd tasted at the Mai Kai, and taught him some tricks of the trade. He dug deeper into the *Trader Vic's Bartender's Guide*, at that point virtually the only book with exotic cocktail recipes from the era, and began to better understand the ingredients and explore the rums.

Jeff quickly learned that getting other recipes from the era was not going to be easy. The first bartender he approached for a recipe was Ray Buhen, owner of the Tiki-Ti, whom he tried to interview. He asked him what was in the Zombie and a few other drinks and was repeatedly given the gruff reply of "rum and fruit juice!" Through Sven, Jeff met Ted Haigh, a cocktail historian. Together they began to drink in old bars and tried to coax bartenders to share their secrets, with a bit more success. Jeff also studied the bartenders closely, which is how he discovered a key ingredient in the Navy Grog—watching Dennis Kwan heat honey to add to the cocktail. Ted introduced him to a wealth of old cocktail books, which sometimes shed light on obscure ingredients, and together they would seek out dusty old spirits in liquor stores, including many old rums.

Jeff was making cocktails at Otto's backyard parties and other events, and it was Otto who encouraged him in 1994 to put together a recipe booklet. Jeff typed out the recipes, used art from his collection of matchbooks, napkins, menus, and postcards for illustration, then handed them out at that year's party. The next year Otto helped him put together a more deluxe version with a color cover, which Jeff sold through *Tiki News*, and at a few LA spots. One of the copies made its way north to publisher Slave Labor Graphics in San Jose, who released *Beachbum Berry's Grog Log* in 1997. Besides *Mr. Boston*, there were few cocktail books coming out at the time, but

*"Nowadays—through Internet, television, and documentaries—
we've become very aware that paradise on earth does not exist.
Even these South Seas islands have their own complex problems and
set of rules and were not as idyllic as the Western World wanted
them to be. But the human being created this illusion because
it has an innate need to believe in paradise on Earth."*

—SVEN KIRSTEN

it was never something Jeff had set out to do. He just saw it as his hobby, saying "I was collecting tiki mugs, tiki shirts, tiki records, and tiki recipes."

Because these recipes weren't usually in books or magazines, Jeff's main source for recipes continued to be conversations with old bartenders, and in the course of his research for the *Grog Log*, and his next book, *Intoxica!*, Jeff had to decipher endless bartender scribbles and shorthand. This ability would be put to the ultimate test when Jennifer Santiago, daughter of former Don the Beachcomber bartender Dick Santiago, gave Dick's 1937 notebook to Jeff. As he recalls it, "I had the Ark of the Covenant in my hands. She gave me a Xeroxed copy of Dick Santiago's Beachcomber recipes. " What many people don't understand or appreciate is that Jeff didn't just reprint these recipes, or find others in an old book or from an Internet search. Having Santiago's notebook was only half the battle. He then had to spend years figuring out and cracking Donn's secret codes listed within. What was Donn's Mix? Spices #4? It wasn't just the Zombie that had to be decoded—there were scores of drinks that he spent years figuring out how to make, interviewing people in order to crack parts of the code, figuring out pieces of the puzzle, testing and retesting.

Since 1998, I've had a growing stack of Jeff's books—well-worn and filled with scribbled notes,

earmarked pages, and a rainbow of cocktail stains—first in my home bars, then in my commercial bars that followed. And in craft cocktail bars of all stripes and on all continents, the fruits of Jeff's research are now being applied to delicious effect—earning him a rightful place among the most respected of cocktail historians. And just as the name "Beachbum Berry" sits at the top of each of his books, it now sits atop a restaurant sign in New Orleans, where since 2014, Jeff and Annene have been welcoming thirsty visitors to their own tiki temple, Latitude 29.

THE EVENTS

Guided by passion, the tiki faithful began to gather in ever-larger numbers in pockets around the country. Maybe the event was held in a plain hotel function room where the exotic atmosphere is created primarily by the good vibes of the guests, or maybe it was held in one of the few surviving tiki bars of the golden era. Events began in fits and starts in the 1990s, and began to coalesce into experiences that would ultimately draw guests from around the world.

The first event I attended outside of someone's home was called Planet Tiki: Bongos by the Bay, produced in 1999 in San Francisco by Otto von Stroheim. It was a lively event and featured a performance from future tiki music mainstays Ape, but well attended though it was, it drew a crowd of mostly locals with many interests and didn't feel especially "tiki." As tiki events grew larger, however, they became more of a destination experience; there's a noticeable change in the energy when attendees are drawn from far and wide . . . and when there's a hotel involved. Attending a large tiki event for the first time can be a feast for the senses. You may enter through a parking lot filled with vintage cars, both meticulously restored and outrageously modified, manned by their owners and enthusiasts sharing tips and tales of automotive exploits. Once inside, pinup models languorously drape themselves across carved idols to the delight of photographers while the rhythmic sounds of chisel and hammer indicate the nearby creation of new idols. Two cocktailians may be overheard debating the finer points of Jamaican rums as well-dressed tiki-philes bob their heads along with the exotica-spinning DJ flipping through the vintage vinyl offered by a variety of vendors.

To be sure, there are traits that conferences of all sorts have in common: registering for your credentials, attending seminars, receptions, and a chance to reconnect with old friends and colleagues who you may see only once a year. Yet, at an event dedicated to a mid-century vision of relaxation, you're bound to find a little bit of dancing, a whole lot of smiles, and a remarkable amount of cocktails. The ubiquity of tiki imagery in the 1950s meant that people didn't congregate to celebrate it during its heyday—popular culture was well saturated. It would be like a convention of Starbucks enthusiasts today. But today's events collect a like-minded cadre of Polynesian Pop fanatics whose passion may be the drinks, the art, the music, or all of the above. Or they may be lovers of Americana, burlesque, lowbrow art, surf, Hawaiiana, or many other subcultures who've heard the tiki calling and are lured to these celebrations of leisure. And they remind us that our love of Polynesian Pop will not be lost as long as there are enough of us to keep it alive and thriving.

Tiki Oasis

Started in 2001 by Otto and Baby Doe von Stroheim, Tiki Oasis has grown from just a few hundred attendees to over three thousand annually, with a changing theme that lures fans of adjacent subcultures like surf and rockabilly to join their tiki brethren. Begun in Palm Springs at the vintage tiki-themed Caliente Tropics hotel, Tiki Oasis moved to the also-tiki-themed Hanalei (now Crowne Plaza) Hotel in San Diego in 2006. Initially with just one or two seminars, it now has several per day, on everything from cocktails to tiki architecture. Dozens of vendors fill rooms across the hotel property. Since my first Oasis in 2002, it's been a joy to attend and watch it grow, while seeing old friends and meeting new enthusiasts. Starting in 2008, I've given the annual keynote seminars on exotic cocktails and rum to large, enthusiastic, and well-informed audiences who have also very kindly tolerated my questionable acting along the way.

CABANA CREW
STRUT AND PHOTOS!

MATCHING
CABANA SET
PHOTO
SHOOT!

SUIT UP &
GET DOWN!

PHOTOGRAPHERS
WANTED TOO!
JOIN US!

PLACE: STARTING BY THE POOL
TIME: 10AM SATURDAY

www.facebook.com/drewgroove

The Hukilau

Started in 2002 in Atlanta, The Hukilau is a perfect example of the way that Tiki Central (see page 90) and the Internet brought tikiphiles together. Christie "Tiki Kiliki" White, Tim "Swanky" Glazner, and Ford Vox were all Tiki Central members who noticed a dire lack of events in the Southeast when compared with the West Coast and were inspired. White and Glazner went on to co-found and organize the first Hukilau event, held at the Atlanta Trader Vic's in 2002. Named for a traditional annual feast held in Hawaiian fishing villages that brings the community together, The Hukilau is, in the words of the organizers, "a metaphorical net thrown out to the entire world, bringing the lovers of 'Polynesian Pop' or 'Tiki'

culture together for our own special celebration." It was a great success from the start, and they were encouraged by several Floridian attendees to move the event to Fort Lauderdale so that it could be centered around the historic Mai Kai Restaurant, where it remains to this day. Like Oasis, it has grown to thousands of attendees, and is now a four-day event full of vendors, seminars, bands, cocktail events, and, as the main event, a night in the Mai Kai with hundreds of tiki fanatics all dressed in their finest aloha wear—a spectacular sight. Being among the old bones of the last great tiki palace while it's filled with those who cherish it is an annual ritual to be savored, and one that you hope will last for decades to come.

Christie "Tiki Kiliki" White

Tiki Kon

In 2003, the Northwest Tiki Crawl appeared in the wilds of Portland, Oregon, with a different approach—rather than conference, bar tour, or pilgrimage to a temple, the crawl sought to find the magic hiding in the garages, basements, and backyards of the faithful. The Crawl's daylong home tiki bar tour introduced many denizens of the Rose City to each other by allowing them to open their doors as hosts, share design and construction notes, and offer a ceremonial toast or two. Since then, the event has grown to be a full three-day weekend now renamed Tiki Kon with vending, live music, cocktail competitions, and more, but its heart still lies in the amazing mid-century homes and the tiki temples within them that are lovingly restored, maintained, and celebrated with a bus tour on the third day of the event.

ANCIENT GODS OF DIAL-UP

The denizens of the tiki nation were rising in numbers around the world in isolated pockets, but in the 1990s, there was little in the way of online resources to connect these distant archipelagos. The first tiki-themed website arrived in 1995 with the Tiki Bar Review Pages, created by touring sound engineer James Teitelbaum, which chronicled his tiki bar visits around the world. It was a valuable resource, but what was still needed was a community.

In 1999, a game developer named Hanford Lemoore was, like many, entranced by the lure of the tiki, but unsure how to connect with like-minded others. In a chat room on Yahoo that year, he started to talk about tiki mugs with another tiki-phile named Jennifer Thompson. In January of 2000, they launched a Yahoo Club called Tiki Central, and immediately attracted the interest of devotees new and old. In 2002, it broke out to its own domain and message board and the user base exploded. Tiki Central expanded into all areas of Polynesian Pop culture, becoming a hub for event planning, buying and selling art and merchandise, sharing details about historic tiki venues, music, art, cocktails, and much more.

Lifelong friendships and relationships have been formed at Tiki Central. Unlike some Internet forums—which provide great information, but perhaps don't necessarily inspire an urge to meet other members—Tiki Central brought together people who, in many cases, shared a mutual love of cocktails and tiki bars, and tended to be pretty social from the get-go. This helped make Tiki Central the means of spreading the word about some of the events that have become pillars of the tiki revival like The Hukilau.

Tiki Central was soon joined by other online resources. In 2002, tiki enthusiast Humuhumu Trott began developing Critiki, which documents images and information on over eight hundred tiki locations around the world, and encourages user reviews of drink quality, music, service, mood, and tikiness, as well as user-contributed photos. Three years later, she launched Ooga-Mooga for the tiki mug collector and enthusiast, allowing users to display and catalogue their collections and share and trade with others. Both sites remain vital databases today.

Fifteen years later, Tiki Central is still an active home to over sixteen thousand users who have contributed nearly 750,000 posts, and remains an invaluable database of historic images and information. Its now gracefully dated interface gives it a certain charm; just like a tiki bar in the modern concrete jungle, it's an anachronism in a world of sleek web 2.0 design. Yet its flickering "OPEN 24 HOURS" logo keeps beckoning to those who wish to form a connection and share a virtual cocktail with anyone on Earth.

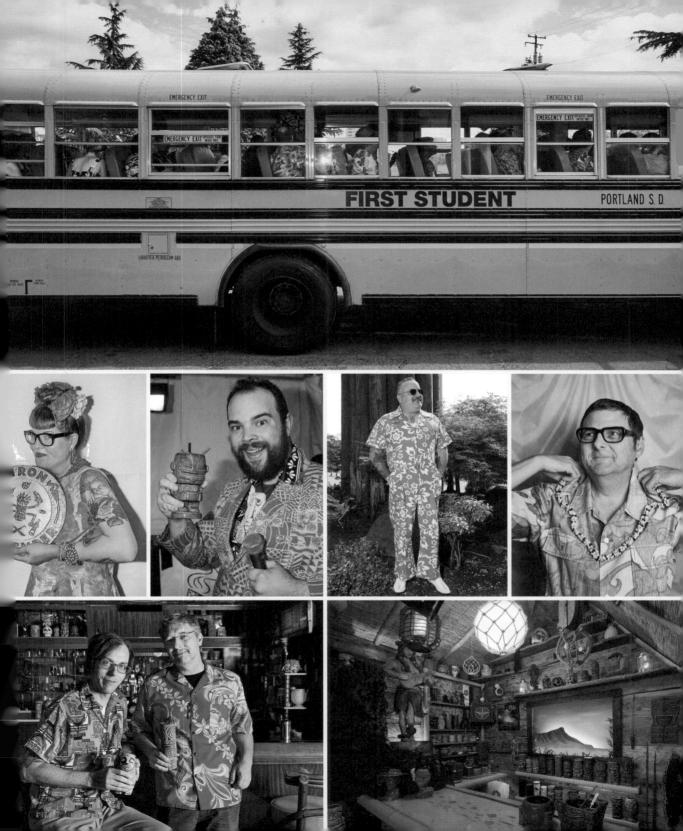

Formidable Dragon

MUNDO PERDIDO

ORIGIN *Created exclusively for Smuggler's Cove by Jeff "Beachbum" Berry, 2009*
GLASSWARE *Chilled coupe*

- ¾ ounce fresh lemon juice
- ¼ ounce SC Cinnamon Syrup (page 327)
- ¼ ounce SC Demerara Syrup (page 324)
- ½ ounce apple brandy
- 1½ ounces black blended rum **5**

GARNISH *None*

Combine all the ingredients in a cocktail shaker with cracked or cubed ice. Shake and double-strain into a chilled coupe.

FORMIDABLE DRAGON

Named for Admiral Vernon's description of drunkenness as "that formidable dragon" in 1740, this concoction was first served at the Tiki Tower Takeover at The Hukilau, 2015.

ORIGIN *Created by Martin Cate*
GLASSWARE *Large (22-ounce) brandy snifter*

- ¾ ounce fresh lemon juice
- ¾ ounce fresh lime juice
- ½ ounce SC Honey Syrup (page 325)
- ¾ ounce SC Molasses Syrup (page 327)
- ½ ounce Amaro Di Angostura
- 1½ ounces blended aged rum **3**
- 1 ounce black blended rum **5**
- ¼ ounce pot still lightly aged rum (overproof) **1**
- 1 ounce seltzer

GARNISH *Edible orchid, multiple mint sprigs, and a swizzle stick*

Add all the ingredients to a drink mixer tin filled with 18 ounces crushed ice and 4 to 6 small "agitator" cubes. Flash blend and open pour with gated finish into a snifter and add garnish.

LEI LANI VOLCANO 2.0 (A.K.A. LEI LANI NOUVEAU)

Created for the Walt Disney Family Museum Tiki Oasis Party, 2013, this updated recipe uses coconut cream and a blended aged rum in place of coconut rum, and uses a guava soda in place of guava nectar for more sparkle.

ORIGIN *Smuggler's Cove original inspired by the Lei Lani Volcano from Walt Disney World, circa 1970s*
SOURCE *Original Lei Lani Volcano was published in* Beachbum Berry Remixed
GLASSWARE *Collins or highball*

- 3 ounces Bundaberg Guava soda
- 1½ ounces pineapple juice
- ¾ ounce lime juice
- 1 ounce SC Coconut Cream (page 328)
- 1½ ounces blended aged rum ❸

GARNISH *Edible orchid*

Add the guava soda to a Collins or highball glass, then add the remaining ingredients to a cocktail shaker and fill with cracked or cubed ice. Shake and double-strain into a Collins or highball glass. Gently add cracked or cubed ice to the glass and then garnish.

TRADEWINDS

If the wind is right, you can sail away and find tranquility with this Jamaican drink from the 1970s.

ORIGIN *Circa 1970s*
SOURCE Beachbum Berry Remixed, *adapted by Smuggler's Cove*
GLASSWARE *Zombie*

- 1 ounce fresh lemon juice
- 1½ ounces SC Coconut Cream (page 328)
- 1 ounce natural apricot liqueur (such as Rothman & Winter Apricot Liqueur or Giffard Abricot du Roussillon)
- 1 ounce black blended rum ❺
- 1 ounce blended lightly aged rum ❷

GARNISH *Lemon wedge speared with a cocktail umbrella turned inside out (as if the wind has gently blown it open)*

Add all the ingredients to a drink mixer tin and fill with 12 ounces of crushed ice and 4 to 6 small "agitator" cubes. Flash blend and open pour with gated finish into a footed pilsner glass. Add garnish.

NOTE For a tasty twist, substitute 2 ounces of London dry gin for the rums.

Tradewinds

PEACHTREE PUNCH 2.0

A modern twist on a Trader Vic's drink from the 1970s incorporating coconut cream, lemon, and seltzer. The original Peachtree Punch was created for the opening of Trader Vic's, Atlanta, hence the celebration of the peach!

ORIGIN *Smuggler's Cove original inspired by the Trader Vic's Peachtree Punch*

SOURCE *The Peachtree Punch was originally published in* Trader Vic's Tiki Party!

GLASSWARE *Double old-fashioned*

> ½ fresh yellow or white peach, pitted, and coarsely chopped into chunks (with skin)
>
> 3 ounces fresh orange juice
>
> ½ ounce fresh lemon juice
>
> 1 ounce SC Coconut Cream (page 328)
>
> ¼ ounce natural peach liqueur (such as Mathilde Peach or Combier Crème de Pêche de Vigne)
>
> 2 ounces blended lightly aged rum ❷
>
> 1 ounce seltzer

GARNISH *Grated nutmeg and peach wedge*

Add the peach chunks, orange juice, and lemon juice to drink mixer tin and muddle the peach. Add the remaining ingredients. Fill with 12 ounces of crushed ice and 4 to 6 small "agitator" cubes. Flash blend and double-strain into a double old-fashioned glass filled with cracked or cubed ice. Garnish with grated nutmeg and a peach wedge on the rim of the glass.

JUNGLE BIRD

A drink from the post-tiki era that has found great popularity coast to coast in saloons of all stripes.

ORIGIN *Kuala Lumpur Hilton, circa 1978*

SOURCE Beachbum Berry Remixed, *adapted by Smuggler's Cove*

GLASSWARE *Collins or highball*

> 2 ounces pineapple juice
>
> ½ ounce fresh lime juice
>
> ½ ounce SC Demerara Syrup (page 324)
>
> ¾ ounce Campari
>
> 1½ ounces black blended rum ❺

GARNISH *Pineapple fronds*

Add all the ingredients to a drink mixer tin. Fill with 12 ounces of crushed ice and 4 to 6 small "agitator" cubes. Flash blend and open pour with gated finish into a Collins or highball glass and add garnish.

GOLDEN GUN

At Tiki Oasis 2012, I taught a seminar about how to structure an exotic cocktail. Attendees were provided with a bunch of exotic cocktail ingredients and challenged to come up with a cocktail. Table Eleven was the winner with this beauty!

GLASSWARE *Collins or highball*

- ¾ ounce fresh lime juice
- ½ ounce fresh grapefruit juice
- ½ ounce SC Demerara Syrup (page 324)
- ½ ounce natural apricot liqueur (such as Rothman & Winter Apricot Liqueur or Giffard Abricot du Roussillon)
- 1 ounce blended aged rum ❸
- 1 ounce blended lightly aged rum ❷
- 2 dashes Angostura bitters

GARNISH *Participants didn't have any garnish at their table, so garnish as you see fit!*

Fill a Collins or highball glass with cracked or cubed ice. Add all the ingredients to a cocktail shaker filled with cracked or cubed ice. Shake and strain into the Collins or highball glass. Your choice of garnish.

HINKY DINKS FIZZY

Created by Trader Vic's for their fiftieth anniversary, this old favorite is rarely seen, but shows that great mixology can transcend even the 1980s.

ORIGIN *Trader Vic's, 1984*

GLASSWARE *Large (22-ounce) brandy snifter*

- 2 ounces sparkling wine
- 1½ ounces pineapple juice
- ½ ounce fresh lime juice
- ½ ounce SC Passion Fruit Syrup (page 325)
- ½ ounce natural apricot liqueur (such as Rothman & Winter Apricot Liqueur or Giffard Abricot du Roussillon)
- 1 ounce London dry gin
- 1 ounce blended lightly aged rum ❷

GARNISH *Mint sprig*

Pour the sparkling wine into a snifter. Add the remaining ingredients to a drink mixer tin. Fill the tin with 12 ounces of crushed ice and 4 to 6 small "agitator" cubes. Flash blend and open pour with gated finish into the snifter. Garnish with a mint sprig.

PART TWO
SMUGGLER'S COVE:
THE MODERN TIKI BAR

"The feeling we try for is this: we make no effort to lure you in. If you want us, you have to hunt us up. We wouldn't have a neon sign outside as a gift. But once you're here, we break our necks to see to it that you're satisfied."

—BUD BACHTOLD, VICE PRESIDENT OF THE BEACHCOMBER CORPORATION, 1948

Creating the Space

The (in)famous anchor at Smuggler's Cove

I RETURNED FROM MY VISIT TO TRADER VIC'S
WASHINGTON, D.C. A CHANGED MAN. MOVING TO
SAN FRANCISCO IN 1996 TO WORK IN THE EXPORT
SHIPPING INDUSTRY PAID THE BILLS BUT DID NOT
SATISFY MY NEED FOR A CREATIVE OUTLET.

I'd visit the historic Tonga Room in the Fairmont Hotel, a forgotten realm in
the bottom of a stately hotel that rekindled my primal urge for escapism, with
its periodic indoor rainstorms and floating bandstand, as well as a scrappy
neighborhood bar down the street from where I was living called Trad'r Sam,
one of the last remaining pre-tiki (see page 26) bamboo bars in the world, both
of which continued to feed my interest in tiki. In 1999, my then-girlfriend (now
my wife), Rebecca, and I decided it might be fun to host a tiki-themed party
at our apartment. Armed with a limited budget, plenty of plastic tablecloths,
Home Depot ferns, and a lava lamp, we managed to create an incredibly
poor "Jungle Room," "Volcano Room," and "Bamboo Bar." My mother served
fried rice in Chinese take-out boxes, while I feebly attempted to make eleven-
ingredient cocktails on the fly, relying heavily on *Beachbum Berry's Grog Log*.
Our guests were patient and forgiving. When we awoke the next day, sitting
among the detritus and leftover rum, we looked around and I thought aloud,
"What are we going to do with all of this crap?"

Rebecca said simply, in a sentence that would unknowingly change the
direction of our lives: "Well, we could put it all in the spare bedroom and make
it a home tiki bar." I rose slowly from the couch, my eyes wide as the gears
began spinning furiously in my mind. "No, no—I was only joking!" she cried,
futilely. "Too late," I replied, my thoughts already drifting to the construction
phase as I wandered into that room. On that day, our humble little home tiki
bar was born. Christened "The Foggy Grotto," it would host many friends over
the next few years.

The lure of the tiki grew more powerful with each passing year. Spending many long and lonely days on the road as an outside sales rep for accounts throughout the Central Valley of California, I'd find myself drifting into antique malls and thrift stores to scour the shelves for old mugs, menus, and other bits of exotic ephemera. Lunches and evenings were spent entertaining clients who looked at me both kindly and quizzically, as I would ramble on about the latest Orchids of Hawaii tiki mug I had unearthed that day. A voice inside was trying to tell me something. But it would be a while longer before I listened.

In 2001, with Tiki Central starting its rise, Hanford Lemoore organized an event to bring the members of Tiki Central together in the real world for the first official event, the San Francisco Tiki Bar Crawl. It began simply with a one-night affair at three or four tiki bars, but for many of us, it was the first time we were able to share drinks and get to know each other. I met many people at the Tiki Crawl who would become longtime friends, and was inspired to start contributing to planning the event. With my passion for excess, I had soon added giant buses, gift bags, and multiple destinations across the Bay Area, ultimately expanding it into a four-day event. I reveled in the role of event planner and host, and found that I loved being a tiki tour guide and experiencing the spirit of aloha that was created as people gathered from around the country to enjoy the Bay Area's great selection of tiki bars. More and more, it seemed that the day job was not to last much longer.

During this same period, my career had become a source of growing frustration with frequent layoffs and no clear path toward advancement. When I was laid off yet again in early 2002, my severance package came with a perk—paid sessions with a therapist who specialized in career transitions. After a few hours on the couch pouring my heart out to her, I had a kind of Eureka moment. I realized that I did have skills I considered myself good at, such as customer service, sales, hospitality, marketing, and organization. Coupled with my personal interest in tiki culture . . . I sat upright and exclaimed, "I think I should open a tiki bar!" My statement was not met with similar enthusiasm, but rather a kind of quiet horror. The color drained from the therapist's face, and in a measured and deliberate way, she calmly replied, "I cannot, in good conscience and with my professional integrity intact, encourage that idea. Have you considered instead, maybe, going into catering?" Our sessions ended soon thereafter.

Two more ill-fated attempts at staying in a straight job led me to something of a premature midlife crisis in 2004. Out of money, Rebecca and I left San Francisco for the suburbs and I spent my days helping organize that year's Tiki Bar Crawl, building a bigger and better home tiki bar, and hatching a plan to build a commercial bar someday. Through the tiki community in the Bay Area, I met Michael and Mano Thanos, two brothers who were experienced owner-operators with a tiki bar of their own who were hoping to expand to a new and larger concept. I had a wealth of ideas for drinks and décor, and I hoped this might be the stage on which I could bring quality ingredients back to tiki. But it would have to wait—while we agreed to go into business together, we could not find a suitable location. After months and months of looking, I decided to pursue an administrative role at a company I admired: Trader Vic's.

I quickly discovered that my dream of working at Trader Vic's Corporate Global Headquarters would remain just that. The bustling, high-rise HQ I'd pictured in my head turned out to be just six people in a quiet office. But it was Victor Bergeron's own granddaughter, Eve, who told me that there was a bartender opening at their newly reborn San Francisco location. I wore my best Hawaiian shirt to the interview,

SMUGGLER'S COVE

The Crazed Mugs, lyrics by Pablus

I came in with the sunset
Ukulele on my shoulder
I'd been traveling for days
The winds and waves'd had their way
I was feeling kind of feral
'til I grabbed an old rum barrel
And into its depths I dove
In the caves of Smuggler's Cove
With the Midnites through the
    mornings
I ignored the west wind's warnings
'cause that tiki torch kept burning
And my spirits kept returning
I began a long and lonely tune
I weaved a tale of travel

From the fragrant mango groves
To the shores of Smuggler's Cove
Now I'm all for the weight of gold
When it's mine to spend it
I buy some respite from the cold
And rum for those befriended
When I'm light I lean on them
And they don't seem to mind it
For gone's the thrill of gold and gem
The moment that you find it
We heard the crack of thunder
As we snapped our cups together
I penned another verse
About some long-forgotten curse
The howling of the wind grew worse

The waves upon the passage burst
Down the mighty rocks they drove
And locked us deep in Smuggler's
    Cove
The tikis smiled in flick'ring light
My song was nearly finished
I bought rum, 'til it was gone
For I knew there'd be no dawn
It wasn't 'til that torch went out
that I scrawled the final stanza
"This is where you'll find our bones
In the caves of Smuggler's Cove."

something that immediately improved upon all my previous interview experiences. I discussed the role with their bar manager, a very serious looking, but darkly funny, man named Jim Shoemake. When he asked for my resume, I slid a blown-up photograph of my home tiki bar across the wood for his review. He picked it up and studied it for a few moments, then simply said, "I think we can work with this." And with that, thanks to the faith of one man, I became a working tiki bartender.

My time at Vic's was short but very productive. As a bartender, I was good, not great. I learned quickly that it was not my destiny. I gained even more respect for bartenders in the process of learning on the job. My direct supervisor, an enthusiastic and dedicated acolyte named Lars Hildebrandt, imported from Vic's Hamburg location, was both an inspiration and a thorn in my side. He pushed me constantly to maintain high standards of service, cleanliness, and efficiency. I, of course, resented him at the time, and only in hindsight can I fully appreciate how much I learned from him and carried with me to future projects. He cared deeply about the legacy of Vic's and the experience of his guests.

Working behind the bar at Vic's on a slow afternoon shift occasionally allowed for a few moments of experimentation. One day my fellow bartender Sonya Runkle tasted a new drink I was working on and suggested that I check out a meeting of the San Francisco chapter of the United States Bartender's Guild (USBG), recently revived by San Francisco bartenders David Nepove, Marcovaldo Dionysos, and Jacques Bezuidenhout. The meeting included two hours of thoughtful discussion and pointed questions about tequila, its production and history, and its styles and applications. It revealed to me an entire community of like-minded professionals in my new industry who were passionate about learning as much as they could about spirits to create better cocktails and experiences for their guests. I promptly handed my first membership dues over to David on my way out, and felt a sense of relief wash over me. For the first time in my adult life, I had no anxiety about what was next, or if I was doing the right thing professionally. I called Rebecca on the way home, energized and more than a little tipsy from the tequila, and exclaimed, "Honey, I've just been to the most amazing meeting. I know what I want to do for the rest of my life."

Less than a year later, Michael and Mano came to see me at Trader Vic's. Mano had found a bar for sale across the bay in the small island community of Alameda. It was an especially filthy dive bar located in a relatively quiet neighborhood. But all of us saw the potential in its bones. Purpose-built as a bar in the 1960s, it had a good layout and was a blank template to dress in bamboo and thatch. We met a few days later, and I presented an outline for my vision of the interior design and how I wanted to execute the drink program. My ideas were almost completely embraced—save for the lousy name I had dreamed up for the place. Instead, Mano came up with an outstanding name that worked perfectly both for location and historic reasons, and the three of us opened Forbidden Island in April, 2006.

I saw this as the opportunity to bring together everything I'd learned up to that point. From Jeff Berry, the decoded alchemy of decades of vintage exotic cocktails and the virtually lost palette of Donn Beach. From Trader Vic's, a different family of drinks and a passion for service. And from my time as a member of the USBG and San Francisco's exploding craft cocktail movement, the principles, ingredients, and techniques that were changing the face of drinking in America coast to coast. And so, with the opening of Forbidden Island, and ultimately, Smuggler's Cove, I was the first to apply the craft cocktail aesthetic to historic exotic cocktails.

Forbidden Island, Alameda, California

Understanding the structure of the historic drinks also allowed me to create better original exotic cocktails using contemporary ingredients, fresh squeezed juices, house-made syrups, unusual bitters, and more. And with the combination of my own practical cocktail skills and Michael's hospitality experience, we were able to execute high-quality exotic cocktails on a large scale.

Almost immediately, people began to take note. Forbidden Island and my cocktails were featured in newspapers and magazines nationwide, and a little bar in Alameda was being recognized for doing something innovative. So while ultimately our business partnership was not to last, Forbidden Island continues to thrive today as a beloved part of the Alameda community and home to great live music and annual events.

THE HUT

The most traditionally tiki space at Smuggler's Cove, the Hut, features a tapa cloth ceiling suspended above traditional woven matting (bac bac) and bamboo walls, and framed by a palm cape roof. Contemporary carvings of weapons, tikis, and more by artist David "Basement Kahuna" Wolfe, Dave "Lake Surfer" Hansen, and Notch Gonzalez line the walls. And the vintage chairs come from the legendary Mai Kai in Fort Lauderdale.

THE BOATHOUSE

At Trader Vic's original San Francisco location, there were several bars within the restaurant, one of which was known as the Boathouse Bar. When I was able to procure the original wooden sign for that bar to hang at Smuggler's Cove, well, the name for our lower level became clear. You'll see it above the bar and flanked on the walls by vintage rum advertisements and memorabilia, finishing off in the back of the room by a ship's wheel that also once called Vic's home.

THE GENESIS OF SMUGGLER'S COVE

Having proved that guests were engaged and excited about enjoying well-made exotic cocktails in a traditional tiki bar setting, I imagined how much further I could take the concept. As tiki was always my first love, I knew that I didn't want to stray from that magical world. But each day, I discovered more and more about the beautiful spirit lying squarely at the heart of the exotic cocktail: rum. While tiki was my passion, rum was quietly speaking to me . . . and it had a long story to tell. The first wave of mid-century tiki bars did much to restore rum's glory and respect—in some ways more glory and respect than it was ever accorded before. They introduced rum's nuances and regional variations to a generation of Americans who had long been weaned off the stuff in favor of whiskey. And Donn's deft hands showed how rums could be employed in ways never before seen. Truly the tiki era was a grand time for the world's rums. But it was, give or take, a forty-five-year span bounded by the birth of Don's Beachcomber on one end and the fall of the great tiki bars on the other. It wasn't enough time to tell rum's three-centuries long story. And that became the guiding principle behind Smuggler's Cove: use the aesthetic of Polynesian Pop and the grandeur of the exotic cocktail to provide a framework for the further discovery of rum.

THE DÉCOR

In order to provide the contractors, designers, and myself with a blueprint and inspiration for a new venue, I begin with creating an imaginary backstory for the space. For example, in the case of Forbidden Island, I imagined the building itself was the hull of a ship, wrecked on a beach ages ago. The survivors patched the damage to the hull with woven matting and made it their home (at least until the rum ran out). I liked to imagine that the wreckage was happened upon many years later and turned into a bar. When we interviewed designers and explained the concept, some seemed confused. But one, Bamboo Ben, simply looked at me and said, "Would they patch the damage on the inside or the outside of the hull?" I knew then that we had found the right designer.

With Smuggler's Cove, even before finding the actual location, I imagined it taking place in a cave. What if, I pondered, there had been a sheltered cove on a tropical island, where smugglers were known to ship and receive goods? And what if, nestled in a rocky hillside in the back of that cove, there was a cave where said smugglers built themselves a private clubhouse decorated with the art, artifacts, and flotsam and jetsam they had traded for rum over the years. They would make it a comfortable space, with the cave walls fortified by old ship's timbers, with bits of the rock projecting through and the occasional spring-fed cascade running through the space. With this template, I knew I could create a space that would showcase both tiki décor and historic rum ephemera. But first to find it a home.

The location of Smuggler's Cove came surprisingly and thankfully quickly: a former neighborhood spot called Jade Bar that I remembered from my time working down the street at Trader Vic's. A strange space, converted from a retail store (and decades before that, ironically, an Alcoholics Anonymous meeting hall), Jade was divided into three floors with a bar on the basement level, a bar at the entry level, and a small mezzanine perched above the entry level. But Jade did have one feature that could not be mistaken for anything but kismet: a waterfall that ran down its levels into a small lagoon in the lower level.

THE MAIN BAR

The carved wooden beams suspended above provide a lattice frame for a spectacular range of décor including: our (in)famous anchor and cannon, both fabricated by Notch, glass float lamps from long-closed Trader Vic's locations, unique vintage pieces from Oceanic Arts, an original "Cannibal trio" carved in 1927 and exhibited in Paris in 2014 at the Musée du quai Branly, and classic tikis from legendary artists like Eli Hedley. Modern artists represented include shell tiki swag lamps built by Kahaka Lamps and tikis by Bosko, set amid ephemera that includes puffer fish, nautical lamps, cargo nets, rigging, World War I and II memorabilia, and much more. Casting your gaze down onto the walls reveals our four illuminated shrines to fallen icons of San Francisco tiki: Matson Lines, Skipper Kent's, Trader Vic's, and Tiki Bob's.

As soon as the keys were in hand on September 1, 2009, work began at a brisk pace. I entrusted the execution of my vision to Ignacio "Notch" Gonzalez of Top Notch Kustomz in San Jose, California. While his day job may be hot rods, Notch is a well-known and respected figure in the tiki community, having wowed the scene with his giant tikis, artfully sculpted and hand-fired tiki mugs, and outstanding private bar. With the help of Matty Najdek of Ore-Cal Construction, we started by covering the street-facing wall of glass. If I was to convince my guests to forget about their jobs and stresses, and redirect their attention toward their friends and the cold drink in their hands, then the world outside had to go.

The next step is to build the decorative foundation, including the walls and ceiling. Foundation itself implies something simple like sheetrock, but in a Polynesian Pop setting, even the foundation should be a layered, visually complex affair to anchor the art and artifacts of tiki and rum décor.

Because of my imagined backstory of Smuggler's Cove, and my desire to emphasize San Francisco's maritime heritage, I decided to focus on nautical tiki décor. Of course, there's a fine line between nautical and pirate décor, and tiki borrows from both. But you'll find no Jolly Rogers or parrots at the Cove. In contrast to piracy, smuggling is about illicit commerce. As we're fond of saying, "We're not a pirate bar, but we're pirate-friendly." My key design influences were the stunning Molokai Bar at the Mai Kai in Fort Lauderdale, its neighbor across town The Wreck Bar, and the late, much-lamented Bahooka

in Rosemead, California. I wanted the seafaring side of tiki to marry with the cluttered and haphazard madness of a bar like the Bahooka. We knew from the start that wooden walls would be part of the story. So Notch and his team set about painstakingly crafting each of the hundreds of wooden planks by hand, grinding the edges into a driftwood-like finish, adding faux termite holes, burning them to bring out the depth of grain, then staining and lacquering them all to a satin finish. Each piece of wood took over two hours each to carefully fabricate, and the result is clear in the undulating detail of the walls.

It is on top of this elaborate canvas that Smuggler's Cove paints a picture of tiki and rum history. While most guests may not fully understand or appreciate the provenance of the art and ephemera that fill Smuggler's Cove, one thing most guests can appreciate immediately is the *authenticity* of the pieces—that they are the *real* works of *real* artists and not plastic reproductions. As San Francisco columnist Herb Caen once said about Hinky Dinks, "Good places, as opposed to stinkers, have a distinctive and mysterious atmosphere—an immediate feeling of quality, dedication, success and self-confidence."

It's my hope that each visit to the Cove will reveal a new facet or item to guests that they may never have noticed before. When the space itself is the entertainment, I'm delighted when it still has the power to entertain.

Ignacio "Notch" Gonzalez at his shop, Top Notch Kustomz

Pampanito

PAMPANITO

Load yer ballast tank and explore the depths! The Pampanito was inspired by a visit to Jamaica and her distilleries. When I spoke with Joy Spence, master blender of Appleton Rum, she said that they loved to take the wet sugar, a rich molasses stew from which the sugar has not been extracted, and use it to make lemonade. "Of course," she added, "we usually put a little rum in there, too." So I used that as my starting point, and added some traditional Jamaican flavors like allspice, and then lengthened it with soda so it wasn't so heavy. It gets its name from the *USS Pampanito* submarine docked in San Francisco, although the story of how that came to be is convoluted and not interesting in the slightest.

ORIGIN *Created by Martin Cate*
GLASSWARE *Collins or highball*

- 1 ounce fresh lemon juice
- 1 ounce SC Molasses Syrup (page 327)
- 2½ ounces seltzer
- ¼ ounce St. Elizabeth Allspice Dram
- 1½ ounces black blended rum ⑤
- 1 dash Angostura bitters

GARNISH *Lemon twist*

Add all the ingredients to a drink mixer tin. Fill with 12 ounces of crushed ice and 4 to 6 small "agitator" cubes. Flash blend and open pour with gated finish into a Collins or highball glass. Garnish with a lemon twist.

MAX'S MISTAKE

Created while I was a bartender at Trader Vic's and named in honor of the Ray's Mistake at Tiki-Ti, this too was an accidental combination of two other drinks. And my mother has always called me "Max." You may not.

ORIGIN *Created by Martin Cate*
GLASSWARE *Large (22-ounce) brandy snifter*

- 1 ounce fresh lemon juice
- 1 ounce SC Passion Fruit Syrup (page 325)
- ½ ounce SC Honey Syrup (page 325)
- 2 ounces London dry gin
- 1 dash Angostura bitters
- 2 ounces Fentimans Victorian Lemonade (or any quality dry sparkling lemonade)

GARNISH *Mint sprig*

Combine all the ingredients in a drink mixer tin. Fill with 12 ounces of crushed ice and 4 to 6 small "agitator" cubes. Flash blend and open pour with gated finish into the snifter. Add garnish.

LA GUILDIVE

ORIGIN *Created by Martin Cate*
GLASSWARE *Chilled coupe*

1 ounce ginger beer

½ ounce fresh lime juice

½ ounce Licor 43

¼ ounce natural peach liqueur (such as Mathilde Peach or Combier Crème de Pêche de Vigne)

2 ounces blended aged rum ❸

Pinch of freshly grated cinnamon

GARNISH *Lime twist*

Add the ginger beer to a chilled coupe. Combine the remaining ingredients in a cocktail shaker and shake with cracked or cubed ice. Double-strain the shaken ingredients into the coupe. Garnish with a lime twist.

THE TWENTY SEVENTY SWIZZLE

Inspired by swizzles of yore, The Twenty Seventy Swizzle came about one night while sitting at the bar with old pal and future Master of the Cove Ron Roumas. I proposed to him that I was going to make the ultimate swizzle based on several classic swizzle recipes. We made several versions and discussed what we liked and disliked about each before settling on a final recipe that incorporated the best of all worlds. The name was inspired by the two rums that I thought really made this drink sing: the heady vanilla of Angostura 1919 and mighty Lemon Hart 151.

ORIGIN *Created by Martin Cate*
GLASSWARE *Collins or highball*

½ ounce fresh lime juice

½ ounce SC Demerara Syrup (page 324)

½ ounce SC Honey Syrup (page 325)

¼ ounce St. Elizabeth Allspice Dram

1 ounce column still aged rum ❹

1 ounce black blended overproof rum ❻

1 dash Herbstura (page 228)

Pinch of freshly grated nutmeg

GARNISH *Swizzle napkin wrap (see page 245), mint sprig, and swizzle stick*

Add all the ingredients to a Collins or highball glass, then add crushed iced until the glass is three-quarters full. Use a bar spoon or lélé to swizzle. Top up with additional crushed ice as needed to fill the glass and garnish.

The Twenty Seventy Swizzle

SHUDDERS IN A WHISPER

When our photographers Dylan + Jeni first came to Smuggler's Cove for our initial meeting and shot some sample photos, they needed some prop cocktails. I whipped up this tasty treat, which served as muse for the day.

ORIGIN *Created by Martin Cate*
GLASSWARE *Large (22-ounce) brandy snifter*

> ¾ ounce fresh lime juice
>
> ½ ounce SC Passion Fruit Syrup (page 325)
>
> ½ ounce natural pear liqueur (such as Mathilde Poire)
>
> ¼ ounce Drambuie liqueur
>
> 2 ounces seltzer
>
> 2 ounces column still aged rum ❹
>
> 2 dashes Peychaud's bitters
>
> 1 dash Angostura bitters

GARNISH *Edible orchid and mint sprig*

Add all of the ingredients to a drink mixer tin. Fill with 12 ounces of crushed ice and 4 to 6 small "agitator" cubes. Flash blend and open pour with gated finish into a snifter. Add garnish.

CUEVAS

ORIGIN *Created by Dane Barca*
GLASSWARE *Chilled coupe*

> ¼ ounce SC Cinnamon Syrup (page 327)
>
> ½ ounce Punt e Mes
>
> ¼ ounce tawny port
>
> 2 ounces blended aged rum ❸
>
> 6 drops Bittermens 'Elemakule Tiki bitters

GARNISH *Maraschino cherry*

Add all the ingredients to a mixing glass. Fill with cracked or cubed ice. Stir and strain into a chilled coupe. Float a maraschino cherry in the center for garnish.

NORWEGIAN PARALYSIS

Chase away the endless night with this marriage of fresh juices, orgeat, and traditional Scandinavian aquavit.

ORIGIN *Created by Martin Cate, inspired by the Polynesian Paralysis*

SOURCE *Polynesian Paralysis* published in Beachbum Berry Remixed, *originally sourced from a 1971 pamphlet called "Drinks of Hawaii" by Paul Dick*

GLASSWARE *Collins or highball*

> 1½ ounces fresh orange juice
>
> 1½ ounces pineapple juice
>
> ½ ounce fresh lemon juice
>
> ¼ ounce SC Demerara Syrup (page 324)
>
> ¼ ounce SC Orgeat (page 330)
>
> 1½ ounces aquavit

GARNISH *Lemon wedge speared with a cocktail umbrella*

Add all the ingredients to a cocktail shaker. Fill with cracked ice. Shake and strain contents into a Collins or highball glass filled with cracked ice. Garnish with a lemon wedge speared with a cocktail umbrella.

JUAN HO ROYALE

Created for Hula's in Santa Cruz, and originally named The Steamer after Steamer Lane, a famous surf spot in Santa Cruz. Hula's wisely realized the name conjured a different image and cleverly renamed it Juan Ho. To capture the azure seas, I make a rare exception for blue curaçao. Revisiting it again recently revealed that it benefitted nicely from a splash of bubbly.

ORIGIN *Created by Martin Cate*

GLASSWARE *Chilled coupe*

> 2 ounces champagne or sparkling wine
>
> ¾ ounce fresh lime juice
>
> ½ ounce SC Orgeat (page 330)
>
> ½ ounce blue curaçao
>
> ½ ounce John D. Taylor's Velvet Falernum
>
> 1½ ounces tequila blanco

GARNISH *None*

Pour the champagne into a chilled coupe. Add the remaining ingredients to a cocktail shaker and shake with cracked or cubed ice. Double-strain into the chilled coupe.

CHARTREUSE SWIZZLE

While it's been a staple of the cocktail renaissance for years now, the structure of this drink owes a debt to the exotic cocktail tradition. Sour, sweet, strong. And if the falernum isn't enough spice for you, how about a hundred or so more in the mix from the Chartreuse?

ORIGIN *Created by Marcovaldo Dionysos*
GLASSWARE *Collins or Zombie glass*

- 1 ounce pineapple juice
- ¾ ounce fresh lime juice
- ½ ounce John D. Taylor's Velvet Falernum
- 1½ ounces Green Chartreuse

GARNISH *Swizzle napkin wrap (see page 245), freshly grated nutmeg and mint sprig*

Combine all the ingredients in a Collins or Zombie glass. Fill the glass with crushed ice until it is three-quarters full. Swizzle with a lélé or barspoon. Top up with additional crushed ice as needed to fill the glass. Add garnish.

ROSELITA

ORIGIN *Created by Martin Cate*
GLASSWARE *Collins or highball glass*

- 1½ ounces seltzer
- ½ ounce fresh lime juice
- ½ ounce SC Orgeat (page 330)
- ½ ounce SC Hibiscus Liqueur (page 331)
- ½ ounce natural pear liqueur (such as Mathilde Poire)
- 1½ ounces column still aged rum ❹
- 1 dash Peychaud's bitters

GARNISH *Edible hibiscus flower on cocktail pick or skewer*

Add the seltzer to a Collins or highball glass. Add the remaining ingredients to a cocktail shaker with cracked or cubed ice. Shake and strain into the glass and carefully add cracked or cubed ice. Garnish with an edible hibiscus flower on a cocktail pick or skewer.

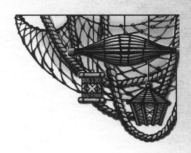

CENTER OF THE GALAXY

The discovery in 2009 that the center of the Milky Way galaxy contains a chemical compound that tastes like raspberries and smells like rum was the inspiration for this cocktail.

ORIGIN *Created by Martin Cate*
GLASSWARE *Chilled coupe*

- ½ ounce fresh lime juice
- ½ ounce SC Demerara Syrup (page 324)
- ½ ounce SC Honey Syrup (page 325)
- ½ ounce St. George Raspberry Liqueur
- 2 ounces blended aged rum ❸
- Pinch of freshly ground cinnamon

GARNISH *Raspberry and a lime wheel*

Combine all the ingredients in a cocktail shaker filled with cracked or cubed ice. Shake and double-strain into a chilled coupe. Float a lime wheel in the center of the drink and rest a raspberry in the center.

CALLALOO COOLER

ORIGIN *Created by Melissa Garcia*
GLASSWARE *Collins or highball*

- 1 ounce seltzer
- ¾ ounce fresh lime juice
- ½ ounce SC Cinnamon Syrup (page 327)
- ½ ounce Cherry Heering
- 2 ounces blended lightly aged rum ❷
- 1 dash Angostura bitters

GARNISH *Grated cinnamon and mint sprig*

Pour the seltzer in a Collins or highball glass. Add remaining ingredients to a cocktail shaker with cubed or cracked ice. Shake and strain into the Collins or highball glass. Carefully add cubed or cracked ice to the glass to fill and garnish with grated cinnamon and a mint sprig.

"The bartender is flailing about like a heavy-metal drummer, desperately beating eight, ten, fourteen ingredients into towering, elaborately garnished concoctions. Strange words fly about—hogo, agricole, solera, orgeat—and the heady perfume of distilled sugarcane fills the air. Tiki. As San Francisco's and perhaps the nation's reigning Tiki bar, Smuggler's Cove draws a crowd almost every night, and you've got to wait outside until there's space. It's worth the wait."

—DAVID WONDRICH, *ESQUIRE'S* "THE BEST BARS IN AMERICA, 2013"

Curating the Experience

Staff of Smuggler's Cove

FROM DAY ONE, THE PLAN WAS TO KEEP THE EXTERIOR AS GENERIC AS POSSIBLE, TO OFFER NO SIGNAGE OR CLUE AS TO WHAT LAY BEYOND THE FRONT DOOR. ONLY A SIMPLE PORT AND STARBOARD LIGHT MARK THE BOUNDARIES OF THE COVE OUT FRONT, AND THE TRANSITION FROM OUTSIDE WORLD TO INTERIOR FANTASIA THUS BECOMES ALL THE MORE DRAMATIC.

The wide-eyed look on the faces of first-time visitors as their eyes adjust and take in the space reminds me why the effort put into the design and the decade of collecting ephemera were worth it. Upon entering, if the place is quiet enough, you might notice the music first. Our playlist is culled from the greats of exotica music both past and present, and just as our concept seeks to broaden tiki through a deeper appreciation of rum, our music is expanded as well with 1960s Jamaican R&B, jazz, bossa nova, and a smattering of Northern Soul. Plus a few goofy novelty songs thrown in to help dispel any notion that I'm a cool guy.

As you enter, you'll be greeted by a staff member who will ask if it's your first visit. If so, they will explain the layout, where to order a drink, and to please watch your step as your eyes adjust. Then you'll be handed a menu.

Once inside Smuggler's Cove, you'll notice a few things missing. Like televisions. Or games. The entertainment is the space, the drinks, and your friends. Smuggler's Cove can elicit a love-it-or-hate-it response, and that's fine. It was never intended to be to everyone's taste. But for those who do love it, and keep coming back, they feel tied to and protective of it. They want to be ambassadors to others and enthusiastically explain to someone new what the place is all about, or offer their favorite drink or rum suggestions. They become more than regulars, they're part of our community.

THE SMUGGLER'S COVE MENU

The Smuggler's Cove menu is a journey through the history of rum, with lengthy drink descriptions, historic notes, and quotes from rum historians and prominent figures. Our menu was the first rum cocktail menu to divide the drinks into historic and regional categories. Icons next to each recipe tell you what kind of vessel it's served in, if we think of it as a house favorite, and if it's particularly strong.

If a guest reviews the menu, and decides they'd rather have a gin and tonic, that's no problem of course, and is always met with a smile. But the menu acts as something of a manifesto. It defines what we do and it also explains why we don't have many common bar ingredients, such as Bloody Mary mix or flavored vodkas. In order for us to offer the best experience possible, we have to jettison the notion that a bar must be all things to all guests. In dining, restaurants are expected to concentrate their energies on one style of cooking or cuisine. It's taken as common sense that the sushi bar has specialized in one concept, so no one is disappointed or angered when they can't get a burrito. But the expectation remains that bars should cater to any whim. I believe that the more a bar can focus on their strengths and specialize within their concept, then they can offer the guest a better product and a better experience.

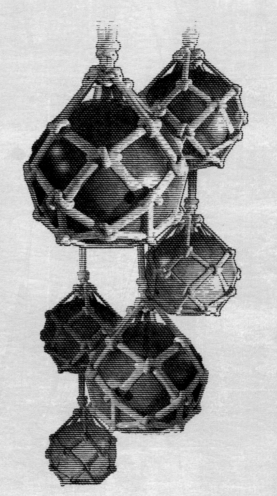

THE CORE OF OUR COCKTAILS

Smuggler's Cove has an ambitious slate of objectives to give you the best experience possible. But of course, at the heart of our bar, lie the cocktails and how we execute them.

Quality Ingredients

Smuggler's Cove goes beyond just using fresh ingredients and quality spirits; we are actively and constantly researching new products, and our mission is to uncover the best ingredients we can.

While it is de rigueur to make as many things in-house as possible for the sake of bragging rights or to impress guests, we try to take a thoughtful approach to the ingredients we make ourselves. We only make our own product if there isn't a commercial one available that is better than what we could make ourselves. For example, I cannot find a demerara simple syrup that exactly matches my preferred sugar blend and mouthfeel, so we continue to produce our own (for a complete list of our house-made ingredients, see page 324). But we don't make products for the sake of it, and pricing rarely comes into the equation. Something that's important for retailers like us to remember is that we don't exist in a bubble; we're part of a spirits industry ecosystem that relies on each other to bring our guests the best products. When there's a great product out there brought to me by someone I can respect, then I'm happy to support it. For example, it would not be hard for us to make an allspice liqueur. But I choose to buy St. Elizabeth Allspice Dram for a couple of reasons. The first is that it's made with Jamaican ingredients and they have the ability to filter it correctly whereas my version retains a lot of unappealing particulate matter. But more importantly, when I buy it, I'm supporting a small importer of craft cocktail products, Haus Alpenz,

that has been able to source or recreate dozens of lost ingredients that greatly benefit cocktail bars of all stripes. So, while I have no use at Smuggler's Cove for one of their obscure Italian amaros, I know plenty of bars that do, and therefore am glad to support that importer's continued efforts.

The Right Rum(s) for the Right Drink

This is one of our most sacred credos. At Smuggler's Cove we like to say that "well is a four-letter word." There's no such thing, as you may have ascertained by now, as a well rum for us. When I'm selecting rums for the cocktails, I'm taking into account a couple of factors—rums that are as close as possible

Custom rums created for Smuggler's Cove

to the historic rums that the recipe originally called for and blends that make sense for the flavor profile we're trying to achieve. It's an ever-evolving process. As new rums come to market and new information comes to light about brands (both good and bad), the rum selected for a drink can and does change. The rums featured in our Mai Tai have changed four times in the six years we've been open. Smuggler's Cove also differentiated itself from the start by having a range of custom rums produced for our exclusive use. Some were born of necessity, some of passion, some of whimsy. Designing a custom rum also allows for us to have a special taste profile that isn't easily reproduced, making your visit to Smuggler's Cove just a little more unique. And with more in the pipeline, we're always poking around the nooks and crannies of the rum world for new treats.

Saving the Exotic Cocktail from Devolution

Throughout the history of cocktails, recipes and techniques have often become bastardized or forgotten with time. Prohibition drove a generation of bartenders out of business or overseas—cocktail bars in Europe and Havana became a refuge for the American cocktail. The fourteen-year Great Experiment damaged our understanding of how to make drinks with repercussions that are still felt today. Yet, despite the huge impact of Prohibition, I argue that no drink category has fallen further or been more debased than the exotic cocktail. In fact, one night on the Bay Area Tiki Bar Crawl several years ago, I walked into a new tiki bar that had a short menu of tiki cocktail classics. I went up to the bar to order drinks for a friend and myself. I said to the bartender, "Hey there—I'd like a Zombie and a Mai Tai. Wait—I think it was a Mai Tai he wanted" and turned back to my friend to double-check his order. "Hey—you wanted a Mai Tai, right?" As I

began to talk to my friend, the bartender cut me off by saying, "Hey man—don't worry about it. It doesn't matter. It's the same drink." And this was at a *tiki* bar. So we struggle with decades of negative perceptions and misinformation. And make no mistake: San Francisco is one of the most sophisticated cocktail markets in the world in terms of consumer education. Our guests are inundated daily with traditional and social media information about spirits and cocktails, and they drink nightly in front of some of the smartest bartenders in the world. And yet there's still resistance when their Mai Tai arrives and it's not pink. Or full of pineapple juice. It's just a vivid illustration of the struggle for acceptance that the exotic cocktail faces. And let's not get started on rum. Actually, better yet, let's.

HI, EVERYONE! MEET RUM.

For so many of our guests, one of their first questions is "You can sip rum?" Indeed, you can! A lot of them! Hundreds of them! For so many people, their only experience with rum is in a cola or floated on some bastardized Mai Tai. They may only be familiar with one or two large brands.

Many people think that the tiki movement taught Americans an appreciation, understanding, and love of rum. However, while Donn and Vic did spread the gospel of the use of rum in cocktails, this did not mean that people were calling for rum neat the way they did other spirits. In fact, spirit lists in the back of the great tiki cocktail menus of the 1950s and '60s almost never include rum as a category, despite following a drink menu of fifty-plus drinks that virtually all feature rum. In his 1974 book, *Rum Cookery & Drinkery*, Trader Vic himself explains that by that time, Trader Vic's restaurants stocked only about twenty rums because most of his American guests just keep right on asking for Scotch, bourbon, gin, and vodka. He says, "Americans haven't yet learned to enjoy rum. I think that the main reason for this is that rum has never really been a liquor that American people bought and drank as a habit." What that tells me is, that despite the best efforts of Donn and Vic over the many years to introduce Americans to the diversity of rum, consumers still only saw it as something to put in punches and exotic cocktails, and not to enjoy on its own.

With over five hundred and fifty rums on our shelves at any time and more than seven hundred varieties having passed through our doors since opening, we aim to change that for good. When you're working with the most diverse spirit on Earth, there's no shortage of tools at your disposal. For some, their first taste of a quality, aged rum is a revelation. For others, we offer an assortment of flights that help show the range of rum styles. Or we showcase rum in a Manhattan or old-fashioned—simple drinks that elevate and accent complex rums. We hope that our efforts (and the efforts of other new rum bars that have followed the Cove) at getting people to enjoy rum on its own terms will be more successful, and that we will be able to look back someday and feel we played a small part in boosting acceptance and appreciation of the category.

And the overall effect is measurable: At this point, rum cocktails and premium rums account for 93 percent of all Smuggler's Cove sales. That leaves just 7 percent for all other spirits, beer, wine, and non-alcoholic drinks combined. Being stubborn about the concept certainly could have backfired, but the results are clear. In addition to encouraging people to use our menus, we drive the sales toward our cocktails and rums with another key tool as well: the Clubs.

PUZZLES, VOYAGERS, AND THE RUMBUSTION SOCIETY: THE GAMIFICATION OF SMUGGLER'S COVE

For years, bars and restaurants have had ways of rewarding guest loyalty though clubs or checklists. And loyalty programs and clubs are more popular today than ever in all aspects of retail. I knew that I wanted to form a club for rum to encourage people to look beyond their favorite brands and try a wider spectrum. So for the opening of Smuggler's Cove, Hanford Lemoore had the idea to create a puzzle game: We announced that Smuggler's Cove was coming to San Francisco, but didn't reveal the location. Rather, we directed people to a website that offered a series of puzzles and games to solve. Hundreds of people competed, and after enough got past the online games, the challenge turned into a scavenger hunt to find hidden locations around San Francisco. Once the four locations were found, they formed an X on a map of San Francisco, with the intersection being the street address of Smuggler's Cove. Hanford's puzzles intrigued and enraged people in equal measure, and got the press excited about following along as well. Once the doors were open, we launched the Voyager of the Cove club, where people can drink their way through the entire menu to earn a special edition logo glass and more. But the most well-known club has become The Rumbustion Society.

Named for a seventeenth-century term for either rum or a kind of unruly brawl (or both!), The Rumbustion Society was my chance to offer a rum club that explored the history and styles of rum from a deeper educational standpoint, and sought to develop smarter consumers who would be able to make educated rum shopping decisions when visiting retailers. This is where we really explore the gamification of drinking, to use a contemporary term. Levels, merit badges, and awards along the journey make learning about rum more engaging and fun (and learning while drinking isn't such a bad way to spend your time off, either). The club has a series of levels:

Level I: Disciple of the Cove

The first level of the club consists of sampling your way through a self-guided tour of twenty examples of rum in one-ounce pours. Guests are given a wallet-size punch card that they keep, and read their way through an on-site guide that offers detailed information about production methods, historic and regional differences, and representative brands. Upon completion, guests are given a basic quiz to see what they've absorbed so far. (The test is famously easy—maybe two questions, open book, and with a lot of help. As I am fond of saying, "What am I going to do, fail you and tell you that you can't drink here anymore? That's not really in my best interest, is it?") Upon your virtually guaranteed passing, you officially earn the title of Disciple of the Cove and are given a Rumbustion Society Membership Card, merit badge, and access to a massive personal checklist of our rums.

Level II: Guardian of the Cove

Disciples can then embark on the second level of the club, which entails a more free-form selection of eighty more rums in full two-ounce pours. Guests can choose their own direction based on some of their favorite flavor profiles. But they also must taste a few of what we lovingly refer to as our Immortal Rums—rums of unique rarity or provenance. After that, they stand eligible as candidates for the title of Guardian of the Cove. At a quarterly convocation where we induct new members, we recite the sacred oath of allegiance to Smuggler's Cove, bestow another

merit badge, and put a brass plate on the wall for all to see. I then crown the new Guardian with the signature Smuggler's Cove crimson fez. Our enfezzed Guardians make quite a sight when gathered in one place. Members at the Guardian level enjoy special benefits including private tasting events with visiting distillers, first tastes of new products, and more. But there are deeper roads to follow.

Level III: Master of the Cove

If members can soldier on for another two hundred rums and more Immortals, they are then awarded

Guardians and Masters of The Cove

with the ultimate journey—a trip to a rum distillery. This nearly unheard of benefit (as brands don't usually cater to consumers in this fashion) has been one of the most talked about features of The Rumbustion Society, and has made a huge impact on our members. The opportunity to trace a rum to its birthplace and witness the production firsthand has allowed us to take small groups around the world to a huge variety of distilleries. Trips to the large facilities open our members' eyes to the scale, efficiency, and modern production methods of some of the most famous names in rum, while usually throwing in a good helping of sun and sand to sweeten the pot. The small

craft distillers allow us to get our hands dirty and see production from a different standpoint, as we often end up helping with the fermentation, draining a barrel, or working the bottling line ourselves. We've even had our own rum made: House Spirits in Portland, Oregon, distilled a small batch rum, called Triumvirate, for our visit that commemorated the first three members of The Rumbustion Society to achieve the title of Master.

I had a hunch that the club would be a popular pastime for many, but I never knew just how much it would connect with people. We've had hundreds of Disciples, over sixty Guardians, and more than thirty

Masters since we opened. And I naively thought that people would sit back with their feet up at that point, but they continue to soldier on. At four hundred rums, Masters receive a limited edition tiki mug that is unique to that level. As drinking four hundred rums is the only way to acquire this mug, we refer to it as the most valuable tiki mug in the world. And still they kept going, which prompted me to create The Black Tassel Brigade for those who have hit five hundred rums. This exalted level includes, as you may have surmised, a black tassel for their fez, a black name plaque on the wall, and . . . well, that's all I can tell you. The Black Tassel Brigade benefits are highly confidential.

Beyond that, who knows? My guests' thirst has outpaced my own creativity. And for that I am both impressed and incredibly grateful.

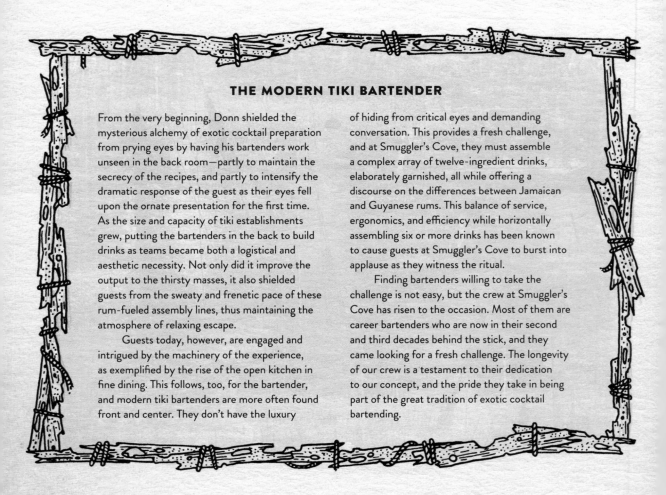

THE MODERN TIKI BARTENDER

From the very beginning, Donn shielded the mysterious alchemy of exotic cocktail preparation from prying eyes by having his bartenders work unseen in the back room—partly to maintain the secrecy of the recipes, and partly to intensify the dramatic response of the guest as their eyes fell upon the ornate presentation for the first time. As the size and capacity of tiki establishments grew, putting the bartenders in the back to build drinks as teams became both a logistical and aesthetic necessity. Not only did it improve the output to the thirsty masses, it also shielded guests from the sweaty and frenetic pace of these rum-fueled assembly lines, thus maintaining the atmosphere of relaxing escape.

Guests today, however, are engaged and intrigued by the machinery of the experience, as exemplified by the rise of the open kitchen in fine dining. This follows, too, for the bartender, and modern tiki bartenders are more often found front and center. They don't have the luxury of hiding from critical eyes and demanding conversation. This provides a fresh challenge, and at Smuggler's Cove, they must assemble a complex array of twelve-ingredient drinks, elaborately garnished, all while offering a discourse on the differences between Jamaican and Guyanese rums. This balance of service, ergonomics, and efficiency while horizontally assembling six or more drinks has been known to cause guests at Smuggler's Cove to burst into applause as they witness the ritual.

Finding bartenders willing to take the challenge is not easy, but the crew at Smuggler's Cove has risen to the occasion. Most of them are career bartenders who are now in their second and third decades behind the stick, and they came looking for a fresh challenge. The longevity of our crew is a testament to their dedication to our concept, and the pride they take in being part of the great tradition of exotic cocktail bartending.

TOP NOTCH VOLCANO

A Top Notch drink inspired by a Top Notch guy. Stare in wonder at the mighty volcano and decide quickly which of your friends should be the first into the fire.

ORIGIN *Created by Martin Cate*
GLASSWARE *Large (32- to 48-ounce) scorpion bowl and long (20-inch) luau straws or other punch bowl or decorative bowl with a ladle and cups.*
SERVES 4

4 ounces fresh lime juice

4 ounces pineapple juice

1 ounce passion fruit puree

3 ounces SC Demerara Syrup (page 324)

1 ounce Luxardo Maraschino liqueur

4 ounces blended lightly aged rum ❷

4 ounces blended aged rum ❸

GARNISH *Fire (see page 245). Otherwise, sliced limes and oranges.*

Add all the ingredients in a drink mixer tin without ice and roll (pour back and forth a few times) with another drink mixer tin to combine ingredients. Divide the contents in half evenly between the tins. Add 12 ounces of crushed ice and 4 to 6 "agitator" cubes to each of the two tins. With each tin, flash blend and open pour with gated finish into a four-person ceramic scorpion bowl. Serve with 20-inch luau straws for easier sharing. Serve on fire!

NOTE Named for the interior designer of Smuggler's Cove, Ignacio "Notch" Gonzalez.

THE NAKED APE

Created in honor of the San Francisco exotica band, Ape, for one of Smuggler's Cove's (incredibly) rare concerts.

ORIGIN *Created by Martin Cate*
GLASSWARE *Ape "Fez Wearin" Monkey Mug (or other tiki mug or double old-fashioned)*

½ ounce fresh lemon juice

½ ounce SC Cinnamon Syrup (page 327)

½ ounce Giffard Banane du Brésil banana liqueur

1½ ounces black blended rum ❺

½ ounce pot still lightly aged rum (overproof) ❶

1 dash Angostura bitters

GARNISH *None*

Add all the ingredients to a drink mixer tin. Fill with 12 ounces of crushed ice and 4 to 6 "agitator" cubes. Flash blend and open pour with gated finish into a tiki mug or double old-fashioned glass.

SWIZZLE FRANÇAIS

ORIGIN *Created by Martin Cate*

GLASSWARE *Collins or highball*

½ ounce fresh lime juice

½ ounce Martinique sugarcane syrup

¼ ounce St. Elizabeth Allspice Dram

2 ounces cane AOC Martinique rhum
agricole vieux **8**

Pinch of fresh ground nutmeg

GARNISH *Swizzle napkin wrap (see page 245)
and mint sprig*

Combine all the ingredients in a Collins or highball glass and fill the glass three-quarters full with
crushed ice. Swizzle with a lélé or barspoon. Top
up with additional crushed ice as needed to fill the
glass and garnish.

SPARKLING MAI TAI

ORIGIN *Created by Martin Cate*

SOURCE *Created for* Sunset *magazine, 2011*

GLASSWARE *Champagne flute or coupe*

¼ ounce fresh lime juice

¼ ounce SC Orgeat (page 330)

½ ounce Pierre Ferrand Dry Curaçao

¼ ounce black blended overproof rum **6**

½ ounce blended aged rum **3**

4 ounces chilled sparkling wine

GARNISH *Lime twist and mint leaf*

Pour all the ingredients except the sparking wine
into a mixing glass. Stir with cracked or cubed ice.
Strain into a chilled champagne flute or coupe and
top with sparkling wine, then garnish.

NOTE To save time, you can batch this recipe
ahead of time. To serve several people, multiply
the ingredient quantities by the number of guests.
Combine all the ingredients except the sparkling
wine and chill for an hour. When you're ready to
serve, pour 1¾ ounces of the chilled mix into each
glass (no need to stir with ice) and top each with
4 ounces of chilled sparkling wine.

THE ERNESTO

ORIGIN *Created by Martin Cate*
GLASSWARE *Double old-fashioned*

- 2 ounces Ting grapefruit soda
- 1 ounce fresh lime juice
- 1 ounce SC Honey Syrup (page 325)
- ½ ounce natural apricot liqueur (such as Rothman & Winter Apricot Liqueur or Giffard Abricot du Roussillon)
- 2 ounces tequila blanco
- 1 dash Herbstura (page 228)

GARNISH *Lime wheel and edible orchid*

Pour the grapefruit soda into a double old-fashioned glass. Add the remaining ingredients to a cocktail shaker filled with cracked or cubed ice. Shake and strain into the double old-fashioned glass. Carefully add cracked or cubed ice to the glass and garnish.

THE SEXPERT

Created in honor of author Susie Bright's book-release party at Smuggler's Cove.

ORIGIN *Created by Martin Cate*
GLASSWARE *Chilled coupe*

- ½ ounce fresh lemon juice
- ½ ounce SC Passion Fruit Syrup (page 325)
- ½ ounce John D. Taylor's Velvet Falernum
- 1½ ounces Peruvian pisco
- ½ ounce gin
- 6 drops Bittermens Burlesque bitters

GARNISH *Edible orchid or hibiscus flower*

Combine all the ingredients in a cocktail shaker and fill with cracked or cubed ice. Shake and double-strain into a chilled coupe and add garnish.

NOTE If you are unable to get Burlesque bitters, substitute other fruit bitters.

Smuggler's Rum Barrel

SMUGGLER'S RUM BARREL

One of the signature cocktails from Smuggler's Cove, and a top seller from day one.

ORIGIN *Created by Martin Cate*
GLASSWARE *SC Rum Barrel or large (22-ounce) brandy snifter*

- 1 ounce fresh lime juice
- 1 ounce pineapple juice
- ¼ ou
- blended overproof rum **6**
- 1 dash Angostura bitters

GARNISH *Freshly grated nutmeg, mint sprig, fresh flower, SC swizzle stick*

Add all the ingredients to drink mixer tin. Fill with 12 ounces of crushed ice and 4 to 6 small "agitator" cubes. Flash blend and open pour with gated finish into a mug or snifter, then garnish.

NOTE We pay tribute to the longstanding tradition of Donn's coded and secret recipes with this drink. Even our bartenders don't know all of the ingredients.

HANA REVIVER

ORIGIN *Created by Martin Cate*
GLASSWARE *Footed pilsner*

- 1 ounce fresh lemon juice
- 1 ounce SC Passion Fruit Honey (page 325)
- ¼ barspoon li hing mui powder (see Resources, page 335)
- 2 ounces seltzer
- 1 barspoon Maraschino liqueur
- 2 ounces pot still unaged rum (see page 197)

GARNISH *Mint sprig and a swizzle stick.*

Add all the ingredients to a drink mixer tin. Fill with 12 ounces of crushed ice and 4 to 6 small "agitator" cubes. Flash blend and then open pour with gated finish into a footed pilsner glass. Add garnish.

KAITEUR SWIZZLE

Named for the breathtaking Kaiteur Falls in Guyana.

ORIGIN *Created by Martin Cate*
GLASSWARE *Collins or highball*

- ¾ ounce fresh lime juice
- ½ ounce Grade A maple syrup
- ½ ounce John D. Taylor's Velvet Falernum
- 2 ounces blended aged rum (Guyana) ❸
- 2 dashes Angostura bitters

GARNISH *Swizzle napkin wrap (see page 245) and mint sprig*

Add all the ingredients to a Collins or highball glass and fill the glass three-quarters full with crushed ice. Swizzle with a lélé or barspoon. Top up with additional crushed ice as needed to fill the glass and garnish.

THE EXPEDITION

The journeys of Donn Beach inspired this cocktail. From Donn's roots in New Orleans, we start with bourbon. As his travels took him to the Caribbean, we add the rum and spices. And as he sets up shop in Southern California, we add the fresh citrus and honey. At the Mai Kai in Fort Lauderdale, Florida, ex–Don the Beachcomber's bartender Mariano Licudine invented one of his most famous drinks, The Black Magic, which uses coffee and citrus. Inspired by The Black Magic, we add Bittermens New Orleans Coffee liqueur, which brings us full circle to Donn's original home.

ORIGIN *Created by Martin Cate*
GLASSWARE *Kuhiko tiki mug or other 16-ounce mug or glass*

- 1 ounce fresh lime juice
- ½ ounce SC Cinnamon Syrup (page 327)
- ½ ounce SC Honey Syrup (page 325)
- ¼ ounce SC Vanilla Syrup (page 326)
- 2 ounces seltzer
- ¼ ounce Bittermens New Orleans Coffee Liqueur
- 2 ounces black blended rum ❺
- 1 ounce bourbon

GARNISH *Edible orchid*

Add all the ingredients to a drink mixer tin with 12 ounces of crushed ice and 4 to 6 small "agitator" cubes. Flash blend and open pour with gated finish into a mug or glass. Add garnish.

The Expedition

THE UNDEAD GENTLEMAN

This is a Zombie that's been simplified slightly and served on the stem, for the sophisticated savage.

ORIGIN *Created by Martin Cate*
SOURCE *Tasting Table, 2011*
GLASSWARE *Chilled coupe*

1 dash absinthe blanc

½ ounce fresh lime juice

½ ounce fresh grapefruit juice (white or pink)

½ ounce SC Cinnamon Syrup (page 327)

½ ounce John D. Taylor's Velvet Falernum

1 ounce black blended overproof rum ⑥

1½ ounces blended aged rum ❸

1 dash Angostura bitters

GARNISH *Intertwined lime and grapefruit twists*

Rinse a chilled cocktail coupe with absinthe blanc. Add the remaining ingredients to a cocktail shaker with cracked or cubed ice. Shake and double-strain into the coupe and add garnish.

THE DEAD RECKONING

Created for the NW Tiki Crawl (now Tiki Kon) in 2007, this has become one of our most popular drinks and has found its way to a few menus around the country.

ORIGIN *Created by Martin Cate*
GLASSWARE *Collins or highball glass*

1 ounce seltzer

1 ounce fresh lemon juice

1 ounce pineapple juice

½ ounce Grade A maple syrup

½ ounce SC Vanilla Brandy (see Note, following)

½ ounce tawny port

2 ounces blended aged rum ❸

1 dash Angostura bitters

GARNISH *Pineapple fronds, mint spring, and lemon spiral*

Add the seltzer to a Collins or highball glass. Add the remaining ingredients to a drink mixer tin. Add 12 ounces of crushed ice and 4 to 6 "agitator" cubes to the drink mixer tin and flash blend. Strain the contents into the glass over the seltzer. Carefully fill the glass with cracked or cubed ice and add garnish.

NOTE To make the SC Vanilla Brandy: Split an 8-inch vanilla bean lengthwise and cut into three roughly equal pieces. Add the vanilla bean pieces to 1 liter of brandy, reseal the bottle, and let rest at room temperature for two weeks. Remove the beans and discard. Add 2 ounces of SC Demerara Syrup (page 324) to the vanilla-infused brandy and mix well. Store in the original brandy bottle for up to 1 year.

The Dead Reckoning

FALINUM

Created for my old pal Falin Minoru, artist and proprietor of Tiki Kaimuki Fine Boozing Vessels, tiki mugs made in Oakland, California.

ORIGIN *Created by Martin Cate*
GLASSWARE *Tiki Kaimuki mug or double old-fashioned glass*

- 1 ounce fresh lemon juice
- 1 ounce SC Coconut Cream (page 328)
- 1 ounce seltzer
- ½ ounce John D. Taylor's Velvet Falernum
- 2 ounces column still aged rum ❹
- 1 dash orange bitters

GARNISH *None*

Combine all the ingredients in a drink mixer tin and fill with 12 ounces of crushed ice and 4 to 6 small "agitator" cubes. Flash blend and open pour with gated finish into a mug or double old-fashioned glass.

HUMUHUMUNUKUNUKUAPUA'A

ORIGIN *Created by Marcovaldo Dionysos*
GLASSWARE *Double old-fashioned*

- ¾ ounce fresh lemon juice
- ¾ ounce pineapple juice
- ½ ounce SC Orgeat (page 330)
- 2 ounces gin
- 2 dashes Peychaud's bitters

GARNISH *Edible orchid and maraschino cherries on a cocktail pick*

Add all the ingredients to a cocktail shaker and fill with crushed ice. Shake and open pour into a double old-fashioned glass. Garnish with an edible orchid and maraschino cherries.

NOTE Substitute a blended aged rum for the gin to make a Lauwiliwilinukunuku'oi'oi.

FINKELGROG

Created for Mai Kai Gents lead singer Judd Finkelstein for his home bar, the Wiki Wiki Grog Shop. Judd's day job as one of the top winemakers in Napa County inspired the ingredients.

ORIGIN *Created by Martin Cate*
GLASSWARE *Double old-fashioned*

½ ounce fresh lime juice

½ ounce fresh grapefruit juice

¼ ounce SC Orgeat (page 330)

½ ounce Napa Wine Syrup (see Note, following)

½ ounce Licor 43

1 ounce blended lightly aged rum ❷

1 ounce black blended rum ❺

1 ounce seltzer

Pinch of freshly ground cinnamon

GARNISH *Zesty conversation*

Combine all the ingredients in a drink mixer tin. Fill with 12 ounces of crushed ice and 4 to 6 "agitator" cubes. Flash blend and open pour with gated finish into a double old-fashioned glass.

NOTE To make the Napa Wine Syrup, place 16 ounces Napa Valley Cabernet Sauvignon in a small saucepan and simmer over medium-low heat until the wine has been reduced by half, about 25 minutes. Add 1 cup of granulated sugar and stir until the sugar has dissolved (about 1 minute). Remove from the heat. Let cool and store in a sealed bottle in the refrigerator for up to three months.

FOR PETE'S SAKE

ORIGIN *Created by Martin Cate*
GLASSWARE *Double old-fashioned*

¾ ounce fresh lime juice

½ ounce SC Demerara Syrup (page 324)

½ ounce SC Hibiscus Liqueur (page 331)

½ ounce Cherry Heering

1½ ounces Peruvian pisco

1 dash Angostura bitters

GARNISH *Maraschino cherry inserted into an edible hibiscus flower speared on a 6-inch black cocktail pick or short swizzle stick*

Add all the ingredients to a drink mixer tin. Fill with 12 ounces of crushed ice and 4 to 6 small "agitator" cubes. Flash blend and then open pour with gated finish into a double old-fashioned glass. Set the cherry-hibiscus garnish across the rim of the glass.

PART THREE

THE SPIRIT OF RUM

"Behold a spirit whose legacy contains all the paradoxes and complexity of the wistfully beautiful region that gave birth to it so long ago."

—BAZ DREISINGER, NEW YORK TIMES

Rum Through the Ages

Martin's home bar, The Novato Grotto

TINKERING IN MY HOME BAR MANY YEARS AGO, AND
FUMBLING AROUND WITH WHAT EXOTIC COCKTAIL
RECIPES WERE AVAILABLE, I'D GET EXCITED WHEN
READING ABOUT A DRINK THAT SOUNDED INTRIGUING
ENOUGH TO HEAD OUT SHOPPING FOR INGREDIENTS,
WHICH OFTEN CALLED FOR A HOST OF ESOTERIC RUMS
FROM AROUND THE WORLD.

But my joy was fleeting once I felt the pain of a gapingly empty wallet after one of these shopping trips. As I would lean back and sip on my drink with a little exotica music playing in the background, I would reflect: but *why* does this cocktail need four rums? So it was back over to the bar for a little tasting of each only to discover (which in hindsight seems obvious) that the four rums in question were *wildly* different. And—they all brought their own unique character to the cocktail. So the question instead soon became *why* are the rums so different? And so began a journey into the labyrinthine world of rum, visits to over a dozen distilleries, and my immersion into an education that never ends.

What follows is by no means intended to be a complete and exhaustive history of rum, which I cannot possibly do justice to in just a few pages. What I hope this will offer you is a kind of "Rum 101" or "Rum Primer"—a way to give you enough to get a general sense, whet your whistle for more, at which point I encourage you to read some of the wonderful books that have been written on the subject, which you can find in the bibliography (page 340).

EARLY ORIGINS, PRODUCTION, AND PIRATES

At its simplest definition, rum is a spirit distilled from sugarcane—from its juice, syrups, or molasses. Sugarcane is a fast-growing grass that traces its origins to Papua New Guinea and through various journeys in the late fifteenth century, made its way to the Caribbean and Brazil.

The prime use of sugarcane originally was to satisfy the insatiable sweet tooth of Europeans. Sugar was the oil of its day—it was a hugely valuable commodity that powered world trade. Unlike Europe, sugarcane thrived in the Caribbean and Brazil, where it got the sun and water it needed. It also, unfortunately, is incredibly difficult to harvest, which means the production of sugar and later of rum emerged on the backs of slaves and prisoners. It is estimated that two-and-one-half million African slaves made the Atlantic crossing just on British ships between 1709 and 1807. In Barbados alone, the population of slaves outnumbered Europeans by more than two to one in the eighteenth century (fifty thousand slaves to just twenty thousand Europeans).

Sugar is made by pressing cane in a mill, then boiling down the juice in a series of vats until the sugar crystallizes. What's left over that doesn't crystallize is molasses. For centuries, it was thought that the molasses by-product of sugar production was fairly worthless, and so it would be discarded, or used as a cheaper sweetener, a fertilizer, or as animal feed. Certainly, both planters and slaves drank fermented cane juice and even fermented molasses during the earliest days of sugar cultivation and production. Possibly as early as the sixteenth century, there was distillation of fermented cane juice in Brazil (known today as cachaça), and perhaps even earlier in India. However, molasses-based rum has its earliest known origins in the Caribbean, with mid-seventeenth century documentation showing rum production on Barbados. Someone, probably a Scottish or Irish indentured servant or a Dutch migrant with some knowledge of distillation (distillation had existed in Europe for hundreds of years), realized that molasses could be diluted and fermented, and subsequently distilled. It was in Barbados that rum was first refined and commercialized, while cachaça continued to be the drink of workers (exportation was not permitted) and was even made illegal in Brazil at various points in the seventeenth and eighteenth centuries.

Given these origins, it is not surprising that, in addition to the early terms rumbullion, kill-devil, and eventually "rum," sugarcane spirit was also frequently called "Barbadoes Waters." According to journalist and author Ian Williams, Barbados, being a fairly flat island with the heat and water needed for sugarcane, made a natural home to the birth of rum not only because of the geography, but also because of a confluence of history. To quote Williams, "The original skills of Neolithic East Asian subsistence farmers, Greek and Arab science, early modern commerce, the Mediterranean abuse of slavery for sugar cultivation, and the Iberian discovery of Africans as readily available slaves were stirred with Protestant enterprise from England and Holland and the Celtic taste for strong liquor and skills in meeting their needs. Together, these streams of history all mixed in one small island to produce the heady cocktail of rum, which was to foment wars, industries, and revolutions around the Atlantic for centuries to come."

Seventeenth-century rum would have originally been distilled in a simple alembic copper pot still like the one pictured opposite, probably holding less than one hundred gallons. The rum produced would have been heavy and full-bodied with many impurities. Early on, the Barbadians began to use double distillation, thereby producing a stronger, yet less toxic, product. Though much of this early Caribbean-produced rum remained there to be

Traditional alembic pot still, Callwood Distillery, Tortola, British Virgin Islands

consumed locally, between the 1660s and the end of the century, rum exported from Barbados grew from roughly 100,000 gallons to nearly 600,000 gallons, making them the leading rum exporter at the turn of the eighteenth century.

During this same period of British colonization and expanded trade, rum began to flow on the islands, among the islands, and north to Colonial America. Caribbean rum producers had the natural advantage of shorter aging times than the newly emerging producers in New England due to their climate (rum ages more quickly in tropical climates, and thus a mature product can be achieved sooner).

Distillation methods for the funky, heavy-bodied, molasses-based pot-distilled rum would also continue to improve, and soon Barbados had heady competition for the export rum market from another British

colony—Jamaica. At least in Barbados and Jamaica, evidence suggests fermentation at this time included not only molasses and water, but also skimmings from atop open vats of sugarcane juice being boiled as part of the production of sugar, and the addition of "dunder" (see page 188). By the end of the eighteenth century, Jamaica was using a ferment with a greater proportion of dunder than other British Caribbean rum producers, and was making a more concentrated (higher-proof) rum. These higher-proof, pungent rums, were the distinctive style for which the country's rum became known.

It was during these early days of rum production and trade that rum caught the eye of an unwanted thirsty consumer: the pirate. Piracy in the Caribbean, and the only slightly more upstanding privateering (government-sanctioned piracy), was especially rampant between the mid-seventeenth and early eighteenth centuries. On both sea and on land, pirates were notorious rum guzzlers, drinking that which they captured, and buying more with their stolen gold. The town of Port Royal, Jamaica, became a lawless drunken "Pirate HQ," home to such famed pirates as Captain Morgan. In the late nineteenth century, the pirate and his bottle of rum would be forever linked by Robert Louis Stevenson in his best-selling book *Treasure Island*.

It is interesting to note that while rum production and rum exports from the British Caribbean expanded in the early part of the eighteenth century, very little went back to Britain itself yet, where gin remained king. This began to change when Britain passed legislation that curbed the local production of gin and lowered taxes on rum imports. However, the demand for rum back home was also spurred on by an important sector of the population: returning seamen.

Sailors receiving their rum ration

UP SPIRITS! BRITAIN AND ROYAL NAVY RUM

As Britain colonized parts of the Caribbean in the mid-seventeenth century, there were more frequent and longer voyages by sea. Leaving Britain with just water and beer on board, the water soon turned bad and the beer was soon drunk, creating a demand for more alcohol rations on board. With several of the British Caribbean islands now producing rum, the navy had an easy solution, and began to purchase vast quantities of it. Over the decades, rum became an acceptable way to keep up morale and discipline on board, for sailors were often press-ganged into service and then served in terrible conditions. An alcohol ration became part of official naval regulations in 1731, and in 1775 rum became integral to those rations through a parliamentary act.

During this era, sailors were getting as much as a half pint a day as their daily rum ration (or "tot") and would frequently end up quite drunk and useless. In 1740, Admiral Edward Vernon, calling drunkenness "That Pernicious Demon" and "The Formidable Dragon," ordered the daily tot diluted with water and split in half. This presumably did not go over well, but it was also Admiral Vernon who suggested that the crew add lime and sugar to their rum ration to make it "more palatable." It wasn't until years later that the link between limes and the prevention of scurvy was discovered, but one can argue Admiral Vernon inadvertently invented the daiquiri. And that "cocktail" earned the somewhat derisive name of grog, short for Vernon's somewhat derisive nickname of "Old Grogham"—so-named for his waterproof cloak made of a fabric called grogham.

By the end of the eighteenth century, the British Royal Navy was one of the biggest rum customers in the world. They needed a high volume of consistent product, and so for nearly 190 years (1784 to 1970), a single broker sourced and blended rums from several British colonies (Barbados, Guyana, Jamaica, Trinidad) of different styles and ages, and distributed the supply to the Royal Navy.

Though the amount of the ration would continue to be cut, and the proof lowered to a measly 109 (!), the daily tot was part of a formal ritual that continued for centuries on board Royal Navy ships, announced daily by the bosun's call of "Up Spirits!" However, while it was one thing to have a bunch of drunk sailors on board eighteenth and nineteenth century ships, it was quite another when, in the twentieth century, those ships became more technologically complex and, more importantly, armed with nukes. After much heated (and hilarious) debate in the British parliament, in which former members of the Royal Navy attempted to defend the tot and its benefits to health, morale, and the ability to fight the enemy, it was determined that the rum ration should be abolished. The dreaded day arrived July 31, 1970, and was nicknamed Black Tot Day, complete with mock funerals and sailors wearing black armbands. Today, only the Queen, a member of the royal family, or the Admiralty itself can call for a rum ration, which it does for special occasions such as a major military victory or royal wedding. This ration is known as "splicing the main brace," which is named for the difficult and dangerous work of repairing the main rigging on the ship (which historically was rewarded with an extra ration).

While the ration may have ended, the style of rum (heavy-bodied, pot-distilled, and high-proof) remained popular primarily in the UK and eastern Canada, and variations of this style are still sold today as "Navy Style" rums. After Black Tot Day, the remaining stocks of Royal Navy rum sat undisturbed in their original imperial gallon flagons in underground British Government warehouses for nearly forty years, making only rare appearances

at important royal and naval functions. A few flagons of this rum were sold to the public, several of which I purchased and sell at Smuggler's Cove. It is immensely special and rare, as this is the exact rum commissioned over fifty years ago for the Royal Navy and contains some rums dating back to the late 1940s. Many of these flagons were purchased in 2009 by Specialty Drinks in the UK, who blended the rum for consistency, and re-packaged it as "The Black Tot."

FERMENTING REVOLUTION: RUM IN COLONIAL AMERICA

Though the drink of choice among Colonial America's early settlers was beer and hard cider, early ties between Barbados and other British colonies in North America meant that when rum began to flow from Barbados in the late seventeenth century, it made its way north to open arms (and mouths). It wasn't long before the New England colonists tried their hand at distilling, making rum as early as the 1660s. Though grain was initially used for whiskies, it was too valuable, both as a food source and to trade, so New Englanders soon turned to their island cousins for an ingredient for their distillation: molasses. By the mid-eighteenth century, distilleries had sprung up throughout New England. The New England style of rum that emerged at the time was generally rough and less desirable than its Caribbean counterpart, but rum production and consumption grew throughout Colonial America. Rum became ingrained in the culture as everything from a mainstay tipple, to a cure for ailments, to its use as actual currency.

Throughout New England the colonial tavern was prevalent, with Massachusetts going so far as to mandate every town have one. It was in these taverns that most rum was consumed, and because it usually wasn't all that palatable neat, it was often diluted with water, and flavored with molasses, sugar, spices, lime, mint, or mixed into early cocktails such as the bounce, flip, or calibogus. However, the most common and popular way to consume rum in Colonial America was most certainly punch. As early as 1682, evidence of punch consumption was widespread, with tax records showing that punch bowls were almost as common as benches and tankards in taverns. A communal drink that celebrated all the most valuable goods in the world, punch was born from the spice trade. The earliest reference to a punch recipe dates to 1596, drunk by English travelers in India with local ingredients including "sugar, lemons, and sundry sorts of spices." The word *punch* stems from the Hindustani word *panch*, which means "five"—the number of ingredients: tea (or spice), lemon, sugar, water, and arrack (an Indonesian distillate of palm sap and red rice, historically quite coarse, and best well diluted). As punch traveled along the trade route—from the East Indies to Europe and then on to New World—recipes took on many variations, including the use of rum as the base in both the West Indies and Colonial America. In the West Indies, the now famous rhyming recipe for a rum punch emerged: one of sour (citrus, usually lime), two of

sweet (sugar), three of strong (rum, obviously), four of weak (local juices), a formula that became critical to the creation of the exotic cocktail.

Rum also played no small part in the American Revolution. Rather than obtaining their molasses from the British West Indies, New England distillers were primarily turning to the French islands where it was cheaper. This didn't go over well with the British, so the Crown then passed the Molasses Act of 1733. It placed heavy taxes on French molasses in theory, but was mostly skirted by the colonists through smuggling and corrupt British customs officials. This led to the more strictly enforced Sugar Act of 1763. A few New England distillers went out of business, and the rest struggled along under the weight of the new expense. The thirteen colonies banded together to complain vehemently to parliament, in part arguing that by damaging New England rum production, the colonies would not have the money to buy goods from English merchants, thus, ultimately, hurting England. The Sugar Act was ultimately revised and tariffs on molasses lowered to an affordable level. But the colonists had now flexed their resistance muscles, priming the pump for full revolution. Rum then literally fueled the Revolution itself, flowing through the

taverns where legislators and militia assembled, and later became part of a daily ration to the soldiers. It is even the case that Paul Revere, on his famous ride, stopped first at a rum distillery, whose owner fortified him for the ride ahead.

After the Revolution, the new United States saw a sharp decline in the production of and preference for rum. For various political reasons, molasses was increasingly difficult to get, and then after the War of 1812, the British began freeing their slaves, meaning that the sugar estates were no longer affordable to run. United States rum distilleries began to shut or change production to the shiny new toy in America—whiskey. Whiskey production was on the rise as the Scots-Irish colonists moved south and west, and found land where corn and rye could be grown in abundance, and distillation could occur far from the eyes of the customs collectors. It was also increasingly the case that whiskey was preferred because it was made entirely in America, with no ties to the Crown. The final nail in rum's coffin came in the second half of the nineteenth century, when the temperance movement began to take hold and unite against distilled spirits, which they collectively (and unfairly, dammit) referred to as "Demon Rum."

"From the galleons of the high seas, to the taverns of Colonial America, to the cocktail lounges of far-distant ports-of-call—over three hundred years of history in a glass."

—FROM THE SMUGGLER'S COVE MENU

MEANWHILE, BACK TO THE ISLANDS . . .

The islands of the French West Indies, including Martinique and Guadeloupe, initially grew sugarcane in order to produce and export sugar, primarily to Europe. Their early distillation techniques were inferior to British Caribbean producers, however, and with little demand for their rum, most of their rum-related exports were in the form of molasses.

In the mid-nineteenth century, French vineyards were ravaged by two blights that devastated wine production and led the French government to lift duties on French Caribbean rum imports. By this point, there was a growth in rum production, especially in the large industrial distilleries making molasses-based rum, primarily centered in the town of Saint-Pierre in Martinique. By the end of the century, exports of rum from Martinique alone had increased from just fifty-six thousand gallons in 1820 to over four million gallons.

During this same period, however, the sugar beet industry emerged and grew in Europe, and Europeans increasingly turned to sugar beets for their sugar needs. This left many smaller sugar producers in Martinique, and other French islands, with a whole lot of sugarcane, and no market for producing sugar, and, with no sugar, there was also no leftover molasses by-product.

Many of these smaller producers then had the idea to make rum directly from the fresh juice of the sugarcane rather than molasses, resulting in the distinctive style known as rhum agricole. When Mount Pelée erupted in 1902, it killed over forty thousand residents of Saint-Pierre, Martinique, and destroyed much of the larger facilities that still made molasses-based rum. The smaller distilleries took this opportunity to expand their production of rhum agricole to fill the void in rum production. Rum that continued to be made from molasses in the French Caribbean was described on the label as rhum traditionnel or, if produced outside of the French Islands, rhum industriel, both terms designed to distinguish it from rhum agricole.

The emancipation of slaves throughout the Caribbean and in the United States in the nineteenth century signaled a massive shift both socially and economically. This, combined with the loss of the European market for sugar, meant that much of British Caribbean rum production also suffered. Two exceptions were Demerara (now Guyana) and Jamaica, both of which remained major exporters, especially to Britain, who reexported about a fourth of this rum to Australia, Africa, and Europe.

THE NOBLE EXPERIMENT AND THE "ISLE OF ENCHANTMENT"

Rum production in the Spanish colonies had been slow to start, as Spain saw rum as a threat to the Spanish wine and brandy market. However, it was difficult for them to stop illicit rum production, and as trade opened up more with French Caribbean and American colonies, the Spanish Caribbean was exposed to more rum, and rum-making techniques. In 1764, rum making became legal in Cuba and Puerto Rico, and Cuban rum began to be exported to the Spanish Americas, and by the 1780s Cuba was exporting both molasses and rum to the newly formed United States. Throughout much of the nineteenth century, however, sugar and molasses for export was the main focus in Cuba, and rum took a backseat. In Puerto Rico, the Dominican Republic, and throughout much of the sugarcane growing areas of Central and South America, rum was produced almost entirely for local consumption.

Column still, Demerara Distillers Limited, Guyana

Historic Cuban rums

In 1832, an Irishman named Aeneas Coffey patented his column (continuous) still, which allowed the production of a lighter bodied, more highly rectified spirit. In Cuba, the Bacardi family bought a distillery in 1862, and started with a pot still that they ran multiple distillations with to create a lighter spirit that was then aged in oak for a few years. They subsequently charcoal filtered the aged spirit to remove most of the color and some impurities, a technique that created a lighter-tasting rum with enough age to smooth out the harsher edges. With the invention of the Coffey still, Bacardi could now more efficiently produce an even lighter rum, and by the early twentieth century chose to switch entirely to column still production.

When Prohibition hit America, thirsty American travelers flooded to Cuba, and discovered and fell in love with the lighter Bacardi rums and the cocktails that featured them, like the world-famous daiquiri. For Americans who had long since abandoned rum in favor of whiskey, or who thought that rum was "coarse," the new style of rum seemed revelatory.

POST-PROHIBITION AND CHANGING TASTES

After Prohibition, Americans once again wanted their rum, though the rum they wanted had changed. Other distillers in Cuba, and then Puerto Rico, quickly followed Bacardi's lead to meet the increased demand of consumers for column distilled "Cuban rum." In the 1930s and early 1940s, Puerto Rico enjoyed favorable tax status as a territory of the United States, and soon they had surpassed Cuban imports, moving from about ten thousand gallons in 1934 to 2.4 million by 1941.

World War II meant that Americans faced a huge shortage of liquor, as domestic production of most spirits was banned, and imported spirits from Europe were hard to come by, for obvious reasons. This left a gaping hole that Caribbean rum could fill. Cheap, quickly made rum flooded the American market, and to such an extent that distributors even (illegally) forced wholesalers to buy three cases of rum for every one case of the much more desirable, and rarer, whiskey. The Andrews Sisters recorded "Rum and Coca-Cola" in 1944, a song about American servicemen enjoying the island girls on Trinidad and drinking rum and Coke. It would sell seven million copies by the end of the decade, and the drink, by extension, was a huge hit as well.

Much of this cheap, unaged rum remained on store shelves and in storage at distilleries after the war was over, and such a surplus meant prices plummeted. Puerto Rico, the largest exporter of rum to the United States, overcame this setback by spending the late 1940s and 1950s investing in improving quality through instituting minimum aging requirements, establishing the Rum Pilot Plant (a government-sponsored rum research program administered by the University of Puerto Rico, that scientifically explored all aspects of rum production), and, possibly most importantly, through an extensive multimillion-dollar marketing and advertising campaign. The rum itself moved even further into the light—rums were designed to meet the palate of 1950s America—a palate that was soon also to be well sated by . . . vodka.

Jamaican rum continued to be 100 percent pot still rum and stayed big and funky until the 1960s. But, at that point, lighter column-distilled rum had become so popular that Jamaica and other producers of full-bodied pot distilled rum felt pressure to change in order to survive. They, as well as other traditional pot-still rum manufacturers, began producing medium-bodied rums made from blending pot and column distillates, and have continued to do so ever since.

Throughout the Caribbean, rum continued to be produced for the local market. In addition, while some of the large, consolidated brands were able to continue to grow and build their own brand outside the Caribbean, many of the Caribbean distillers in the 1960s and 1970s were producing rum in bulk to serve the needs of large European and Canadian brands who were blending and bottling the bulk rums.

The 1980s brought spiced rum to the U.S. market, and the introduction of coconut, orange, and other flavored rums, many of which were simply cane-neutral spirit with chemical additives, and hadn't seen anything resembling actual spices, coconut, or fruit. Despite their artificial nature, flavored rums became popular, particularly with younger drinkers. As with the devolution of the exotic cocktail, so, too, seemed to be the way of rum.

TODAY: THE RISE OF PREMIUM RUM

In the last few decades, we've seen a welcome resurgence in rum. From 2000 to 2010, some estimates suggest that global rum consumption has grown as much as 40 percent. Along with increased consumption of rum in general, there has been growth in the production and consumption of premium rums. Rum producers in the Caribbean have begun to bottle and brand their rums, rather than continue to just produce bulk product. Rum brands large and small began to emphasize that an aged rum can be sipped and enjoyed the same way as other quality spirits, and even attempted to borrow language and categories from other respected spirits, cognac and Scotch, to help market their products. The exploding market of premium cigars in the last twenty years has been a wonderful partner in rum's journey, creating a demand for good rums to sip with them.

At the same time, the booming cocktail renaissance has also sent professional and home enthusiast bartenders and mixologists on a quest to better understand rum, and to have the choice of a wider flavor palette to play a more significant role in their cocktails. There is also an increased desire among contemporary mixologists for honest products that, if flavored or spiced, are done so by adding real flavors and real spices.

With this demand, and the rise of the micro-distillery in the United States in the last few decades, there is also now an exciting renaissance in domestic rum production. Because of their size, the micro-distiller almost always uses a pot still, with the column still being prohibitively expensive and space consuming. This means, however, that micro-distillers are being creative in their source ingredients, fermentation and distillation techniques, and how they age and finish their rums.

There has also been the welcome introduction of several domestic and international rum shows, drawing thousands of visitors, both industry professionals and the public, to sample rums and learn more about their history, production, and the culture of rum-producing lands.

And in those Caribbean countries that have produced rum for centuries, today rum is a vital part of their economies and offers both employment and global recognition. While rum will never be able to separate itself from its terrible history in many lands, rum is now a celebrated part of Caribbean culture; from the rum shops of everyday life to toasting important occasions, rum provides the flavor. And as each country steps further out onto the world stage, with many only knowing independence for less than a century, they take pride in remarkable premium rums that they now consider their own and no longer defined by the names of the countries whose flags once flew over their lands.

ARRACK PUNCH

ORIGIN *Created by Smuggler's Cove, inspired by traditional colonial-era punch recipes*

SOURCE *Traditional arrack punch recipes are published in* Punch: The Delights (and Dangers) of the Flowing Bowl

GLASSWARE *Small (32-ounce) punch bowl or other decorative bowl with a ladle and cups*

SERVES 4

2 ounces fresh lemon juice

2 ounces fresh lime juice

3 ounces SC Demerara Syrup (page 324)

6 ounces Batavia arrack

2 ounces pot still lightly aged rum (overproof) ⓘ

6 ounces Carbonated Chai Tea (see Note, following)

GARNISH *A few slices of lemons and limes*

Add all the ingredients to a drink mixer tin and roll (pour back and forth a few times) with another drink mixer tin to combine the ingredients. Divide the contents evenly between the two tins. Add 12 ounces of crushed ice and 4 to 6 "agitator" cubes to each of the two tins. With each tin, flash blend and open pour with gated finish into the serving bowl. Float a few lemon and lime slices on the punch for garnish.

NOTE To make the Carbonated Chai Tea, steep 1 teaspoon chai tea leaves in 1 cup water for 5 minutes. Strain then carbonate with a home soda maker (such as an iSi Soda Siphon or SodaStream).

EL DRAQUE

Named for famous "local" privateer Sir Francis Drake, this was the great-great (x 14) grandfather of the mojito. Originally a slurry, room-temperature mess, we've refined its fiery character with aged cachaça, Demerara sugar, fresh lime, and mint.

ORIGIN *Created by Smuggler's Cove, inspired by a traditional recipe*

SOURCE *Traditional recipe described in* Rum: Yesterday and Today

GLASSWARE *Chilled coupe*

5 fresh mint leaves

¾ ounce SC Demerara Syrup (page 324)

¾ ounce fresh lime juice

2 ounces pot still aged cachaça

GARNISH *Lime wheel with sword cocktail pick*

Muddle the mint with the syrup and lime juice in a cocktail shaker. Add the cachaça and cubed or cracked ice. Shake and double-strain into a chilled coupe. Garnish with a lime wheel speared on a pirate sword cocktail pick.

Grog

GROG

To be a sailor in the British Royal Navy in the 1700s was not what anyone would call a life of leisure, but at least there was the daily rum ration to look forward to, even if it was diluted with brackish water. In 1740, Admiral Edward "Old Grogram" Vernon told his sailors they could exchange their salt and bread for limes and sugar and, not being fools, they perhaps became the first to see the wisdom in forsaking food for a good cocktail. And so Grog was born.

ORIGIN *Traditional recipe, adapted by Smuggler's Cove*
SOURCE *Described in* And a Bottle of Rum: A History of the New World in Ten Cocktails
GLASSWARE *Old-fashioned*

> ½ ounce fresh lime juice
>
> ½ ounce SC Demerara Syrup (page 324)
>
> 2 ounces rum (see Note, following)

GARNISH *None*

Add the ingredients to a cocktail shaker filled with cracked or cubed ice. Shake and strain into an ice-filled old-fashioned glass.

NOTE If you want to truly mimic a grog from the 1700s, use a pot still unaged rum or a black pot still rum. (And skip the ice. And the clean glass. And maybe add some brackish water. Maybe not.) If you're looking for a nineteenth-century–style grog, try a black blended rum. For a more refined grog, as we serve at Smuggler's Cove, choose a blended aged rum.

RUM FLIP

The original tavern flip of rum and beer gradually evolved. Egg was added, and then beer dropped altogether from the mix. A lovely drink to finish off the night, but don't let us tell you when to enjoy it.

ORIGIN *Traditional recipe*
SOURCE How to Mix Drinks, or the Bon-Vivant's Companion
GLASSWARE *Chilled coupe*

> 1 medium egg
>
> ¼ ounce SC Demerara Syrup (page 324)
>
> 2 ounces blended aged rum ❸

GARNISH *Freshly grated nutmeg*

Add the ingredients to drink mixer tin and dry flash without ice for 10 seconds (see page 229). Fill with 12 ounces of crushed ice and 4 to 6 small "agitator" cubes. Flash blend and double-strain into a chilled coupe glass. Top with freshly grated nutmeg.

Clockwise from bottom left: Bombo, Calibogus, Rum Flip (page 165)

BOMBO

From discriminating pirates aboard ship, to the electorate of colonial Virginia who found themselves plied with the stuff courtesy of a young George Washington during his campaign bid for the House of Burgesses, Bombo was enjoyed for hundreds of years. As cocktail historian David Wondrich says, "[Bombo] is a simple drink in the same way a tripod is a simple device: Remove one leg and it cannot stand, set it up properly and it will hold the whole weight of the world." Ours is a kind of proto-old-fashioned, made with Demerara Syrup for a more refined molasses flavor.

ORIGIN *Traditional recipe, adapted by Smuggler's Cove*
SOURCE *Described in* And a Bottle of Rum: A History of the New World in Ten Cocktails
GLASSWARE *Old-fashioned*

¼ ounce SC Demerara Syrup (page 324)
2 ounces blended aged rum ❸

GARNISH *Freshly grated nutmeg*

Stir the rum and syrup in a mixing glass and strain into an ice-filled old-fashioned glass. Top with grated nutmeg.

NOTE At Smuggler's Cove, the house style is to use a blended aged rum in this recipe. However, for a closer historical approximation of colonial-era drinks, you may wish to choose a pot still unaged rum or pot still lightly aged rum. Those produced today in New England especially mimic the rums of the day, albeit with much improved quality!

CALIBOGUS

Popular in colonial taverns in both the United States and Canada, Calibogus was traditionally a heady mixture of spruce beer, molasses, and rum.

ORIGIN *Smuggler's Cove modern original, inspired by traditional flavors*
SOURCE *Traditional recipe described in* And a Bottle of Rum: A History of the New World in Ten Cocktails
GLASSWARE *Collins or highball*

3 ounces seltzer
¼ ounce fresh lime juice
¾ ounce SC Molasses Syrup (page 327)
1 drop spruce beer soda extract (see Resources, page 335)
¾ ounce Zirbenz Stone Pine liqueur
1¼ ounce blended aged rum ❸

GARNISH *Swizzle stick*

Add the seltzer to the bottom of a Collins or highball glass. Add the remaining ingredients to a cocktail shaker and shake with cracked or cubed ice. Strain into the glass and carefully add cracked or cubed ice and garnish.

MARY PICKFORD

Created to honor Mary Pickford, the legendary actress and founder of United Artists, while she was shooting a film in Cuba, this cocktail was a staple of Cuban bars and nightclubs serving thirsty Americans.

ORIGIN *Prohibition-era recipe, adapted by Smuggler's Cove*
GLASSWARE *Chilled coupe*

- 1½ ounces pineapple juice
- 1 barspoon SC Grenadine (page 328)
- 6 drops Luxardo Maraschino liqueur
- 1½ ounces blended lightly aged rum ❷

GARNISH *None*

Add all the ingredients to a cocktail shaker. Add cracked or cubed ice, shake, and then double-strain into a chilled coupe.

NOTE The Smuggler's Cove house style for the Prohibition-era cocktails is to use a blended lightly aged rum for more body and to mimic the less-efficient distillation methods of the day. Alternatively, you may wish to use a column still lightly aged rum, but we suggest using one with a slightly higher proof to maintain an era-appropriate "pop."

DAIQUIRI NO. 1

The most elegant, simple, and famous of all Cuban cocktails, the Daiquiri and its variants were set in stone by legendary barman Constante Ribalaigua of the famous Floridita bar in Havana.

ORIGIN *Prohibition-era recipe, adapted by Smuggler's Cove*
SOURCE Bar La Florida Cocktails, *1935 reprint*
GLASSWARE *Chilled coupe*

- ¾ ounce fresh lime juice
- ½ ounce SC Demerara syrup (page 324)
- 2 ounces blended lightly aged rum ❷

GARNISH *None*

Add all the ingredients to a cocktail shaker. Add cracked or cubed ice, shake, and then double-strain into a chilled coupe.

"The moment, now, had arrived for a Daiquiri. . . . It was a delicate compound . . . but still a revelation, and I was devoutly thankful to be sitting, at that hour in the Inglaterra, with such a drink. It elevated my contentment to an even higher pitch; and, with a detached amusement, I recalled the fact that farther north prohibition was formally in effect."

–JOSEPH HERGESHEIMER, SAN CRISTÓBAL DE HABANA, 1920

From left: Mary Pickford, Hotel Nacional Special (page 171), Daiquiri No. 1

Daisy de Santiago

HOTEL NACIONAL SPECIAL

ORIGIN *Prohibition-era recipe,*
adapted by Smuggler's Cove
SOURCE The Gentleman's Companion
GLASSWARE *Chilled coupe*

> 3 or 4 (1-inch-square) pineapple chunks
>
> ¾ ounce fresh lime juice
>
> ½ ounce SC Demerara Syrup (page 324)
>
> ½ ounce natural apricot liqueur
> (such as Rothman & Winter Apricot Liqueur
> or Giffard Abricot du Roussillon)
>
> 1½ ounces blended lightly aged rum ❷

GARNISH *None*

In cocktail shaker, muddle the pineapple chunks with
the lime juice and syrup. Add the apricot liqueur and
the rum, then fill with cracked or cubed ice. Shake
and double-strain into a chilled coupe.

DAISY DE SANTIAGO

A "lovely thing, indeed" and one of food and cocktail
writer Charles H. Baker's favorite drinks from his
travels through Cuba.

ORIGIN *Prohibition-era recipe,*
adapted by Smuggler's Cove
SOURCE The Gentleman's Companion
GLASSWARE *Double old-fashioned*

> 1 ounce fresh lime juice
>
> 1½ teaspoons SC Demerara Syrup (page 324)
>
> 1 ounce seltzer
>
> ½ ounce Yellow Chartreuse
>
> 1½ ounces blended lightly aged rum ❷

GARNISH *Mint sprig*

Add all the ingredients to a cocktail shaker. Add
cracked or cubed ice. Shake and strain into a double
old-fashioned glass filled with crushed ice. Add
garnish.

EL PRESIDENTE

This drink honors a Cuban president, but there are differing accounts as to exactly which one it was. Yet he must have been a good one to get his name on a drink this tasty. A sadly forgotten classic, it's described by author Wayne Curtis as "part tropical treat, part sophisticated lounge drink, and wholly Cuban."

ORIGIN *Prohibition-era recipe, adapted by Smuggler's Cove*
GLASSWARE *Chilled coupe*

  ½ teaspoon SC Grenadine (page 328)
  ¾ ounce dry vermouth
  ½ ounce Pierre Ferrand Dry Curaçao
  1½ ounces blended lightly aged rum ❷

GARNISH *None*

Add all the ingredients to a cocktail shaker. Add cracked or cubed ice, shake, and then double-strain into a chilled coupe.

TWELVE MILE LIMIT

Sailing beyond the U.S. government's Prohibition-era reach of 12 miles off-shore to load up on hooch is certainly a great inspiration for a drink name. This heady combination of rum, rye, and brandy shows that rum plays well with others. Though not a Cuban drink, it certainly belongs to the era and the theme.

ORIGIN *Prohibition-era drink, created by journalist Tommy Millard*
SOURCE *Vintage Spirits and Forgotten Cocktails*
GLASSWARE *Chilled coupe*

  ½ ounce fresh lemon juice
  ½ ounce SC Grenadine (page 328)
  1 ounce blended lightly aged rum ❷
  ½ ounce rye
  ½ ounce brandy

GARNISH *Lemon twist*

Add all the ingredients to a cocktail shaker. Add cracked or cubed ice, shake, and then double-strain into a chilled coupe.

El Presidente

PARISIAN BLONDE

ORIGIN *Adapted by Erik Ellestad*
SOURCE The Savoy Cocktail Book
GLASSWARE *Chilled coupe*

- 1 ounce Pierre Ferrand Dry Curaçao
- 1 ounce blended aged rum ❸
- 1 ounce sweet cream (see Note, following)

GARNISH *Freshly grated cinnamon*

In a mixing glass, stir together the curaçao and rum with cracked or cubed ice. Strain into a chilled coupe. Carefully pour the sweet cream over the back of a spoon to float on top. Garnish with freshly grated cinnamon.

NOTE To make the sweet cream, in a drink mixer, blend 6 ounces of heavy whipping cream with 1 ounce of SC Demerara Syrup (page 324) until slightly thickened but still pourable (a few seconds).

CORA MIDDLETON

ORIGIN *Adapted by Smuggler's Cove*
SOURCE The South American Gentleman's Companion
GLASSWARE *Chilled coupe*

- 2 teaspoons egg white
- 2 ounces blended aged rum ❸
- ¾ ounce fresh lime juice
- ¼ ounce SC Demerara Syrup (page 324)
- ½ ounce Small Hand Foods Raspberry Gum Syrup

GARNISH *1 dash Angostura bitters*

Combine the egg white and rum in a drink mixer tin and dry flash without ice for 10 seconds (see page 229). Transfer contents to a cocktail shaker and add and the remaining ingredients, then shake with cracked or cubed ice. Double-strain into a chilled coupe. Drop 1 dash of bitters on top of the surface of the drink for garnish.

MILLIONAIRE COCKTAIL (NO. 1)

A larger than life drink from *The Savoy Cocktail Book*.

ORIGIN *Adapted by Smuggler's Cove*
SOURCE The Savoy Cocktail Book
GLASSWARE *Chilled coupe*

¾ ounce fresh lime juice

1 dash SC Grenadine (page 328)

¾ ounce natural apricot liqueur
(such as Rothman & Winter Apricot Liqueur
or Giffard Abricot du Roussillon)

¾ ounce black pot still rum (see page 198)
or blended aged rum ❸

¾ ounce sloe gin

GARNISH *Lime wheel*

Add all the ingredients to a cocktail shaker with cracked or cubed ice. Shake and double-strain into a chilled coupe. Garnish with a lime wheel.

BATIDA DE MARACUJÁ E COCO

A national treasure in Brazil, *batida* is Portuguese for "shaken" or "milk shake" and is a sweet and creamy blend of cachaça, condensed milk, and your choice of either coconut milk (Batida de Coco), passion fruit nectar (Batida de Maracujá), or both (Batida de Maracujá e Coco).

ORIGIN *Traditional Brazilian recipes, adapted by Smuggler's Cove*
GLASSWARE *Old-fashioned*

¾ ounce passion fruit puree

2 ounces coconut milk

1 ounce pot still aged cachaça (see page 199)

1 ounce sweetened condensed milk

GARNISH *Mint sprig*

Add the passion fruit puree, coconut milk, and cachaça to a drink mixer tin. Add 6 ounces of crushed ice, and then the condensed milk (if you put condensed milk in first, it can get too cold and stick to the tin before integrating). Flash blend and open pour with gated finish into an old-fashioned glass.

NOTE If you want to leave out the coconut for a "Batida de Maracujá" then increase the passion fruit puree to 1 ounce.

WRAY & TING

A delicious Jamaican staple, simple and refreshing. Pot still Jamaican overproof rum is finely balanced with crisp, refreshing Ting grapefruit soda from Jamaica, and a squeeze of lime

ORIGIN *Traditional Jamaican drink*
GLASSWARE *Collins or highball*

> 1½ ounces Wray & Nephew White Overproof Rum
>
> 4 ounces Ting grapefruit soda

GARNISH *Lime wedge*

Fill a Collins or highball glass with cracked or cubed ice. Add the rum. Top with grapefruit soda and stir. Squeeze a lime wedge and drop in.

HIBISCUS RUM PUNCH

A lovely and delicious twist on a Jamaican Christmas tradition.

ORIGIN *Smuggler's Cove original, based on traditional recipes*
GLASSWARE *Collins or highball*

> 2 ounces seltzer
>
> ½ ounce fresh lime juice
>
> 1 ounce SC Hibiscus Liqueur (see page 331)
>
> ⅓ ounce SC Demerara Syrup (page 324)
>
> 1½ ounces blended aged rum (Jamaica) ❸

GARNISH *Edible hibiscus flower on a plastic pick or lime wheel*

Add the seltzer to a Collins or highball glass. Add the remaining ingredients to a cocktail shaker. Fill with cracked or cubed ice. Shake and double-strain into the glass. Carefully add cracked or cubed ice to the glass and garnish.

NOTE Fun marketing fact: This drink was originally called a Sorrel Rum Punch on our menu, as hibiscus is called sorrel in the Caribbean. Customers didn't know what sorrel was, and so no one ordered the drink. We changed the name to Hibiscus Rum Punch and sales tripled. There is an art to menu copy, and I won't pretend to have mastered it.

Hibiscus Rum Punch

Ti' Punch Vieux

TI' PUNCH / TI' PUNCH VIEUX

The beautiful and traditional way to enjoy a Martinique rhum agricole is like this, with just a hint of lime and Martinique cane sugar. In Martinique, you are frequently given all of the ingredients to make the drink yourself, including a full bottle of rhum. (Since they only give you one slice of lime, there's no chance you'll tear through the whole bottle. Also, they assume you're a decent person.) This tradition is referred to with the phrase, "chacun prépare sa propre mort" which, roughly translated, means "each prepares his own death."

ORIGIN *Traditional Martinique recipe*

GLASSWARE *Old-fashioned*

1 teaspoon Martinique sugarcane syrup

2 ounces cane AOC Martinique rhum agricole blanc ❼ (substitute an élevé sous bois, or rhum vieux ❽ for a Ti' Punch Vieux)

1 small rounded chunk of fresh lime (cut from the side of the lime, approximately the size of a quarter, with some pulp attached)

GARNISH *None*

In an old-fashioned glass, add the sugarcane syrup and rhum. Swizzle with a barspoon or lélé. Squeeze the lime round over the drink and drop it into the glass. (The squeeze should yield 6 to 10 drops of lime juice.)

BARBADOS RUM PUNCH

ORIGIN *Smuggler's Cove original based on traditional recipes*

GLASSWARE *Footed pilsner*

1 ounce fresh lime juice

1 ounce SC Demerara Syrup (page 324)

2 ounces blended aged rum (Barbados) ❸

1 dash Angostura bitters

GARNISH *Freshly grated nutmeg*

Fill a footed pilsner with cubed or cracked ice. Add all the ingredients to a cocktail shaker. Fill with cubed or cracked ice. Shake and strain into the glass. Top with grated nutmeg.

JAMAICAN MILK PUNCH

This drink was described in 1873 in *The Brooklyn Daily Eagle* as "the surest thing in the world to get drunk on, and so fearfully drunk, that you won't know whether you are a cow, yourself, or some other foolish thing."

ORIGIN *Smuggler's Cove original, inspired by traditional recipes*
GLASSWARE *Double old-fashioned*

1 ounce whole milk

1 ounce heavy whipping cream

½ ounce SC Demerara Syrup (page 324)

1 ounce black blended rum (Jamaica) ❺

6 drops vanilla extract

1 dash Angostura bitters

GARNISH *Freshly grated nutmeg*

Add all the ingredients to a drink mixer tin. Fill with 12 ounces of crushed ice and 4 to 6 "agitator cubes." Flash blend and open pour with gated finish into a double old-fashioned glass. Top with grated nutmeg.

CORN AND OIL

ORIGIN *Traditional Barbados recipe, adapted by Smuggler's Cove*
GLASSWARE *Old-fashioned*

½ ounce John D. Taylor's Velvet Falernum

2 ounces blended aged rum (Barbados) ❸

2 to 4 dashes Angostura bitters

GARNISH *None*

Add all the ingredients to an old-fashioned glass and fill with crushed ice. Stir to combine until frost forms on the outside of the glass.

NOTE Old Barbadians confirmed a preference for crushed ice. And please—use Barbados rum.

QUEEN'S PARK SWIZZLE

Named after the green oasis in the heart of Trinidad's Port of Spain, Trader Vic described this drink, created at the Queen's Park Hotel, as "the most delightful form of anesthesia given out today."

ORIGIN *Traditional Trinidad recipe*
SOURCE *Trader Vic's Bartender's Guide,*
adapted by Smuggler's Cove
GLASSWARE *Collins or highball*

- **4 mint leaves**
- **½ ounce fresh lime juice**
- **½ ounce SC Demerara Syrup (page 324)**
- **2 ounces black blended rum ⑤**
- **2 dashes Angostura bitters**

GARNISH *Swizzle napkin wrap (see page 245)*
and mint sprig

Gently muddle the mint leaves with the lime juice and syrup in a Collins or highball glass. Add the rum and bitters. Add crushed ice until the glass is three-quarters full, then use a barspoon or lélé to swizzle. Top up with additional crushed ice as needed to fill the glass. Add garnish.

NOTE Rum was not produced on a large scale in Trinidad until after World War II, so despite the drink's Trinidad origins, we suggest a black blended rum, the likely choice when the drink was created. We also believe that even though the bitters look pretty when floated on top, the drink tastes much better when they are swizzled with the rest of the ingredients.

"One of the main reasons for the past unpopularity of rum has been due to the lack of knowledge about the various types to be used, its various flavors and its proper use. No one bothers to explain that there is a rum for every purpose."

—TRADER VIC, *TRADER VIC'S BOOK OF FOOD AND DRINK*, 1946

Understanding Rum

Interior, Smuggler's Cove

I FREQUENTLY HEAR PEOPLE SAY THAT "RUM ISN'T REALLY FOR ME," OR "RUM AND I DON'T GET ALONG," OR SIMPLY, "I DON'T LIKE RUM." I ALWAYS COUNTER WITH "THERE IS A RUM FOR EVERYONE. YOU JUST HAVEN'T MET THE RIGHT RUM YET."

Rum is unquestionably the most diverse spirit in the world. It is made in at least sixty countries from different raw materials in different kinds of stills, aged at different temperatures and in different kinds of wood.

The very thing that makes rum such an exciting spirit—its diversity—is also what makes it the most confusing for the consumer. With the exception of particular sectors within rum, such as the Appelation d'Origine Contrôlée (AOC) designation for rhum agricole from Martinique (see page 189), there are few strict rules about production or aging, and what rules there are vary from country to country. In recent years, there has been a growing effort to change this. Organizations such as the West Indies Rum and Spirits Producers' Association Incorporated (WIRSPA), founded in the 1960s, have developed an Authentic Caribbean Rum (ACR) *marque*, a visual symbol used to help distinguish Caribbean rum of quality. However, they continue to face the challenge that, unlike tequila, Scotch, or cognac, for example, the WIRSPA members each have their own regional traditions and rules, some literally going back centuries. It is far trickier regulating a spirit with so many varying geographical origins and methodologies. Of course, many producers also say that too much regulation in rum would stifle the creativity and individuality in their products.

In the past, the simplest categorization system stemmed from the colonization of rum-producing lands. From this history, rums were categorized into 1) "English" style: the fuller-bodied molasses-based rums produced from pot stills, made in the former British colonies of Jamaica, Barbados, and Guyana, among others; 2) "Spanish" style: the lighter-bodied molasses-based rums produced with column stills, made in the former Spanish colonies of Cuba, Puerto Rico, Nicaragua, and the Dominican Republic; and 3) "French" style rums: grassy and aromatic rums made from fresh cane juice on the French Caribbean islands of Martinique, Guadeloupe, and others.

However, these designations, while still widely used, are no longer particularly useful. First, it is difficult for rum to grow and evolve if it continues to be pigeonholed into categories that stem directly from centuries-old colonial beginnings.

Second, with technological advances in distillation equipment and methods, there is far greater diversity in rum production today than there once was. By the 1960s, for example, traditionally "English-style" producing countries such as Jamaica and Trinidad, started producing lighter rums to meet changing market tastes. (For example, in 1967 Tate and Lyle introduced a new light rum from Trinidad that they boasted was "whiter than whitish," marketing jargon that was unsettling for several reasons.) Many producers now blend distillates from column and pot stills in their rum production, which gives them the flexibility to create a range of products, many of which do not adhere to the "style" their country traditionally produced. Some Venezuelan producers (which would ostensibly fall under the "Spanish" umbrella) have pot stills. Trinidad (formerly an "English-style" rum producer) now only produces column-still rum. French islands, home of "French style" rhum agricole, still make some molasses rum.

Third, having these styles is confusing because it also leads the consumer to think there might be an influence of the growing region—that the actual sugars themselves differ by country of origin, and impart an influence of terroir. As we'll discuss below, with the exception of rums made from fresh-pressed sugarcane juice, this is rarely the case.

Lastly, many rum producers do not distill a drop of rum—they import actual distillate from elsewhere, and then blend and age it. In this case, the country where the rum was "produced" may have little to do with its actual country of origin.

Another common categorization for rum that is used somewhat arbitrarily by the US Alcohol and Tobacco Tax and Trade Bureau (TTB), and is widely used in rum marketing, as well as in rum competitions I have judged, is by color: "White," "Gold" (or "Amber"), and "Dark." However, describing rum by color is as useless as describing all wine as "red" or "white." A rum may be white because it is unaged, or white because it has been aged and filtered. The rum may include a distillate that's been double-distilled in a pot still, and therefore retains some of that characteristic funk, or it may be produced entirely with a multicolumn still setup and have a very light, nearly neutral character. An unaged or lightly aged rhum agricole will taste completely different than an unaged molasses-based rum despite both being "white." A rum may be "golden" from the addition of color or through actual aging. And, again, a heavy-bodied, pot-distilled "gold" rum will be entirely different than a column-distilled "gold" rum from Puerto Rico, or a "gold" rhum vieux from Martinique. With the spread of the column still and coloring agents, color no longer has a direct relationship to rum's flavor profile—if it ever did. Other spirits have recognized the problem with these categories: gold tequila has become a bad term because it signifies a mixto tequila, i.e., not 100 percent agave. And frankly this has never even been an issue with most other spirit categories: Ever ask for a gold Scotch? Or a dark bourbon?

To add to the above confusion, there remains little transparency in the rum world about how particular rums are made and, on top of that, how the way a particular rum is made may change over time. Some rum producers and brands are outright dishonest about their methods, and some simply hold their cards very close to their chest. I have watched some rum brands change their distillation methods, their source ingredients, how they finish the rum, and even what country the rum is produced in. As rum writer, importer, and expert Ed Hamilton says, "If you haven't tasted a rum every six months, you haven't really tasted it." I do the best I can with the knowledge and research I have access to, but learning about rum is an ongoing process.

With all this in mind, it is virtually impossible to come up with a way to categorize rum that everyone can agree on. But my hope is that the information in the pages that follow will help inform you, the consumer, about what you are buying and imbibing. I have created categories based on what I see as the most important factors influencing a rum's taste, character, and value: production methods, raw material, and aging. (It's worth mentioning the vital role fermentation plays in production, but detailed information about fermentation is hard to find and frequently considered a trade secret.) At the end of this chapter, I offer a list of rums by category, and how to use them with the recipes in this book. These rums can also make excellent substitutions for other spirits in classic cocktails, and many are best enjoyed on their own, to be slowly savored as you celebrate all of life's moments. Whether you're closing on a new home or just putting on a pair of pants, there's always an occasion for rum.

"My favorite rum is the one in my hand."
—ED HAMILTON

THE KEY FACTORS

The Raw Material

All rum comes from sugarcane and its by-products. "By-products" can mean fresh cane juice, sugarcane syrup, evaporated cane juice, various crystalized sugars, and, as is the case with most of the world's rum, molasses. Rums made from fresh sugarcane juice, such as rhum agricole, can contain the distinctive influence of terroir. The soil quality, climatic conditions, and availability of water all influence the characteristics of the sugarcane juice, and therefore, the final flavor of the rum. In contrast, most molasses rum distillers source molasses from multiple lands, thus making it unlikely a particular country's terroir would be able to come through in the final product. Differences in distillation and fermentation techniques further dilute terroir's influence, such that differences in even a single-sourced molasses, if perceptible to begin with, would not come through in the finished rum. I often tell people that in a molasses rum, the beauty of the final product is less in its raw material, and more in the skilled hands of the distiller and blender, for there is still quite a bit of art alongside the science.

At its most basic, rum production involves adding yeast to a sugar source. The combination of the particular yeast strain used and length of time it is left to act on the sugars, converting them to alcohol (fermentation), produces particular compounds that create part of the rum's final flavor and aroma. The longer the fermentation, the more congeners (a parent term for the aromatic and flavorful substances created during fermentation including esters, tannins, aldehydes, etc.) are produced in the "wash"—the liquid that will ultimately be distilled. Fermentation may last as short as twenty-four hours (typically for a lighter, column-distilled rum) or as long as two weeks (for a very high ester pot-distilled rum). While some rum producers use wild, naturally occurring yeast strains, many rum producers are highly protective of their cultivated yeast strains, some of which have been carefully propagated over decades to produce particular flavor compounds. Bacardi, for example, keeps some of its original yeast in a climate-controlled vault in Switzerland, in case any of the cultures at its distilleries become corrupted.

A few Jamaican rum producers are known for using "dunder pits," a traditional process involving bacteria and wild yeast strains, which results in a higher concentration of powerful esters and helps give Jamaican rums their distinctive "funky" flavor and aromas. Dunder pits are historically wood-lined pits hidden in the ground, into which leftover wash from a previous distillation and, sometimes, skimmings from the sugar boil (or rotting bananas and other fruit, or both) are added. This pungent-smelling concoction is left to age for months, and creates a substance with highly concentrated acids and esters called "dunder." Dunder is then added to fermented molasses and distilled. These ultra high-ester rums are rarely bottled by themselves today, but rather blended in with other rums to add depth and complexity.

Distillation/Production Method

POT (BATCH) STILL

For hundreds of years, the only production method for rum was the pot still, the same technology used to produce all other spirits of the day. A pot still is in essence a large kettle, and because alcohol has a lower boiling point than water, the spirit vapors rise and are condensed and collected. Simple enough. The pot still, with its exotic shape and bright copper finish, today may seem like a romantic affectation—but in fact, its shape affects the taste of the finished product, which can be quite complex. Some of that complexity is due to the evolving nature of the wash as it rises in proof, initially rising in strength due to reflux (spirit vapors dropping back into the fermented wash) and ultimately falling as available spirit is transferred and finally captured in the condenser. A second pass through the pot still is required to bring the collected spirit up in proof to a usable level of approximately 70 percent alcohol by volume. At this point, the spirit retains a large amount of congeners and is very full-flavored and full-bodied. The bold flavors can take time to mellow, either by resting in stainless tanks or by aging on oak. Further distillations in the pot can lighten and increase the proof of the rum, but at an added cost—pot distillation is inefficient, and a great deal of energy and much more raw material is required for the finished product. And yet, the rums created through batch distillation create aroma and flavor compounds that cannot be exactly replicated through continuous distillation. There is a reason that a technology that traces its roots back over one thousand years is still widely in use today, just as it is in whiskey, cognac, and a host of other spirits.

COLUMN (CONTINUOUS) STILL

Born from the creative energies of the Industrial Revolution, the column still transformed the production of spirits around the world. From its inception, it had several advantages over the pot still. Chiefly, it is able to produce spirits much more efficiently—less raw material and much less energy are required to yield a greater volume of distilled spirit. It also operates without interruption—rather than having to replace a batch of fermented wash with each distillation in a pot still, the column still is fed a continuous supply of wash, which greatly improves its output. And the spirit produced by column stills is much lighter-bodied and achieves a higher proof more quickly. With the refinement of Aeneas Coffey's two-column design, rum producers who preferred the lighter style and improved efficiency took advantage of the new technology to create rums using column stills. As demand grew globally and brands grew in turn, some producers moved to ever larger stills, adding more trays to improve rectification and ultimately, some would replace their Coffey stills with multicolumn facilities to ultimately increase production efficiency and yield an ever lighter distillate with fewer congeners. Some of these facilities produce a spirit so neutral as to be virtually indistinguishable from ethyl alcohol. It has become the preferred style among some producers to make a separate, heavier rum on a single column and blend it back into the lighter multicolumn distillate, either pre- or postaging, to create their final products.

BLENDED POT/COLUMN

As discussed in the previous chapter, economic pressures combined with consumers' changing tastes contributed to the implementation of a new style of rum in the early to mid-twentieth century. Following the lead of the Scottish, who had discovered the benefits of marrying pot and column distillates to produce blended Scotch whisky nearly a century earlier, rum producers took to producing blended rums and created a new medium-bodied style of rum. In some instances, the pot and column rums are blended

AOC MARTINIQUE RHUM AGRICOLE

In Martinique, there is now a designation for rhum agricole as an Appellation d'Origine Contrôlée (AOC) product just like champagne and cognac (labeled: Appellation d'Origine Contrôlée Martinique Rhum Agricole). To earn this designation, the rhum agricole must be made from the fresh juice of sugarcane, and adhere to strict rules about when and how the cane is harvested, pressed, and how the sugarcane juice is fermented and distilled, including the regulation that the cane juice must be distilled using a single-column still. Since there's so little variation in how rhum agricole is produced, it's perhaps the best style in which to appreciate terroir in rum—the north and south of Martinique have different soil conditions and annual rainfall. It's worth mentioning here that there is a common misperception that spelling rum as "rhum" automatically means you are talking about rhum agricole. This is not true. "Rhum" is simply the French word for rum, so any rum produced or sold in a French-speaking country is labeled rhum, having nothing to do with its ingredients or production methods. It will always be appended on the label with the word *agricole* (made from fresh cane juice) or *traditionnel* (made from molasses), and additionally reference "AOC Martinique" if it's made from fresh cane juice in Martinique and adheres to standards of that governing body.

prior to aging, and in others they are aged separately, then blended.

Blended rums offer many advantages. By adjusting ratios in the blends, a wide range of products can be produced that have multiple profiles and applications. Blended rums also take advantage of a phenomenon called persistence—pot-still rum can have such complexity and depth of character that not only does a little go a long way in a blended rum, but it also allows a blended rum to be smoother on the palate at a younger age, just as the blended Scotch makers discovered years before.

Aged or Unaged

Aging rum can affect the spirit through two means. First, if aging in a barrel, the wood used will impart its own qualities (which vary depending if the wood is new or used), including vanillin, tannins, and color, as well as some influence from any spirit that previously aged in the barrel (bourbon, sherry, etc.) and charring done to the barrel's interior prior to contact with the rum. Second, over time, compounds that were produced in the yeast fermentation and remain in the distilled spirit oxidize and produce sweet and fruity aromas (even a rum aged in a steel tank will change some with time).

Another important consideration to the aging of rum is the climate in which the rum is aged, with more rapid aging occurring in warmer equatorial climates like the Caribbean. It is estimated that a rum in the Caribbean ages two to three times faster than a spirit in a cold climate. This means that a much younger rum can achieve comparable maturity to a twenty-year Scotch or cognac. This also means that, at least for now, rum is a relative bargain, as it takes much less time to produce a mature product, and it can be offered at a lower price than many other aged spirits.

A bottled rum may reflect a blend of rums of varying ages. For example, some rum producers in Central and South America and a few Caribbean islands use a variation of the solera method (which is used to make sherry in Spain), in which older rums are added to younger rums in the cask and allowed to mature together.

I have noticed there is understandable confusion among consumers about the relation between the color of a rum and its age. For example, many rum consumers think that white rums are unaged—the rum equivalent of vodka. This is not the case. Very few rums on the market are totally unaged, and many are aged long enough to take on color, but have had the color filtered out of them as part of their style. Similarly, a rum with a golden color is not necessarily aged longer, if at all—color may be added to rum, or even neutral spirit, for the appearance of age.

This may lead a consumer to turn instead to the age statement on the bottle. However, this, too, can be at best confusing, and at worst misleading. Some countries such as Puerto Rico and Venezuela only allow a spirit to be called rum if it has aged for a minimum number of years. In some countries, including Barbados, Jamaica, and Guyana, age statements refer to the youngest rum in the bottle, but the age statements of solera producers typically refer to the oldest rum in the bottle, while still others use an average age. Some countries have strict definitions for their age terminologies, while others have terms that imply age ("aged," "añejo," "XO," "Extra Old,") but don't enforce strict aging guidelines. Others may forgo any age statement at all and declare their rums "aged to perfection," feeling confident that their product has enough oak influence, and enough mellowing to offer the consumer a well-rounded and balanced expression. It's worth noting that it *is* possible to age a rum to the point where it's overoaked. Plus, you may find that your taste preferences lead you to enjoy a more youthful spirit that speaks more to the flavors of its distillate. In all cases, explore, discover, and find your own preferences.

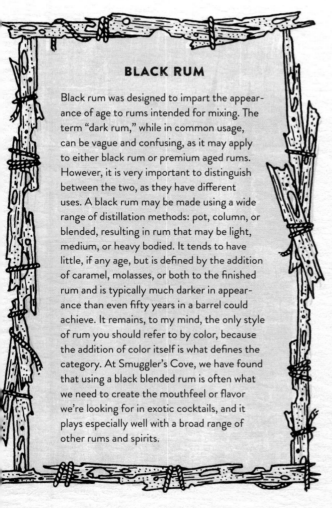

BLACK RUM

Black rum was designed to impart the appearance of age to rums intended for mixing. The term "dark rum," while in common usage, can be vague and confusing, as it may apply to either black rum or premium aged rums. However, it is very important to distinguish between the two, as they have different uses. A black rum may be made using a wide range of distillation methods: pot, column, or blended, resulting in rum that may be light, medium, or heavy bodied. It tends to have little, if any age, but is defined by the addition of caramel, molasses, or both to the finished rum and is typically much darker in appearance than even fifty years in a barrel could achieve. It remains, to my mind, the only style of rum you should refer to by color, because the addition of color itself is what defines the category. At Smuggler's Cove, we have found that using a black blended rum is often what we need to create the mouthfeel or flavor we're looking for in exotic cocktails, and it plays especially well with a broad range of other rums and spirits.

HOW TO TASTE RUM

Relaxing with a glass of beautifully made rum is surely one of the great pleasures in life, as enjoyable an experience after a satisfying dinner as it is after a satisfying bowl of corn flakes. But sitting down to really taste, appreciate, and understand a rum requires a bit more concentration. I've been judging at rum competitions across the United States, Europe, and the Caribbean for almost a decade,

and I've seen a wide range of product categories, settings, techniques, and glassware. There are quite a few variables, but a few constants as well.

When you approach a rum for thoughtful analysis, make sure you're in a brightly lit space with still air, free from outside aromas. Don't wear any strong scents yourself. Even hours later, the last thing you ate can affect your taste and perception, so choose blander foods for the meal prior. I shouldn't have to say don't smoke anything either, but I will: don't smoke. (We'll talk about rum and cigars later.)

Start with the bottle itself. Studying the bottle for information can help manage and shape expectations . . . provided the producer has supplied a reasonable amount of information. Knowing that you're about to drink a column-distilled product from Puerto Rico gives you many clues about what to expect, so you won't be disappointed if it doesn't taste like pure pot-still rum from Jamaica.

Pour it into your tasting glass, and always pour enough to reach the widest interior diameter of the glass. And never judge a rum cold or on ice as it inhibits the aromatics. There are several schools of thought on the kind of glass. Some things are certain: nothing tall, or anything that keeps your nose more than just a couple of inches from the spirit. A straight-sided glass works well only if it's especially short and has a wide surface area. I also would avoid anything where the overall glass flares outward as it lets too many precious aromatics dissipate, but if a glass has an especially wide diameter but a very narrow opening at the top, it can overly concentrate the more volatile alcohol evaporating off the sample, making it harder to appreciate the more delicate aromatics. My preference is for what's called a sherry copita, as it has only a very gently tapered side, and allows you to appreciate the aromatics and observe the spirit—however, I also suggest experimenting with two other commercial glasses, the Glencairn and the NEAT glass.

Tilt the glass to the side to create a thin edge and look for a slight green hue where the spirit ends. This indicates more age. Don't be as obsessed with the "legs" on the glass as they more often indicate alcohol content and the uneven interaction between alcohol and water rather than quality or age.

Smell that beautiful rum! Swirl the rum first to enhance evaporation and release more aromas. My preferred nosing technique is to put my nose deeply into the glass then breathe in with my mouth outside of the rim rather than my nose. You will find that even when breathing in with the mouth, your body will still breathe in through your nose at the same time, only at a much reduced rate, allowing you to avoid any sharp burn on the nose. Are you enjoying the aroma? Does it conjure up fond memories or evocative destinations with inviting scents?

To "condition" your mouth, sip a small amount of the rum and let it roll down all sides and coat your mouth. Then spit it out. I know, it's hard for me, too. Now take a larger taste and let it remain on your tongue while you note how the flavors evolve. Then swallow and see how it further evolves in the aftertaste. Do the flavors linger? Or is the finish short? Was the overall experience complex with different notes of oak, molasses, spices, and fruits? Did the rum take you on a pleasurable journey?

Some elements of analyzing rums can be quantified. You can readily assess color, proof, and, with more detailed laboratory analysis, the exact chemical structure. But what is harder to quantify is each person's organoleptic response. Every person experiences taste uniquely, and factors such as recent meals, your health, and even the weather can play a part. It may be worth revisiting a rum later that you may not have initially enjoyed. What's the worst that can happen? You have to drink more rum? And consider tasting with friends—compare notes and see what elements work for some people (or not). Compare a rum side-by-side with a "reference" rum of a similar style—if there's a light, dry column still aged rum that is currently your favorite, use that to decide if there's something else you'd rather be pouring.

Oh, and if you're tasting a few rums in a sitting, have some plain unsalted crackers and water handy to help keep the palate fatigue at bay.

Rum's best friends that aren't named lime and sugar are named cigar and chocolate. Pairing either of them with rum can be a sublime experience. Their flavor characteristics often overlap, making them highly complementary. However, both—cigars especially—can obscure nuance in rum. But when the "hard work" of analyzing your rums is done . . . by all means. Some rum blenders have told me that the best way to pair rum and chocolate is to match sweeter rums with dark chocolate with a high cacao percentage and drier rums with milk chocolates. Others have told me exactly the opposite. I suggest you start your own extensive clinical trials and try your favorite pairings over and over again to ensure you can replicate the results.

Above all, enjoy yourself! Rum is a delight and a luxury and should be savored. No other spirit can match a fine rum's combination of sophistication and

"I like rum. I like the drinks it makes and everything about it. I think it's better booze right straight along for all purposes."

—TRADER VIC, *TRADER VIC'S BOOK OF FOOD AND DRINK*, 1946

joie de vivre. When the marketing types tell you rum can be enjoyed like a fine cognac or tastes like a great whiskey, you tell them, "No, it tastes like a *great rum.*" Defend rum, for rum stands on its own.

A WORD ABOUT SPICED RUM

Spices have been added to rum since its birth, and when you travel in the Caribbean you will find all kinds of rums in street markets that have been infused with local spices. Early on it was done to cover up the harshness of poorly made spirit, but the tradition has continued. Most Americans were introduced to spiced rum through the launch of Captain Morgan in the early 1980s, and therefore it is worth noting that there is not a single recipe from the golden age of tiki that calls for spiced rum. The spices in those drinks were added with syrups, liqueurs, and . . . spices. My simple rule for spiced rum: Is it real? Has the rum ever seen a real spice? I only carry brands at Smuggler's Cove where I have personally seen physical spices being infused and not synthesized flavors from a lab being added. As such, I don't have very many at all. (However, it's worth noting that today's American micro-distilled rums are good about adding real spices.) But here's the very best thing about spiced rum: It couldn't be easier to make it yourself. Do you really like cinnamon? Add more! It's your rum! The only real rule is that you only get out what you put in, so start with a quality rum and then use organic spices. I can promise you that you will produce something superior to a mass-produced brand. We offer our own Smuggler's Cove house recipe here, which has proven to be very popular over the years. Try it, but also think of it as a starting point for your own explorations and adventures . . . and don't hesitate to try other spices we've never tried.

SC HOUSE SPICED RUM

Makes two (750 ml) bottles

- 2 (750 ml) bottles blended aged rum ❸
- 1 (8-inch) vanilla bean (split lengthwise)
- 1 (5 by 1½-inch) strip of orange peel (with as little white pith as possible)
- 6 allspice berries
- 1 (8-inch) cinnamon stick
- 6 whole cloves
- ¼ teaspoon freshly grated nutmeg
- 10 whole black peppercorns
- 2 slices fresh ginger (unpeeled), cut into quarter-size coins
- ⅓ cup SC Demerara Syrup (page 324), optional

In a half-gallon glass jar, combine the rum, vanilla bean (scraped seeds and pod), orange peel strip (you may wish to expel the orange peel oil a little as you add it), allspice, cinnamon stick, cloves, nutmeg, peppercorns, and ginger; seal airtight. Let the sealed jar of rum rest in a dark room for 72 hours, stirring once daily. Line a wire-mesh strainer with cheesecloth and set over a large bowl. Strain the spiced rum through the cheesecloth into the bowl. Add the SC Demerara Syrup (if desired, adjusting amount as you like; your chosen base rum may be plenty sweet as is) and stir to blend. Transfer to bottles and seal well. The spiced rum will keep for several months at room temperature.

A WORD ABOUT SUGAR IN RUM

There is a common misperception that somehow rum is more caloric because its raw material is sugarcane or a sugarcane by-product. This isn't true—sugar does not travel through the distillation process. There is as much sugar in rum as there is in bourbon, vodka or tequila. Remember that ALL spirits come from sugar of some kind—sugar is what the yeast feeds on to create alcohol. That sugar can come from sugarcane, or fruits such as grapes and apples, or grain starches that have been converted to sugar in the case of whiskeys and vodkas. When you taste a really well-distilled rum (and this is regardless of raw material or distillation method), there should be a perceptible sweetness to the product. But this sweetness is not sugar in the distillate, but rather the result of a skilled distiller making choices to retain flavors and characteristics that honor the raw material. Just as you would still taste the vegetal agave flavor in young tequila, or a grain flavor in genever, you will taste fresh pressed cane in an unaged agricole, or molasses in a pot still rum.

However, having said all that, several rum producers on the market today do willingly add sugar to their final product after distillation. There are many reasons for this decision, some noble, some not so noble. Adding sugar can act as a flavor enhancement. But, much like salt, it operates on a curve. A little bit can accent the underlying flavors, but too much can quickly overwhelm and "deaden" the spirit.

For some brands, like Plantation Rums, which are blended and bottled in Cognac, France, the use of sugar is based on the tradition of adding sugar to cognac, called *dosage*. Plantation believes that their own blends of excellent well-aged distillates, finished in Cognac with dosage, benefit from the sugar accenting the flavors of their products. I mention Plantation because they are one of the few brands that are fully transparent about their use of sugar.

Be wary of marketing jargon, or stories about how using a sweeter raw material leads to a sweeter final product—nonsense. Information on which brands have sugar added can be found on the public websites of a few European governments and a few enthusiasts who have taken to analyzing the products themselves. I encourage you to be an informed consumer and make your own decisions, and if you find that sweeter rums meet your taste and mixing preferences, then by all means, enjoy.

But the danger of the addition of sugar, especially when a brand is not honest about it, is twofold: One is that sugar can be added to mask a very young rum and give a consumer the impression that it is more "premium" than it is. Secondly, the use of sugar is clearly affecting consumer tastes. There is increasingly an association that a sweeter rum means finer rum, because there is a growing belief that sweetness equals "smoothness." Smoothness (which must be noted is not a flavor and is a pretty nebulous term as it is) would more traditionally be used as a descriptor when the distillate you're tasting is well-made, rounded, and balanced—through the quality of the distillation, the aging, the blending, or any combination of those. The addition of sugar can obscure that distinction.

> *"The old colonial rum culture resulted in producers not having the confidence to sell their product to the world as the great drink it is. If rum is to achieve its potential, it must stop being a commodity, and start being a brand. The twenty-first century should be the one in which rum finally divests itself of its colonial trappings and stands proud."*
>
> —DAVE BROOM, *RUM*, 2003

A WORD ABOUT FLAVORED RUM

According to DISCUS, the Distilled Spirits Council of the United States, spiced and flavored rums now account for 53 percent of the U.S. market—a majority for the first time. I've been asked many times why rum isn't taken more seriously, and in my opinion, this category weighs rum down and keeps it from achieving its full potential. Flavored rums are easy and fast to produce, often using the most neutral of distillates, able to bypass local aging requirements, and filled with usually synthetic flavors. Does a spirit steeped in as much history as rum deserve to be treated with the contempt of bubblegum-flavored rum? (In fairness, cinnamon, honey, and apple whiskey are all poised to ruin the whiskey category as well.)

Here's a great way to make mango rum: combine mangoes and rum. Try real fruit in your recipes. This allows you to use a significantly more interesting rum with some flavor and body, and your entire drink will taste better and more complex. Ask a chef: There are no shortcuts to fine dining. Real cooking takes accuracy, skill, care, and good ingredients. So do great rums and great rum cocktails. If you think that flavored rums are more "fun," then I ask you to look at the drinks throughout this book: Do they not seem like fun? I sure have a hell of a lot of fun making and drinking them.

You are the new rum lovers. Despite my sugared, spiced, and flavored screeds above, there has never been a better time to be a rum consumer in America. Old brands have returned, new brands are starting all the time, and historic styles are being painstakingly reconstructed. It's up to you to vote with your wallet: Support the bars, restaurants, and retailers that carry quality rum brands. Tell your friends about quality rums and encourage them to do the same. The category is diverse—encourage that diversity by spreading the love to brands both big and small. The future of rum is in your hands and in your glass.

RUM CATEGORIES

Beyond the colonial names, beyond the meaningless colors, what follows is the Smuggler's Cove classification system for rums, which emphasizes how the rums are made, not what they look like.

I also had a more practical objective in mind when I designed this system: if you want to make your own "speed rack" at home, you can buy one rum from each category with a numbered icon, and then you're ready to tackle any recipe (see page 18 for more information on stocking your home bar). If you're like me—you don't just need rum, you want rum—you can always buy multiple in each category.

The Fine Print

The following rums are readily available in the United States and chosen from a variety of rums that range on my personal scale between "strongly endorse" and "happily tolerate." Several very small lovely rums and independent bottlers did not make this list because of limited supply or regional availability. New rums will appear and favorites will change or go away, so this list will always be in flux. Note that independent bottlers sell rums from nearly all of these categories, so you must check your labels carefully for mention of distillation method. Rums from independent distillers are listed in the Pot Still Aged category because independent bottlers are one of the only sources for this category of rum.

Molasses and evaporated sugarcane products are combined as one category. Most of the world's rums are molasses, of course, but there are a handful of producers using variants like sugarcane syrup, evaporated cane juice, and unrefined turbinado sugar. Some of these products have the advantage of containing more fermentable sugar for higher yields, and may also contain less sulphur and heavy mineral content than molasses, but the distinction is one of taste—all are produced by the transformation of the cane juice to a syrup or a crystalline form through heating, and as a family they are distinct from fresh-pressed cane juice.

You will notice that in the Prohibition-era cocktails and in exotic cocktails that might normally call for "light Puerto Rican rum," we do not use column still lightly aged rum as one might expect. The house style at Smuggler's Cove calls for category 2 instead, as we believe that a blended, lightly aged rum with a hint more body better captures a more historic taste profile. But if you prefer a lighter taste, then you can easily substitute.

Here's how we define our age ranges:

- **Lightly Aged:** 1 to 4 years old. Limited wood influence allows the well-rested spirit to shine through. Some of these may have charcoal filtration to remove their color, but some wood character will remain.

- **Aged:** 5 to 14 years old. Definite and noticeable oak influence adds more depth and nuance to both the spirit and cocktails as spice, vanilla, leather, and woody notes develop. Lovely in a variety of applications. You will see rums listed as "Aged" that may have higher age statements on their labels, but when produced by a solera method, we prefer to categorize them by something more closely resembling their average age.

- **Long Aged:** 15+ years old. Rums best enjoyed neat. I always say you should sip any damn rum you want, but note that the "long aged" category features rums that were designed by their producers to enjoy on their own, and some of the depth and subtlety of those products would be lost in a complex cocktail.

MOLASSES AND EVAPORATED CANE RUMS

POT STILL UNAGED
Hamilton Jamaica Gold (Jamaica)

Owney's New York Rum
(New York, USA)

Pritchard's Crystal
(Tennessee, USA)

Privateer Silver Reserve
(Massachusetts, USA)

Rum Society #40 (Guyana)
and #62 (regional blend)

Sammy's Beach Bar Rum
(Hawaii, USA)

Sergeant Classick White
(California, USA)

Wray & Nephew (overproof)
(Jamaica)

POT STILL LIGHTLY AGED ❶
Ballast Point Three Sheets Aged
(California, USA)

Diablo's Shadow Navy Strength
(overproof) (California, USA)

House Spirits Aged Rum
(Oregon, USA)

Journeyman Road's End Organic Rum
(overproof) (Michigan, USA)

Maggie's Farm Queen's Share Rum
(overproof) (Pennsylvania, USA)

Montanya Oro and Platino
(Colorado, USA)

Pritchard's Fine
(Tennessee, USA)

Privateer Amber
(Massachusetts, USA)

Ragged Mountain Rum
(Massachusetts, USA)

Richland Georgia Rum
(Georgia, USA)

Rum Society #65
(regional blend)

Smith & Cross (overproof) (Jamaica)

Sun Rum Barrel Aged
(Washington, USA)

Thomas Tew Single Barrel
(Rhode Island, USA)

POT STILL AGED
Berry Bros & Rudd
(independent bottler, various)

Cadenhead
(independent bottler, various)

Duncan Taylor
(independent bottler, various)

El Dorado Single Barrel PM (Guyana)

Hamilton St. Lucia (St. Lucia)

Mezan
(independent bottler, various)

Plantation
(independent bottler, various)

Samaroli
(independent bottler, various)

St. Nicholas Abbey 5 Year (Barbados)

POT STILL LONG AGED
Appleton Estate 50 Year (Jamaica)

Diplomatico Ambassador and Single
Vintage (Venezuela)

The Black Tot (regional blend)

BLENDED LIGHTLY AGED ❷
Appleton Estate Signature Blend
(Jamaica)

Banks 5 Island and 7 Island
(regional blend)

Cartavio Selecto 5 (Peru)

Chairman's Reserve Silver
(St. Lucia)

Cockspur Fine (Barbados)

Denizen (regional blend)

Diplomatico Añejo and Blanco
(Venezuela)

El Dorado 3 Year (Guyana)

Mount Gay Eclipse (Barbados)

Plantation 3 Star (regional blend)

Real McCoy 3 year (Barbados)

Santa Teresa Claro (Venezuela)

BLENDED AGED ❸
Appleton Estate Reserve Blend
and Rare Blend 12 (Jamaica)

Cadenhead Green Label (regional
blend)

Cartavio Selecto 12 and 18 (Peru)

Chairman's Reserve and Forgotten
Casks (St. Lucia)

Cockspur 12 (Barbados)

Denizen Merchant's Reserve
(regional blend)

Diplomatico Reserva and Reserva
Exclusiva (Venezuela)

Doorly's 5 Year, 12 Year,
and XO (Barbados)

Dos Maderas 5+3 and 5+5
(regional blend)

El Dorado 5 Year, 8 Year, and 12 Year (Guyana)

Kaniché XO (Barbados)

Mount Gay Black Barrel and XO (Barbados)

Plantation 5 Year Grand Reserve and 20th Anniversary (Barbados)

Providencia (regional blend)

Pusser's (regional blend)

Real McCoy 5 Year and 12 Year (Barbados)

RL Seale 9 Year Port Cask Finish and 10 Year (Barbados)

BLENDED LONG AGED
Appleton Estate 21 (Jamaica)

Banks The Endeavour (regional blend)

Cartavio XO (Peru)

El Dorado 15 Year, 21 Year, and 25 Year (Guyana)

Mount Gay 1703 (Barbados)

Pusser's 15 (regional blend)

Santa Teresa 1796 (Venezuela)

Smooth Ambler Revelation Rum (Jamaica)

St. Lucia Distillers 1931 (St. Lucia)

COLUMN STILL LIGHTLY AGED
Bacardi Heritage 1909 (Mexico)

Caliche (Puerto Rico)

Caña Brava (Panama)

Crusoe Organic White (California, USA)

Cruzan Estate Diamond (U.S. Virgin Islands)

Don Q Cristal (Puerto Rico)

Facundo Neo (Bahamas/Puerto Rico)

Flor de Caña Extra Dry 4 Year (Nicaragua)

Ron Del Barrilito 2 Star (Puerto Rico)

Scarlett Ibis (Trinidad)

COLUMN STILL AGED ❹
Admiral Rodney (St. Lucia)

Angostura 1824, 1919, 5 Year, and 7 Year (Trindiad)

Bacardi 8 and Reserva Limitada (Bahamas/Puerto Rico)

Brugal 1888 and Extra Viejo (Domincan Republic)

Caña Brava 7 Year (Panama)

Cruzan Single Barrel (U.S. Virgin Islands)

Don Pancho Origines 8 (Panama)

Don Q Añejo and Gran Añejo (Puerto Rico)

El Dorado Single Barrel EHP and Single Barrel ICBU (Guyana)

English Harbour 5 and 10 (Antigua)

Facundo Eximo, Exquisito, and Paraiso (Bahamas/Puerto Rico)

Flor de Caña 12 (Nicaragua)

Kirk & Sweeney 12, 18, and 23 (Dominican Republic)

Ron Abuelo 12, 7, Centuria (Panama)

Ron Botran Reserva and Solera 1893 (Guatemala)

Ron Cenenario 9, 12, 20, and 25 (Costa Rica)

Ron Del Barrilito 3 Star (Puerto Rico)

Ron Matusalem 15 (Dominican Republic)

Trigo (Puerto Rico)

Westerhall Plantation (Grenada)

Zacapa 23 and XO (Guatemala)

Zafra (Panama)

COLUMN STILL LONG AGED
Don Pancho Origines 18 and 30 (Panama)

English Harbour 25 (Antigua)

Flor De Caña 18 and 25 (Nicaragua)

Reserva de la Familia Serrallés 20 Year Old (Puerto Rico)

BLACK POT STILL
Hamilton Jamaica Black (Jamaica)

BLACK BLENDED ❺
Coruba (Jamaica)

Goslings's Black Seal (regional blend)

Hamilton Guyana 86 (Guyana)

Kohala Bay (Jamaica)

Lemon Hart 80 (Guyana)

Pampero Anniversario (Venezuela)

Newfoundland Screech (Jamaica)

Blackwell's Black Gold (Jamaica)

Skipper Finest Old Demerara (Guyana)

BLACK BLENDED OVERPROOF ❻
Hamilton Guyana 151 (Guyana)

Lemon Hart 151 (Guyana)

Plantation O.F.T.D. (regional blend)

FRESH CANE JUICE RUMS

CANE COFFEY STILL AGED
Rhum Barbancourt 5 Star and Estate
Reserve (Haiti)

CANE POT STILL UNAGED
Capovilla Agricole PMG (Marie
Galante)

St. George California Agricole
(California, USA)

CANE POT STILL AGED
Capovilla Rhum Liberation 2010
(Marie Galante)

St. George California Reserve
Agricole (California, USA)

**CANE AOC MARTINIQUE RHUM
AGRICOLE BLANC** ❼
Clément Première Canne and Canne
Bleue (Martinique)

Duquesne Blanc (Martinique)

La Favorite Blanc (Martinique)

Neisson Blanc, Le Rhum, and L'Esprit
Overproof (Martinique)

Rhum J.M White 100 proof
(Martinique)

**CANE AOC MARTINIQUE RHUM
AGRICOLE VIEUX** ❽
Clément V.S.O.P., 6 Year Très Vieux,
and 10 Year Très Vieux (Martinique)

Duquesne Élevé Sous Bois
(Martinique)

La Favorite Coeur de Ambré and
Vieux (Martinique)

Neisson Élevé Sous Bois and Réserve
Spéciale (Martinique)

Rhum J.M E.S.B. Gold and V.S.O.P.
(Martinique)

**CANE AOC MARTINIQUE RHUM
AGRICOLE LONG AGED**
Clément Cuvée Homere (Martinique)

Neisson 15 Year and 18 Year
(Martinique)

Rhum J.M 1994 and 1997
(Martinique)

POT STILL UNAGED CACHAÇA
Avuá Prata (Brazil)

Novo Fogo Silver (Brazil)

POT STILL AGED CACHAÇA
Avuá Amburana (Brazil)

Novo Fogo Gold (Brazil)

The Chadburn

THE CHADBURN

If you're looking for a change of speed, give this combination a try.

ORIGIN *Created by Martin Cate*
GLASSWARE *Chilled coupe*

- ½ ounce tawny port
- ½ ounce natural pear liqueur (such as Mathilde Poire)
- 2 ounces blended aged rum ❸
- 6 drops Bittermens Xocolatl (Chocolate) Mole bitters

GARNISH *None*

Add all the ingredients to a mixing glass. Fill with cracked or cubed ice. Stir and strain into a chilled coupe.

NOTE The Chadburn (named for the Chadburn telegraph) is quite sweet and makes a fine after-dinner drink. But it's easily converted to a more preprandial version by decreasing the amount of port and pear liqueur to ¼ ounce each.

A WISH FOR GRACE

Created for the celebratory event at the Smithsonian, Washington, D.C., in honor of the two hundredth anniversary of "The Star-Spangled Banner." Our own Steven Liles could be found there serving his delicious concoction. It is for this reason we recommend a rum in the style of a traditional New England rum.

ORIGIN *Created by Steven Liles*
GLASSWARE *Chilled coupe*

- ¾ ounce fresh lemon juice
- ½ ounce 2:1 Simple Syrup (page 324)
- ½ ounce Pierre Ferrand Dry Curaçao
- 1½ ounces pot still lightly aged rum ❶ (New England)
- ¾ ounce Blandy's 5 Year Verdelho Madeira
- 1 dash Angostura bitters

GARNISH *Lemon twist*

Add all the ingredients to a cocktail shaker filled with cracked or cubed ice. Shake and strain into a chilled coupe and garnish.

HOT BUTTERED RUM

The most famous way to ward off the chill of a cold night, a hot spiced rum appeared in the 1862 Jerry Thomas *Bartender's Guide*.

ORIGIN *Smuggler's Cove original, adapted from historic recipes*
GLASSWARE *8½-ounce Irish Coffee glass*

> 3 barspoons SC Hot Buttered Rum Batter (recipe follows)
>
> 1½ ounces blended aged rum ❸
>
> 6 ounces hot water

GARNISH *Cinnamon stick*

Add the batter and rum to the mug. Top with hot water and stir well. Add garnish.

NOTE Always feel free to play with the proportions. Another twist is the Wilford Brimley, created by our bartender Dane Barca: Add 2 barspoons of batter, 1 ounce of SC Coconut Cream (page 328) and substitute 1 ounce of black blended overproof rum to the mug before topping with hot water. Top with 1 ounce of sweet cream (see Parisian Blonde, page 174) and grate nutmeg on top.

SC HOT BUTTERED RUM BATTER

MAKES *about 4 cups batter; about 48 servings*

> 1 teaspoon freshly ground cinnamon
>
> 1 teaspoon freshly ground nutmeg
>
> 1 teaspoon freshly ground black pepper
>
> ¾ teaspoon ground cloves
>
> ½ teaspoon ground allspice
>
> ½ teaspoon ground anise seed
>
> 2 cups salted butter
>
> 4 cups packed golden brown sugar
>
> 2 tablespoons Brer Rabbit Mild Molasses
>
> 1 teaspoon vanilla extract

Combine the cinnamon, nutmeg, black pepper, cloves, allspice, and anise seed in a small bowl and set aside. Melt the butter in a saucepan over low heat. Add the sugar and stir. Add the molasses and vanilla extract and stir. Finally, stir in the spice mixture. At first, as you stir to combine, the butter will form a separate layer. Continue to stir over low heat until all the ingredients combine, including the butter, about 15 minutes. Remove from the heat. Let cool slightly. While still warm and malleable, pour the batter into a storage container. Let cool completely, then seal airtight, and store in the refrigerator where it will keep until the expiration date of the butter used to make it; note that date before you start the recipe.

NOTE When possible, it is always best to use fresh spices, but if you don't have a small pepper mill to grind the anise seeds, allspice, and black pepper, I would suggest buying ground versions.

ABRICOT VIEUX

ORIGIN *Created by Martin Cate*
GLASSWARE *Chilled coupe*

½ ounce natural apricot liqueur
(such as Rothman & Winter Apricot Liqueur
or Giffard Abricot du Roussillon)

2 ounces cane AOC Martinique rhum
agricole vieux **8**

1 dash Angostura bitters

1 dash orange bitters

GARNISH *Orange peel oil*

Combine all the ingredients in a mixing glass filled
with cracked or cubed ice and stir. Strain into a
chilled coupe. Express orange peel oil over the drink
and discard the peel.

PANIOLO OLD-FASHIONED

The sweet and savory taste of li hing mui makes a
pretty accent to a lovely rum in a simple presentation.

ORIGIN *Created by Martin Cate*
GLASSWARE *Old-fashioned*

1 teaspoon Li Hing Mui Syrup (page 332)

2 ounces blended aged rum **3**

1 dash Angostura bitters

GARNISH *Orange peel*

Add all the ingredients to a mixing glass filled with
cracked or cubed ice and stir. Strain into an old-
fashioned glass over a large single ice cube or ice ball.
Express oil from the orange peel over the drink and
drop the peel into the drink.

PORT ROYAL

Savory, food-based spice blends can add a surprising complexity to cocktails, and Jamaica's treasured jerk seasoning certainly has fun with its fellow countryman Wray & Nephew Overproof rum.

ORIGIN *Created by Martin Cate*
GLASSWARE *Chilled coupe*

¾ ounce fresh lime juice

¾ ounce SC Jerk Syrup (page 329)

1½ ounces blended lightly aged rum ❷

½ ounce Wray & Nephew white overproof rum

5 drops SC Hellfire Tincture (page 332)

GARNISH *None*

Add all the ingredients to a cocktail shaker. Add cracked or cubed ice and shake. Double-strain into a chilled coupe. Top with five spread-out drops of Hellfire Tincture on the surface of the cocktail.

KINGSTON PALAKA

A rummy riff on a contest-winning cocktail from a long time ago.

ORIGIN *Created by Martin Cate*
GLASSWARE *Chilled coupe*

½ ounce fresh lemon juice

⅛ teaspoon li hing mui powder
(see Resources, page 335)

1 ounce Drambuie

1½ ounces blended aged rum (Jamaica) ❸

GARNISH *Lemon peel*

Combine all the ingredients in a cocktail shaker. Shake and strain into a chilled coupe and add garnish.

Clockwise, from top right: Kingston Palaka, Paniolo Old-Fashioned (page 203), Port Royal

DONN DAY AFTERNOON

ORIGIN *Created by Martin Cate*
GLASSWARE *Double old-fashioned*

- ½ ounce fresh lime juice
- ½ ounce SC Cinnamon Syrup (page 327)
- 4 ounces chilled Stiegl-Radler Grapefruit Beer
- 2 ounces cane AOC Martinique rhum agricole blanc ❼

GARNISH *Grapefruit peel*

Add all the ingredients to a double old-fashioned glass. Gently add cracked or cubed ice and stir. Express oil from the grapefruit peel and then drop the peel into the drink.

BAIE DU GALION

Named for the beautiful waters on the leeward side of Martinique, this cocktail uses cane AOC Martinique rhum agricole in a contemporary stirred cocktail where all the ingredients have grassy or herbaceous notes. Another reminder that rhum agricole is not limited to the Ti' Punch.

ORIGIN *Created by Martin Cate*
GLASSWARE *Chilled coupe*

- ½ ounce Green Chartreuse
- ¼ ounce Drambuie
- 2 ounces cane AOC Martinique rhum agricole blanc ❼

GARNISH *Lemon twist*

Add all the ingredients to a mixing glass. Fill with cracked or cubed ice. Stir and strain into a chilled coupe. Add garnish.

Baie du Galion

Agricole Guava Cooler

AGRICOLE GUAVA COOLER

Inspired by the spices and flavors found in the farmers' market of the capital city of Martinique, Fort-de-France, this refreshing cooler mixes tropical fruit, Caribbean spices, and cane AOC Martinique rhum agricole.

ORIGIN *Created by Martin Cate*
GLASSWARE *Collins or highball glass*

2 ounces Bundaberg guava soda

¾ ounce fresh lime juice

¾ ounce Licor 43 spiced liqueur

2 ounces cane AOC Martinique rhum agricole blanc ❼

2 dashes Angostura bitters

GARNISH *Mint sprig, cinnamon stick, and lime wheel*

Add the guava soda to a Collins or highball glass, then add the remaining ingredients to a cocktail shaker with cracked or cubed ice. Shake and strain into the glass. Gently add cracked or cubed ice to fill the glass, then add garnish.

RICHARD SEALEBACH

Named for Richard Seale, distiller and owner of Foursquare Distillery in Barbados.

ORIGIN *Created by Rebecca Cate, inspired by the classic Seelbach cocktail from the Seelbach Hotel*
GLASSWARE *Champagne flute*

½ ounce Pierre Ferrand Dry Curaçao

1 ounce R. L. Seale 10 Year rum

7 dashes Angostura bitters

7 dashes Peychaud's bitters

4 ounces chilled champagne

GARNISH *Lemon twist*

Combine all the ingredients except the champagne in a mixing glass filled with cracked or cubed ice. Stir and strain into a champagne flute and top with chilled champagne. Add garnish.

COSA NOSTRA #2

Per Dane, "Polite yet deadly."

ORIGIN *Created by Dane Barca*
GLASSWARE *Footed pilsner*

> ¾ ounce fresh lemon juice
>
> 1½ ounces Amaro Averna
>
> 1 ounce blended lightly aged rum ❷
>
> 1 dash Angostura bitters
>
> 2 ounces real ginger ale

GARNISH *Lemon twist and swizzle stick*

Add all the ingredients except the ginger ale to a footed pilsner glass. Add cracked or cubed ice. Top with ginger ale and stir very gently to combine, then add garnish.

SPONTANEOUS RUMBUSTION

A rummy hot toddy by way of a Blue Blazer.

ORIGIN *Created by Dane Barca*
GLASSWARE *8½-ounce Irish coffee or other heat-resistant glass*

> ¾ ounce fresh lemon juice
>
> ½ ounce SC Honey Syrup (page 325)
>
> 1½ ounces black blended overproof rum ❻
>
> ½ ounce pot still lightly aged rum (overproof) ❶
>
> 4 ounces boiling water

GARNISH *Long lemon peel*

Combine the lemon juice and honey in an Irish coffee glass. Add both rums to a Blue Blazer mug (see Resources, page 335). Add the boiling water. Use a lighter to ignite the liquid and pass that flaming liquid back and forth from one Blue Blazer mug to a second Blue Blazer mug for a few seconds. When the flame turns orange, immediately pour the flaming contents of Blue Blazer mug into the Irish coffee glass and put out the flame by placing mug on top of the glass. Garnish with and express a sizable lemon peel long enough to rest on top of the Irish coffee glass.

Spontaneous Rumbustion, created by Dane Barca

PART FOUR
EXOTIC COCKTAILS:
MYSTIQUE AND TECHNIQUE

"Welcome aboard and up anchor! You're off and away for a legendary cruise to the world's most mysterious and glamorous destinations . . . Rare rums, herbs, spices and fruits have been gathered for the pleasure seekers of the Kon Tiki Ports. These are the necessary ingredients for the exotic fare you will presently find listed within . . . So, to the sounds of the wild cry of gulls, the creaking of the rigging and the wash of salt spray across the bow—set sail!"

—KON-TIKI PORTS MENU

the Theater of the Exotic Cocktail

Bartender Steven Liles and his drink mixer

MAKING YOUR OWN FRESH SQUEEZED EXOTIC COCKTAILS AT HOME IS NOT MAGIC. IT'S NOT EVEN THAT MUCH WORK. THERE IS NEVER A REASON TO BUY A PREBOTTLED COCKTAIL, ARTIFICIALLY FLAVORED SPIRITS, OR LIME JUICE IN THOSE LITTLE GREEN PLASTIC BOTTLES.

I am always struck by the lengths people will go to in order to prepare a fresh, home-cooked meal. They'll watch cooking shows on TV, pour over recipes online, shop for esoteric spices and produce, and spend hours cooking for themselves or guests. And then, when it's time for their predinner cocktail, they'll reach into the freezer or cupboard, and pull out some artificially flavored spirits or sour mix. If you can chop an onion for dinner, you can juice a lime for a cocktail.

And there's no better way to understand the heart and soul of a great exotic cocktail than by making it yourself. For me, taking my first fumbling steps nearly twenty years ago opened my eyes to the rewards. The trial and error as you struggle for balance in cocktails, and that first sip as the freshness and layers of flavor come rushing through the straw and you realize you've nailed it is the unforgettable eureka moment. There's a pride in the achievement, and an anxiousness to share it with your friends. Handing a beautifully garnished fresh exotic cocktail to your guest with a smile on your face is one of the great pleasures of hospitality.

So whether you're following an old recipe, or inventing your own, here are some great tips to making perfect exotic cocktails at home.

BUT . . . WHAT IS AN EXOTIC COCKTAIL?

During the golden era of tiki bars in the United States, the siren call that would lure you through the bamboo doors most often included the words "exotic cocktails." "Tropical drinks," "tiki cocktails," or "Polynesian cocktails" may also have been used, but the romantic in me still prefers the term "exotic cocktail" because it so neatly captures the time period and desire to escape to somewhere mysterious.

We celebrate exotic cocktails today, and rightfully so, as a unique and important chapter in the history of the American cocktail—but there remains confusion about what, exactly, they are. A fantastic modern cocktail may have unusual tropical ingredients, but being served over ice and having an interesting garnish doesn't make it an exotic cocktail. Having nine ingredients doesn't qualify, either. Clearly, a definition is needed—not only to help quantify the category, but also to provide a structure for developing new drinks.

But let's be clear: *I'm* not the one declaring what an exotic cocktail is. The definition that follows belongs to Donn Beach, and those in the 1940s and 1950s who did their best to imitate Donn.

Since Donn is the father of this revolution, we can safely start to define the exotic cocktail template the way he did: as an elaboration of the traditional planter's punch formula balancing sour, sweet, spirit (rum), weak, and spice components.

Let's look at the palettes Donn, Vic, and the later pioneers were painting with. Thanks to the work of Jeff Berry, we have much more insight into what these early "building blocks" of tiki are. As Jeff points out, through his "turbo-charged" planter's punches, Donn laid the foundation on which all other tiki drinks were built.

When all the primary ingredients are laid out like this, the first thing you notice is that there are simply not that many. The sour component is very straightforward: lime, grapefruit, and orange. The only "tropical" things are pineapple (shipped to California) and passion fruit (cultivated commercially in Southern California). There is no papaya, mango, or guava. Coconut doesn't make the list (it appeared only as a dehydrated powder in one recipe, and later in one drink served in a fresh coconut). The state of commercial refrigeration and shipping meant only the heartiest imported tropical fruits would make it to the mainland. So Donn crafted cocktails with the harvest that was around him.

Given that the palette he worked with was so limited, what made his drinks so diverse? First up was the sour: using vibrant fresh citrus gave his drinks their bright sparkle and made them balanced and refreshing. Secondly, the sweet. Of course he could just use sugar, but he found that blending or substituting in additional sweeteners like honey and maple syrup lent earthy depth to his concoctions. Thirdly, the rums. What rums they were! During Prohibition, production of American spirits had been severely curtailed, but in the Caribbean and elsewhere, rum production had continued unabated, and when the floodgates opened at the end of 1933, high-quality, long-aged rum was plentiful and cheap. (Much is made of how rum allowed Donn to build an empire on cheap hooch, but imagine if Scotch were the cheapest spirit on the market—island-themed Scotch cocktails would not have worked conceptually. Clearly, the choice of rum was of passion, not of price.)

Donn began experimenting with blending rums of several styles in the same drink. If, he would reason, a drink made entirely with heavy Jamaican rum was too bold, why not make it lighter and more complex with the introduction of a light Cuban rum, or perhaps a touch of smoky Demerara rum? It may not strike an imbiber today as particularly innovative,

THE DONN PALETTE (1930s)

SOUR/CITRUS	TROPICAL FRUITS & JUICES	SWEET	SPIRITS & LIQUEURS	SPICE & BITTERS	OTHER
Lime	Pineapple (chunks and juice)	Sugar/simple syrup	Rums	Angostura	Soda water/ seltzer
Grapefruit	Passion fruit juice/ syrup	Brown sugar	Pimento dram (allspice liqueur)	Herbsaint/ Pernod	Butter
Orange (used only in conjunction with lime and/or grapefruit)		Honey	Falernum	Cinnamon/ cinnamon syrup	Milk
		Maple syrup	Blackberry brandy	Vanilla/vanilla syrup	Fresh mint (as an ingredient)
		Grenadine	Cointreau	Nutmeg	
			Peach liqueur and brandy	Clove	
			Apricot liqueur and brandy	Almond extract	
				Sarsparilla	
				Ginger syrup	
				Ginger beer	
				Coffee (chilled, hot, and as a syrup)	

but there was certainly no one making martinis with three gins, nor would the residents of one Caribbean island have considered adding another island's rums to their own drinks.

Donn's real secret weapon was the spice. People in the Caribbean had been spicing rums and liqueurs for centuries, but after the colonial era, it was uncommon in America. He had a gift for taking the spices out of the baking pantry and blending them into cocktails in exciting new ways. Unlike the punch of early, Colonial America, Donn did not use spice to cover up the harshness of poorly made rum. Flavors like cloves, cinnamon, ginger, and nutmeg, when blended with other ingredients and out of context,

made a drinker furrow their brow and ask themselves, "I know what that is, but I just can't quite place it . . ."

So using just Donn's palette alone in a baroque version of a planter's punch gives you everything you need to produce the original generation of exotic cocktails. And now to this framework, we add the innovations of the man who was, in Donn's words, his "greatest imitator," Trader Vic.

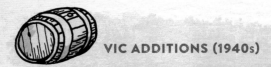

VIC ADDITIONS (1940s)

SOUR/CITRUS	TROPICAL FRUITS & JUICES	SWEET	SPIRITS & LIQUEURS	SPICE & BITTERS	OTHER
Lemon	Banana	Orgeat	Tequila		Italian vermouth
Cranberry		Raspberry or cranberry syrup (rarely, and often substituted with grenadine)	Okolehao		French vermouth
			Gin		
			Pisco		
			Scotch		
			Brandy		
			Applejack/ Calvados		
			Maraschino liqueur		
			Southern Comfort		
			Crème de cacao		
			Crème de cassis		
			Drambuie		

Vic began with attempts to reverse-engineer what he had tasted at Donn's bar alongside the drinks he enjoyed in Havana. Most of the Cuban drinks were a success thanks to published recipes in souvenir guides sold at bars like La Florida. His efforts at Donn's drinks yielded more uneven results. But it was part of his journey, and he soon landed upon a house style. Trader Vic added lemon, which had a longer California growing season and more availability than lime, and was an ingredient Donn never liked or did much with. He also added banana—it was, remember, his Banana Cow that made him realize the power of the exotic on his guests at Hinky Dinks. But perhaps Vic's most important contribution was the French ingredient orgeat, a lightly floral almond syrup he knew from his French upbringing, which

would become a signature ingredient in many of his most famous drinks. Vic rarely turned to spices at all, opting instead for the occasional dash of Angostura bitters for depth. He also added ingredients he'd experienced in Havana like sweet vermouth, maraschino liqueur, and white crème de cacao. In addition to blending rums, as Donn did, he also innovatively blended other base spirits with the rum, such as gin and brandy. Notice also that at this point there is still no vodka, which would not rise in popularity in American until the 1950s.

With the spread of tiki across America, a few more ingredients expanded the exotic cocktail palette during the golden era. Better transportation networks meant more of the expected tropical fruit juices, and blue crept into the tiki menu by way of

THE GOLDEN ERA ADDITIONS (1950s AND 1960s)

SOUR/CITRUS	TROPICAL FRUITS & JUICES	SWEET	SPIRITS & LIQUEURS	SPICE & BITTERS	OTHER
Guava		Confectioners' sugar	Vodka	Galliano	Cream
Lychee nut juice			Bourbon	Kummel	Crème de menthe
Mango		Coconut cream	Aquavit	Van der Hum liqueur	
Peach			Triple sec		
Papaya			Cognac	Tia Maria	
Tamarind			Blended whiskey	Rose's Lime Cordial	
Guanabana			Blue Curaçao		
Tangerine			Benedictine		

the curaçao-laced Blue Hawaii, invented by Harry Yee in 1957 at the Hawaiian Village Hotel in Waikiki. Coconut began its rise with the commercialization of Coco Lopez coconut cream in 1954, removing prior transportation and labor hurdles. What's still noticeably absent is spiced rum, which wasn't broadly popular in the United States until the introduction of Captain Morgan in 1984.

So, the template established by Donn and built on by Vic still held fast through tiki's golden era, albeit a little battered by changing tastes.

THE METHOD TO THE MADNESS: THE DRINK MIXER

Donn's arsenal of ingredients came together with the aid of a very special tool: the drink mixer. The drink mixer, which you may know as a milk shake machine or spindle blender, started coming into use in cocktails in the 1920s and was popular in Havana before being largely replaced by the more modern blender, the first of which was introduced by Waring in 1938. When Don's Beachcomber Café opened in 1933, it was the drink mixer in the back room that prepared Donn's famous Rhum Rhapsodies. Close inspection of a portrait of Donn working in the back bar of his original restaurant reveals that not only was there no blender, there was no cocktail shaker in sight either. (Trader Vic, on the other hand, did find use for the blender, not surprisingly given his visit to Havana where it was in use, and deployed it to excellent effect in some of his riffs on Cuban cocktails. At Vic's remaining locations, the drink mixer and blender operate side by side, and he noted the distinction in their uses in his 1947 *Bartender's Guide*.)

Use of the drink mixer continued through the entire tiki era and is in use today at all of the surviving origial tiki bars. This is because nothing else matches the results of the drink mixer. In just three or four short seconds of "flash blending," it will effectively chill, perfectly dilute, and aerate your cocktail, making it frothy, waking up the citrus, and pushing the aromatics to the surface of the drink as the air in the cocktail rises. It's also ideal for working with egg whites, eliminating the traditional dry shake, and when using seltzer water in drinks to create additional froth without using a closed shaker tin and causing pressure to build up. Tough ingredients to work with, like condensed milk, are no match for the drink mixer, and you'll save the wear and tear on your own body from shaking. In short, there's no substitute.

What the drink mixer isn't is a blender. A drink mixer will not make you a frozen drink. There are no frozen cocktails in this book, and the decision was made for both style and space reasons that from day one, Smuggler's Cove would serve no frozen cocktails. As late as the early 1960s, as we progress to menus with photographs of cocktails rather than illustrations, it's still clear to see that the exotic cocktails aren't frozen.

So does it mean that an exotic cocktail shouldn't be frozen? I don't think so. To my mind, it's the exotic cocktail template and the palette that are the most important. Following those, and using quality ingredients and skillful proportioning, means that a shaken, flash blended, or frozen drink can be an exotic cocktail.

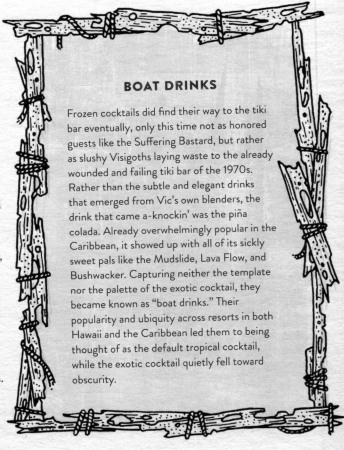

BOAT DRINKS

Frozen cocktails did find their way to the tiki bar eventually, only this time not as honored guests like the Suffering Bastard, but rather as slushy Visigoths laying waste to the already wounded and failing tiki bar of the 1970s. Rather than the subtle and elegant drinks that emerged from Vic's own blenders, the drink that came a-knockin' was the piña colada. Already overwhelmingly popular in the Caribbean, it showed up with all of its sickly sweet pals like the Mudslide, Lava Flow, and Bushwacker. Capturing neither the template nor the palette of the exotic cocktail, they became known as "boat drinks." Their popularity and ubiquity across resorts in both Hawaii and the Caribbean led them to being thought of as the default tropical cocktail, while the exotic cocktail quietly fell toward obscurity.

CREATING THE TIKI "PALETTE"

Now that you understand the tiki ingredient palette from which to paint your cocktail masterpiece, it's time to start stocking ingredients. On pages 324 to 333, you'll find recipes for ingredients we make ourselves. That said, if there is an honestly made product on the market (that is, no chemicals or high fructose corn syrup in them, for example), and you are thirsty and don't feel like making your own orgeat or grenadine, go ahead and purchase it (see Resources, page 335, for some ideas). Do note that the recipes in this book are all formulated to work with the Smuggler's Cove house-made ingredients, so if you are using commercial versions, you may need to play around with ingredient ratios to get the flavors right.

The Sour: Juices

CITRUS

It takes a team of two people over three hours a day just to prep the fresh juices and garnishes for Smuggler's Cove, but it is absolutely essential. Even pasteurized citrus juice is no substitute for fresh squeezed in an exotic cocktail—by heating the juice, however gently, you are in effect cooking it, and it loses that essential sparkle. Never use shelf-stable citrus juice. Part of what made Southern California the natural birthplace of tiki was the availability of wonderful fresh citrus.

A few tips:

Choose citrus that feels heavy for its size and has as thin a skin as possible that has some "give" when you squeeze it in your hand. Best to buy your fruit within a day or two of when you plan to juice it.

You must juice your fruit the day you are going to use it, as it has a very short "shelf" life once it is juiced—basically only a few hours at most, after which it begins to become bitter rather than sour.

There is some evidence to suggest that lime juice is actually at its peak three to four hours after it is juiced, because the pH has decreased slightly, resulting in greater perceived acidity. Lemon and grapefruit can also hold up fairly well for several hours, but oranges decline fairly rapidly, so juice them last. Plus they're a little easier on the ol' juicin' hand.

The "juice from one lime" or "juice from half a lime" instruction is common in Trader Vic recipes. The problem is that limes come in a variety of sizes and their juice yields vary, even within the same size of lime, depending on country of origin, ripeness, season, etc. And the limes that Vic was using in the 1950s were almost certainly smaller than today's. So we have translated the lime juice in his recipes into more exact amounts.

It is preferable to use a tannic and more bitter grapefruit such as the white or pink varieties that were available to Donn, rather than the much sweeter Ruby Red. Donn's recipes were created with white and pink grapefruits, depending on seasonal availability. Although the Ruby Red varietal was created in Texas in 1929, it's not clear if it was shipped to California in the 1930s for people to work with. And subsequent cultivation of Ruby Red over the decades has made it much higher in sugar content. You can always add sugar later, but you can't "unsweeten" a grapefruit that is too sweet.

PASSION FRUIT

Passion fruit is a staple of the exotic cocktail, adding wonderful tartness, mouthfeel, and complexity whether as a puree or as part of a syrup. But passion fruit is messy and not always readily available year round, and most commercial passion fruit syrups do not contain real sugar *or* real passion fruit. I find that packaged passion fruit puree—as long as it is nearly 100 percent fruit, and is a natural product without high fructose corn syrup or chemicals added (see Resources, page 335, for suggestions)—is a totally acceptable substitute for fresh. I also use this puree to create my own passion fruit syrup (page 325).

The Sweet: Sugar and Other Syrups

SUGAR SYRUPS

A one-to-one simple syrup (equal parts sugar and water) is, of course, not wrong—it is just not the house style of Smuggler's Cove. I have always chosen to make my simple syrups in a two-to-one ratio (two parts sugar to one part water) because there is less water added to the drink that way, and I have found that a richer syrup contributes the right sweetness, mouthfeel, and body to exotic cocktails. In addition, at Smuggler's Cove a portion of our house simple syrup (SC Demerara Syrup, page 324) is made of demerara sugar, which is less refined than white granulated sugar, and therefore retains additional molasses. You can feel the difference in the touch—demerara still retains a stickiness or tackiness to the touch, which tells you it is only partly refined. (Note that demerara sugar is different than brown sugar, which is fully refined white sugar that has had molasses added back into it for flavor.) I have found that demerara sugar adds additional depth to exotic cocktails, while also being useful to mimic the less refined sugar that would have likely been used in Colonial American and historic Caribbean punches and other drinks that are part of our menu. However, you will notice that for our other house-made syrups that include sugar, the recipes call for just a refined white sugar simple syrup as the base. This is because in those cases we *don't* want the added flavors/dimensions of the demerara in the syrups. We just want to highlight the flavor of syrup being made (coconut, cinnamon, vanilla, passion fruit). A final tip to consider is the addition of a pinch of salt to enhance sweetness, a trick we employ in a few of our housemade syrups.

ORGEAT

Originally from France, orgeat is an almond-milk sugar syrup with orange flower water and rose water, and adds a divine floral dimension and mouthfeel to exotic cocktails. I hear this word massacred more than nearly any other ingredient. I met with an orgeat producer in France and he told me it is pronounced "ore-zha," (think Zsa Zsa Gabor), so I'm stickin' with it. We choose to make our orgeat with blanched, untoasted almonds, a style sometimes referred to as "blanche orgeat." Some commercial orgeat producers use whole almonds (with the peel), some toast the almonds, and some add apricot kernels to create a more marzipan-like flavor profile. Some orgeats have a much stronger floral note than ours, even verging on perfume-y. All of these decisions create interesting and unique orgeats, and I encourage you to find the right orgeat for you. If buying a commercial product, do make sure it is made from real almonds (not almond flavoring), and avoid the usual enemies (artificial flavorings, high fructose corn syrup, etc.). And, I feel I have to mention, there is no substitute. Amarettos (Italian almond liqueurs) or almond extract can't fill in for orgeat.

PASSION FRUIT SYRUP

As mentioned previously, we use a packaged passion fruit puree as the base of our syrup (page 325). You will also notice that a few of our recipes call for both passion fruit nectar and and honey syrup. One interesting alternative in these cases is to make a passion fruit honey (page 325), which will bring a more intense passion and honey flavor to the drink.

MAPLE SYRUP

Maple syrup comes in a few categories, which indicate when it has been harvested, which influences the syrup's color and flavor. Smuggler's Cove uses a

Grade A dark amber maple syrup, but you may want to experiment with a Grade B syrup for its more intense flavor.

GRENADINE

Grenadine is (or rather *should* be) a pomegranate and sugar syrup that first hit the United States in the late nineteenth century. But, when grenadine really hit its stride in the early twentieth century, commercial grenadine syrups made without pomegranate were so ubiquitous that it is likely that a lot of exotic cocktails were formulated with imitation grenadine. There is some hint of this in Trader Vic's *Book of Food and Drink* where Vic has recipes that call for "pomegranate syrup (or grenadine)." Sometimes, not everything from the past is a good thing. Do NOT use artificial grenadine. It is made from a bunch of chemicals and high fructose corn syrup and not only doesn't include pomegranate or even essence of pomegranate, it doesn't even taste like pomegranate. See Resources, page 335, for suggestions on quality grenadines that are available, or page 328 for our recipe.

COCONUT CREAM

There are several coconut creams on the market, but you have to be very cautious, as a lot of them are filled with chemicals and flavoring and have barely, if ever, seen a coconut. I strongly encourage people to make their own (page 328). It is not difficult if you start with an honest quality unsweetened coconut milk.

The Strong: Choosing Your Rum

If a cocktail recipe simply called for "rum," you could end up with one hundred versions of the drink depending on the rum you chose. The daiquiri showcases this perfectly. Try this fun experiment at home with friends. Choose one rum from each of five different categories outlined in our rum chart

(pages 197–99). Then make five simple daiquiris (recipe on page 168) and change only the rum. What do you notice? If you use a molasses-based, column-distilled, lightly aged rum, you might get a dry, crisp drink, very similar in character to what would have been served in Prohibition-era Cuba. But without being guided as to a style of rum, you could easily have chosen a rhum agricole blanc and your drink would taste similar to a ti' punch, very grassy, heavier bodied, and with an extra heat from the higher proof. See? Science is fun!

In the 1930s, early cocktail guides started to call for particular rum styles in their recipes in a way that isn't done with other spirits (with the exception of distinguishing between Genever, Old Tom, Plymouth, and London Dry gin). For example, the 1930 *Savoy Cocktail Guide* often called specifically for Bacardi rum, Jamaica rum, or St. Croix, but only ever called for "Scotch" and not Scotch from a particular region, like Islay or Speyside. There are no historical bourbon, or vodka drinks that "just wouldn't be the same" without a particular style or brand.

However, the people we really have to thank for spreading the gospel of "the right rum for the right drink" are Donn and Vic. An excellent illustration of Vic's passion and knowledge about rum is his 1946 *Book of Food and Drink*. In addition to recipes that call for twelve different types of rum throughout its pages, the book has a twenty-page "About Booze" section of which fifteen are devoted to rum. Whereas Vic recommends the home bartender stock one brand of bourbon, gin, rye, and Scotch, he breaks rum into four categories (Puerto Rican or Cuban, Jamaican, Demerara, and Haitian), and suggests a brand for each.

Many contemporary rum and tiki bars have rediscovered the Trader Vic and Don the Beachcomber philosophy of blending rums. Many now have their own "house rum blend" that they use throughout their menu, thus giving their recipes a signature taste. This is great, as long as you always remember two things: 1) Use only quality rums in your blend. Blending poorly made rum with good rum does not raise the quality of the poorer rum. 2) Be thoughtful in your house blend so that it can be versatile for use in a few different drinks.

While there may have been little access to rhum agricole in the heyday of the tiki era, to dismiss the category wholesale would be to miss out on beautiful, complementary flavors. Similarly, just because there were few American rums during that time, the many emerging American craft rums available in the United States today should certainly be used and experimented with in your exotic cocktails.

The Weak

PINEAPPLE

In many ways, pineapple is your secret weapon of juice when it comes to an exotic cocktail. Even canned pineapple will add a pleasant froth to your drink, and can add body and length to your cocktail without making it too sour. However, make sure you use 100 percent unsweetened, not-from-concentrate, pineapple juice. The Smuggler's Cove blend is a combination of one-quarter fresh to three-quarters canned pineapple juice. This gives us consistency in terms of acidity and sweetness from the canned, but adds the sparkle and additional froth of fresh juice on top.

SELTZER

The purpose of adding small amounts of seltzer to most exotic cocktails isn't to make the drinks fizzy, but rather to gently dilute them, improve mouthfeel when using several syrups, and provide a visually appealing frothy head on the drink when using the drink mixer (see page 221).

Ice

Though technically belonging to "the weak" category of the palette, ice gets its own category, as its varieties are such a critical component to the exotic cocktail. I recommend you purchase a standard metal 12-ounce scoop. Most of our recipes call for 12 ounces, so it will be a quick way to tell you have the right amount.

CUBED ICE

Cubed ice from your home freezer is recommended for use in shaking or stirring drinks. I do not recommended cubed ice for drinks made with a drink mixer as it makes it harder for the spindle to operate correctly. If you're having a small gathering and want to serve stirred or shaken drinks, you will need to plan ahead to have enough cubed ice. In the week leading up to the gathering, freeze trays of cubes each night and store the finished cubes in large ziplock bags.

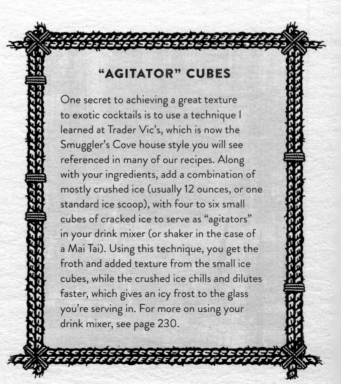

"AGITATOR" CUBES

One secret to achieving a great texture to exotic cocktails is to use a technique I learned at Trader Vic's, which is now the Smuggler's Cove house style you will see referenced in many of our recipes. Along with your ingredients, add a combination of mostly crushed ice (usually 12 ounces, or one standard ice scoop), with four to six small cubes of cracked ice to serve as "agitators" in your drink mixer (or shaker in the case of a Mai Tai). Using this technique, you get the froth and added texture from the small ice cubes, while the crushed ice chills and dilutes faster, which gives an icy frost to the glass you're serving in. For more on using your drink mixer, see page 230.

CRACKED ICE

Cracked ice refers to uneven, smaller pieces of ice than cubed (think bagged party ice), which provides quicker chilling and dilution. It is the ideal ice to use for your "agitator" cubes (see page 226), and to make your crushed ice (see below). Though cubed ice is preferred for shaken or stirred drinks, cracked ice is large enough to use instead, making it an ideal ice for larger gatherings because it means you can have one ice play a few different roles. Note, however, that if using cracked ice for this purpose, you will want to shake or stir for less time than you would with cubed ice to avoid making those drinks overly watery. Using store-bought party ice for your cracked ice is perfectly fine. People tend to be dismissive of grocery store cracked ice, but the truth is the water used is very pure, and the freezers inside grocery stores are set to extremely cold temperatures to compensate for your travel time. Nevertheless, I recommend bringing a quality cooler with you to the grocery store, buying your ice last, and transferring it immediately to the cooler. Also, take a quick look at the ice, and make sure it doesn't look like it's been at the store a hundred years or been melted and refrozen.

CRUSHED ICE

Crushed ice is used in swizzles and heavily concentrated drinks like grogs. Crushed ice dilutes quickly, but if it's packed into a glass, the combined coldness will slow down that melting so you have the best of both worlds—a drink that stays nice and cold for a long time, but continues to improve as the ice slowly dilutes. Your goal for crushed ice is small, granular, pellets that are about 5 millimeters in diameter. For home use, I have had a good experience with a home ice crusher (see Resources, page 335). If you need a lot of crushed ice (i.e., for more than a few people), however, go to your local meat or fish counter and ask them nicely (and offer a little cash) to fill up a cooler for you. Save your crushing arm for hoisting cocktails! If you're having people over, do your crushing ahead of time to speed up drink makin'. And keep it in a dedicated cooler that has no other objects or odors in it.

"SNOW" ICE

This ice is finer than crushed ice, and is the type of ice used for making snow cones or Hawaiian shave ice. In the exotic cocktail world it is used primarily for ice garnishes (see page 241). The easiest way to make snow ice is to put crushed ice through a food processor. If you don't have a food processor, there are also several retail model snow cone machines available.

Spices and Other Essentials

Use fresh spices—whole nutmeg, whole cinnamon sticks, and whole vanilla beans—in your syrups and to top your drinks. Note when grating your own spices that "1 dash" equals approximately 5 grates with a Microplane.

FALERNUM

A critical ingredient in your tiki arsenal, falernum has been an exotic cocktail recipe staple since the earliest Don the Beachcomber days. Falernum originated in Barbados, and is a rum, sugar, and lime-based liqueur with a variety of spices, including (but not limited to) cloves, almond, ginger, nutmeg. As it was traditionally homemade, family recipes vary widely. At Smuggler's Cove, we use John D. Taylor's Velvet Falernum. It has been made in Barbados for decades by a Barbadian-owned company, which also means that my money goes back into the Caribbean economy. But homemade falernums are very popular, and there are many recipes available online to try. However, do note that if your particular falernum is overwhelmingly clove-y or ginger-y, then it can quickly overpower many recipes.

PIMENTO DRAM (ALLSPICE LIQUEUR)

A traditional ingredient from Jamaica, pimento dram is a liqueur made from rum infused with allspice berries (which come from the pimento tree, hence the name). While pimento dram used to be nearly impossible to find without going to Jamaica, we are now fortunate to have a few brands on the market, including our preferred, St. Elizabeth, which is made from Jamaican ingredients. Again, as with falernum, you can certainly make your own, but the cocktail recipes in this book that call for pimento dram have been formulated around St. Elizabeth.

"HERBSTURA"

One of Donn's secret weapons in his drinks is his great combination of spices. A staple for him was the combination of Herbsaint (an anise-flavored liqueur) and Angostura bitters. So much so, that Don the Beachcomber locations would combine them in a dasher bottle, which we also do at Smuggler's Cove. You won't need much—a small (1½- to 3-ounce) bitters or dasher bottle will serve you for quite some time. Add equal parts Herbsaint and Angostura bitters to the dasher bottle and shake well to integrate.

BITTERS

As staples in your bar, stock Angostura bitters and a quality orange bitters. However, just substituting a different bitters, changing the volume of bitters, or adding bitters to drinks that never had them can make dramatic and exciting changes to a cocktail, so be sure to experiment with the scores of other great bitters on the market today. At Smuggler's Cove, we use Angostura bitters in the commercial-size (16-ounce) bottle. In our testing, this bottle has shown to yield a much heavier dash than a 4-ounce Angostura bottle or Japanese glass dasher bottle. In effect, if you are using a smaller Angostura bottle or Japanese dasher, you might need to dash more than the recipes in this book call for. Or, if you find some of these drinks too heavy on the bitters for your liking, you might want to use a smaller bottle to scale back the bitters.

EGGS

It's important to keep eggs (and egg whites) in the refrigerator, and only take them out when you are ready to use them in a drink. Because of this, and because raw eggs can be harmful for someone who is pregnant or immune compromised, eggs are a less-than-ideal party ingredient. When a drink calls for a whole egg, crack the egg to order. However, when making individual egg-white drinks, you should "prime" your egg whites ahead of use: crack and separate your eggs and pour the whites into your mixing tin without ice and flash blend them for two to three seconds to break up the proteins. These egg whites should either be used immediately, or poured into a clean plastic squeeze bottle and immediately refrigerated for use in a few hours after the well-known "wet dog smell" that develops has a chance to dissipate. Once your egg whites are ready for use, you will note that our recipes call for a "dry flash." Rather than using a cocktail shaker for the traditional "dry shake," we have found that using a drink mixer works especially well to generate a strong, foamy, lasting head on your cocktail.

To dry flash, flash blend your primed egg whites along with any 80-proof or higher spirits included in the recipe, without ice, for ten seconds. Then add the ice and the rest of your ingredients and proceed with your regular few-second flash blend.

The rough recipe equivalency for "the white of 1 egg" is ½ ounce.

BUILDING YOUR TIKI TOOLKIT

There are many excellent bartending books that will teach in more detail about general tools and basic techniques (such as stirring, shaking, or making a lemon twist), so please refer to my list of recommended books that I encourage you to read and have handy (see Bibliography and Recommended Reading, page 340). What I want to focus on here is what you need to know to create a great exotic cocktail.

The Jigger and Measuring

Number one rule of thumb when making an exotic cocktail: measure your ingredients. This is important for bartending in general, but exotic cocktails are particularly unforgiving if your quantities are out of whack. This was an edict handed down from the Trader himself in his 1947 *Bartender's Guide*: "My best advice is to make every drink as though it were to be the best you've ever made, and you can't do this if you don't measure." As for what you use to measure, this is entirely up to you, but I suggest choosing a jigger with the most-used measurements: I like one that is 1, 2, and 3 ounces on one side and ½, ¾, and 1½ ounces on the other because it covers almost all your bases.

The Drink Mixer, Flash Blending, and the Open Pour

I feel strongly that the drink mixer is an essential cocktail tool for the creation of many of the drinks in this book (see page 221 for more on why). However, just to be clear, you don't have to rush out and buy the commercial, weapons-grade version we use at Smuggler's Cove. We've tested three levels of drink mixer, pictured on page 231, and they all yield virtually identical results. The light-duty version—the

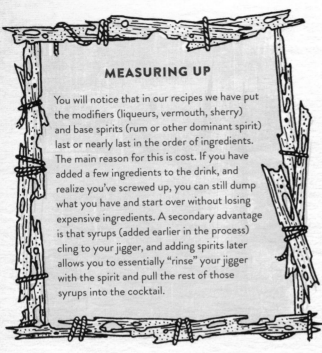

MEASURING UP

You will notice that in our recipes we have put the modifiers (liqueurs, vermouth, sherry) and base spirits (rum or other dominant spirit) last or nearly last in the order of ingredients. The main reason for this is cost. If you have added a few ingredients to the drink, and realize you've screwed up, you can still dump what you have and start over without losing expensive ingredients. A secondary advantage is that syrups (added earlier in the process) cling to your jigger, and adding spirits later allows you to essentially "rinse" your jigger with the spirit and pull the rest of those syrups into the cocktail.

Hamilton Beach 760C Classic DrinkMaster Drink Mixer—costs less than a nice cocktail shaker or a bottle of good rum, so go ahead and get one and try it out. If you are just playing around now and then, this will probably be all you ever need. For more frequent use, or for entertaining, or to truly embody the spirit of Donn and Vic, step up to the more durable medium-duty model—the Waring PDM series Drink Mixer, or the weapons-grade version—the Hamilton Beach Single-Spindle Drink Mixer HMD200 Series.

Any model drink mixer will be a welcome addition to your home bar. You'll even find vintage designs that serve as their own décor—they will naturally look cool in your tiki bar because they have always been in tiki bars. Still need a reason to buy one? Milk shakes for the kids!

You will see that many of the recipe instructions say to "flash blend" with your drink mixer. Here, you should give a quick three-to-four–second pulse with the drink mixer that will aerate, dilute, and chill the drink but leave much of the ice intact. In some cases, this ice will be strained out, and the liquid contents poured over fresh ice in the glass. However, in most cases, you will be pouring the entire contents (ice and all) into the glass you are serving in—a technique we have dubbed the "open pour." When using the open pour, you should give your tin an added swirl to be sure and capture as much of the ice as possible, before employing a "gated finish" (see page 232) to ensure your drink will fit in your serving glass.

In many modern craft cocktail bars, serving a drink with the ice used to mix it is often derisively referred to as a "dirty dump." But in the tradition of the exotic cocktail, the technique makes sense for a few reasons, including the use of heavy syrups that require additional dilution, and the ability to bring a visually appealing frost to the surface of the serving vessel more quickly. I've always found that it creates just the right mouthfeel and temperature in exotic

Bartender
Melissa Garcia

cocktails. One added bonus to the open pour is that you don't have to worry about a phenomenon food science writer Dave Arnold has termed "holdback," in which, by straining, you can lose as much as 25 percent of your precious cocktail that remains stuck to your ice after mixing.

(Please note: You must *always* use a stainless steel mixing cup with a drink mixer. NEVER use glass—the spindle blades will shatter it and your cocktail will taste like human blood.)

The Shaker and Shaking

Which shaker you choose is a matter of personal preference. However, I'd recommend a "tin on tin" (aka "cheater tin") setup. This is similar to the classic Boston shaker (stainless steel metal tin used with pint glass), but is lighter weight, seals more easily, and avoids the dangers inherent in working with glass. The "tin on tin" setup consists of a larger metal tin (28 ounces) that, instead of being used with a pint glass, is used with a smaller-sized metal tin (18 ounces—the "cheater" tin) that fits inside the larger tin. Having a two-piece setup also gives you the flexibility to use a Hawthorne strainer and "gated finish" (see following).

Strainers, Double-Straining, and the "Gated Finish"

Whichever strainer you use, be aware of the afore-mentioned "holdback," the amount of cocktail lost due to straining. One tip from Dave Arnold to drasti-cally reduce holdback is to be sure, after you think you have finished straining, to sharply snap your chilling vessel (tin or glass) down, right the vessel, and then strain one last time.

We recommend three different strainers, each of which has a specific use:

JULEP STRAINER

Preferred for stirred, spiritous cocktails such as the Manhattan or martini, which do not involve fruit juice or ice shards from shaking and therefore merely need a strainer that blocks the ice as you pour from your mixing glass.

HAWTHORNE STRAINER AND "GATED FINISH"

Used with shaken and flash-blended cocktails, which typically involve fruit juice and other ingredients. Beyond blocking larger pieces of ice, the spring of the Hawthorne strainer will also hold back pulp, ice shards, or other solid matter that you don't want in your drink. A tab on the strainer's back serves as "gate control"—it controls the amount of small ice shards that are allowed through with the liquid. Typically, you will keep the gate tight to avoid those ice shards. For drinks in which, after flash blending or shaking, you are pouring everything (including ice) into the serving glass ("open pour"), you will sometimes have more contents than properly fit the glass. The Hawthorne strainer will also allow what I've termed the "gated finish": after an open pour of about seven-eighths of the contents of your tin into the serving glass (being sure to give the tin a good swirl partway through to capture a lot of the ice in those contents) pour the remaining one-eighth of the contents using your Hawthorne strainer with a tight gate in place to block any remaining ice, thereby straining just the remaining liquid into the glass. This is the technique you will see in service at classic tiki bars.

FINE-MESH STRAINER AND "DOUBLE-STRAINING"

The fine-mesh strainer is used in combination with another strainer (typically a Hawthorne) for the purposes of double-straining your cocktail. When a drink instructs you to double-strain, it is generally for two reasons: 1) The drink has been shaken to chill the ingredients, but the final cocktail is being served up neat so you want to remove any remaining ice shards, both for mouthfeel and so the drink doesn't dilute any further, and 2) the drink includes pulp, spices, egg white, or particulate matter that is small enough to get past your Hawthorne strainer. To double-strain, hold the fine-mesh strainer over your serving glass and then pour the liquid from your shaker or drink mixer tin (with strainer in place), so that it passes through the fine-mesh strainer. Periodically, tap your shaker against the side of the fine-mesh strainer to hasten the flow of the liquid through it.

The Juicer and Juicing

Even though we've begun to win the war for fresh juices, there's still one battle left to wage: overzealous juicing, which pulls a lot of bitterness into the citrus juice. The resulting cocktail has the sparkle and zest of freshness, but doesn't actually taste that good.

At Smuggler's Cove, we solve this problem with a commercial juicer that extracts just the internal portion of the fruit—the juice and juice sacs. It keeps both the peel, and, more importantly, the white albedo (or "pith") out of the process.

However, just because you don't have a spare ten thousand dollars to spend on a juicer doesn't mean you can't adhere to the philosophy behind it. No matter the juicing method, the secret is to GO EASY. I know limes can be pricey and you want to get your money's worth, but trust me. Buy a few extra and show them a gentle touch. When using a handheld citrus squeezer or manual stand juicer, stop just short of closing it all the way, or when using an electric juicer, stop just short of pushing all the way down on the electric juicing spindle. When you pull away the spent fruit, the pulp should still be intact and look fairly healthy, not like it's been squeezed within an inch of its life.

A few other tips:

- Check your recipes ahead of time, and see if any of them call for lime garnishes—you will want to be sure to set some good-looking limes aside for this. It's easy to get juice-happy and forget.

- There has been a longstanding debate about whether, if you roll your fruit on the counter before juicing, or keep it at room temperature, or even heat it slightly, it will yield more juice. Recently, bar owner and author Jeffrey Morganthaler did an experiment comparing lemons stored/prepped different ways, and found none of this to be true. So keep your fruit fresher longer in the fridge, and when it's time to juice, you don't need any extra acrobatics.

- Precut all of your fruit just before juicing, so that you can juice more quickly. See the nub where the fruit used to be attached to its tree stem? Cut perpendicular to that.

- Bottle your juices in glass bottles or plastic squeeze bottles and label them. I typically will use old booze bottles that have been well cleaned.

- As you are juicing, or afterward, it is important to pour your juice through a mesh strainer prior to bottling. This will get rid of unwanted pulp and seeds that will clog your mixer, your pour spouts, your dishwasher, and your pretty cocktail.

- Keep your bottled juice refrigerated and sealed prior to service and, once in service, keep it on ice. Unfortunately, as mentioned earlier, at the end of the night, you should go ahead and throw out the extra as fresh citrus does not last.

PINEAPPLE CORING AND JUICING

When choosing your pineapples, look for fresh, healthy, and firm fruit. You can tell in part by feel (slightly soft to the touch), smell (fresh and not overripe), and the condition of the leaves on top (unbroken, not browned or shriveled). Look for the eyes to be uniform from top to bottom.

A pineapple corer is an invaluable tool for extracting pineapple fruit for juice or garnish (see page 241). Number one rule: the plastic ones do not last. Spring the extra couple of bucks and get yourself a stainless steel corer (most kitchen supply stores have these, or they're available online.)

Note: If you want to use your pineapple to create a lovely vessel for your drink, there are other tips and techniques to follow (see page 238).

However, if all you care about is the fruit or juice, you can cut off the top and bottom of the pineapple, insert the corer, twist the corer a few times and pull out your fruit. To core the pineapple manually, remove the top and bottom, cut along the outside of the skin, removing any brown patches left over from the eyes—then slice the fruit in half and quarters again, being sure that the core of the pineapple is removed, as you do not want this for either juicing or garnishing.

Once you have your fruit extracted, your best bet for juicing pineapple is a good high-speed (centrifugal) juicer. The key is to have a detachable pulp collector, and watch it carefully as you juice. Pineapples yield lots of juice and pulp, and I've been caught off-guard on many an occasion with an overflowing pulp collector.

Swizzle Stick and Swizzling

A "swizzle" is a style of drink defined by how it is made (with ingredients whisked together with crushed ice using a swizzle stick), rather than by which ingredients go in it. A swizzled cocktail and corresponding "swizzle stick" made their debut sometime in the late 1860s, when ice became more widely available in the Caribbean. At the time, cocktails were often "frothed" or "frisked into effervescence" by putting a stick—called a *bois lélé*—into the glass and rubbing it between one's palms. This long wooden stick

with a starburst cluster of short prongs at the end, made from the Caribbean *Quararibea turbinata* tree (aka the "swizzlestick" tree!), is still found on Martinique today, and is commonly used in the making of the ti' punch (see photo on page 178 of a lélé and a ti' punch). Plastic versions are available, and in a pinch a barspoon or bar whisk can be used, but online you can now get the real deal, and we recommend you do, as nature made it best. Or, better yet, it seems like a good excuse to travel to Martinique and bring back a bunch (see Resources, page 335).

To properly swizzle a drink, add the ingredients to a tall glass you will be serving in, like a Collins or a Zombie and fill the glass about three-quarters full with crushed ice. Take the lélé (or barspoon or bar whisk), push the end toward the bottom of the glass, and place the handle between the palms of your hands. Briskly roll the handle between your palms, rotating the end in the drink while raising the stick up and down the length of the glass (see photo, page 227). Continue until the outside of the glass is well frosted, then top with additional crushed ice.

ADDING THE MAGIC

The Menu

Great menus were a part of the escapist experience of a tiki bar and were home to some of the most purple prose ever put to paper. Be inspired to continue this tradition with your own bar's menu. Take the Hawaii Kai menu as an example, in which you would read, "As you cross our threshold, you become part of the romantic Polynesian world jealously guarded by Tiki Gods. Delight your senses with lyrical waterfalls and glorious lava rock gardens. Inspect our bamboo huts flown in from the distant Islands. See our captive Manu birds display

their colorful plumage as they 'serenade' you with a cacophony of song." Adding to the mystery and enchantment of the tiki experience were the drink names and descriptions themselves. Write-ups were often vague and told you next to nothing about what was in the drink, but would pique your curiosity and offer you an enticing illustration. Some brought up the soothing escape of the islands, like Kona Kai's description of their Aku Aku: "Fresh pineapple filled with liquid sunshine and the fragrance of the jasmine," or the Outrigger's description of their Birds of Paradise, "Bibulation Exotica! . . . A Taste of Paradise with a Capital P!" Other descriptions suggested danger and intrigue, such as Kon-Tiki's warnings about their Coral Reef cocktail, "A challenge for all navigators, dangerous at low tide," or Steve's Rum Barrel, "Before ordering a third one, better check with your insurance man."

The Vessel

Striking vessels were used to serve exotic cocktails even before the tiki mug. Donn's drinks began using elegant glassware—unusual shapes, repurposed pilsner glasses, and a few styles of his own design. Thanks to the efforts of Jeff "Beachbum" Berry, two classic glasses, the swizzle cup made of lightweight stainless steel, and the lovely, elegant, rippled pearl diver glass, are once again available through Cocktail Kingdom (see Resources, page 335). There were also drinks served out of pineapples and coconuts (see page 238), and later even bamboo, both real and ceramic. Have fun with your glassware. Even though you may have trouble finding tiki mugs, thrift and antique stores remain an excellent source for other inexpensive but beautiful glassware of all shapes and sizes.

TIKI MUGS

The menu at Kon Tiki Ports suggested, "When you have partaken of this delicious brew; the forbidden water of the islands; take its ceramic container, 'KANOA' home with you to ward off evil spirits and make you return for more." The tiki mug was a reminder of adventures and misadventures, when the rum may have made many of the details of your evening a bit . . . fuzzy.

At the peak of the tiki craze, mug designs came in all shapes and sizes and glazes, and a large restaurant might have several different mugs on offer, with different drinks served in each. Orchids of Hawaii would not only design mugs for a restaurant, but would also illustrate the restaurant's drink menu so it could include images of the various mugs. Mugs were often tikis, but those ranged from Ku to Moai in design, and from fierce to cartoonish. To keep them company were ceramic hula girls, skull mugs, buddhas, pirates, rum barrels, coconuts, pineapples, and bamboo.

While Trader Vic was likely the first to offer a special ceramic drinking vessel, his early versions included South Seas themes and a skull mug. It isn't clear which bar was the first to use an actual tiki in its mug design, but there is some reason to believe it may have been Tiki Bob's in San Francisco. This mug remains coveted to this day—so much so that the one I had cemented in place at the Cove went missing in the middle of a busy weekend night of service. This is a picture of the replacement Tiki Bob mug at Smuggler's Cove today, safely secured.

In addition to their great advertising and souvenir properties, the tiki mug has another distinct advantage—it hides what's in your glass. As you'll quickly discover as you delve into the world of exotic cocktail mixology, a lot of these tasty drinks are, quite simply, ugly. When made with real ingredients and well-aged rums, they can be the color of a muddy

river, and aren't especially appetizing. What better solution than to pour them into a colorful and attractive vessel?

In the mid-1990s, Southern California artist Bosko Hrnjak, after collecting tiki mugs from long-lost bars for years, had the idea to try his hand at manufacturing his own, and the commercial tiki mug tradition was reborn. Most tiki bars that are part of the tiki revival have continued the tradition of having souvenir mugs manufactured for their guests creating an opportunity for the return of large-scale production by firms like Tiki Farm and Munktiki, both launched in 2000. At Smuggler's Cove, we have had over twenty original mugs designed, and have sold over eighteen thousand of them since we opened our doors.

Having six or eight tiki mugs at the ready to serve cocktails to your guests is a fun addition to any home bar. However, in addition to the cost, I need to warn against serving cocktails out of vintage mugs—many were made before the FDA regulated lead levels in the glazes of ceramics, and so tiki mugs made before 1970 are no longer considered food-safe. What is particularly problematic with lead-laden glazes is contact with anything highly acidic like, say, exotic cocktails, which leaches the lead out of the glaze much faster than other foods. There are home lead-testing kits you can buy that will tell you for sure, but considering how valuable old mugs are anyway, I would suggest you leave your old mugs on the shelf. Instead, find yourself a few modern mugs for your parties. Ideally, these would come from a trip to your friendly local tiki bar or artist in your area, but if that's not in the cards, there are lots of online options (see Resources, page 335).

Beware, however: Once you buy a handful of mugs, it can become kind of addicting. It is also often the gateway drug to a full home tiki bar. After all, you're going to need somewhere to display all those mugs. To quote mug collector and author Duke Carter, "A desire to create a Tiki room of one's own to house these Tikis in a manner befitting a god becomes an overriding concern. One quickly moves from a collector to a curator, a designer, a bartender, a host, and historian sharing tales of Tiki palaces young and old and stories of the most recent acquisitions."

DRINKS IN PINEAPPLES

Talk about a crowd pleaser. Get ready to do a lot more of them once guests see the first one go out. Cut the top off your pineapple about one inch from the base of the fronds, and set aside. You will need to use a pineapple corer to core your pineapple rather than doing it manually, as you need to have an intact pineapple shell. As you're coring, have a few fingers wrapped around the pineapple approximately one inch from the base, and feel for the moment when the corer blade is inside the pineapple parallel to your fingers and stop—you want to make sure not to go too far down lest your pineapple cease to be water tight. It's also a good idea to test the pineapple by filling it with water before serving, just to make sure you didn't cut through the bottom, or there will be drink sadness.

Cut the remaining core at the base (again, not too far down) and discard. A curved grapefruit knife works well for this. Take the top of the pineapple and cut a small triangle out of the edge (or two triangles, one out of each edge, if serving a drink for two). Fill the pineapple with your delicious concoction of choice, and place the pineapple top back on as a lid. You can remove the fronds if you don't like them tickling your nose, or use a longer straw. A cocktail umbrella inserted through the lid into the side of the pineapple is a decorative way to help keep the lid in place. Insert straw in the triangle hole, and serve to smiling guests.

THE COCONUT

While it isn't difficult to get into a mature (brown) coconut to drink out of it (using an ice pick or drill to pierce two out of the three holes on the top will do the trick), it is much harder to get a drink *into* it. We've found that the best mature coconuts to serve out of are the ceramic kind. However, what is very doable is to open a young Thai coconut (the kind sold in grocery stores or Asian markets that has a white husk, and often a conical top). The easiest and safest way is with a Coco Jack tool (see Resources, page 335).

The Garnish

The garnish. The finishing touch. Window dressing, flavor accent, conversation starter—all of the above.

Opening a Thai cocunut

Donn Beach, tiki godfather, was not a fan of over-the-top tropical garnishes. In the early years of tiki, tropical garnishes were still fairly traditional—pineapple, cherries, mint, twists—albeit with a bit more flair. A great example is the horse's neck: typically a spiral-cut length of wide orange or lemon peel that runs up the inside of the glass, it got its name from having the top of the orange peek out over the rim of the glass, like a horse's head outside the door of a stable. But in the world of tiki, the innocent horse's neck suddenly became a deadly viper—ready to strike the drinker. And so was born the sidewinder's fang, "the Scorpion of the Islands—for the brave and bold . . . a banisher of trouble," the house specialty at the long-gone Lanai in San Mateo, California.

Eventually, tiki garnishes started to get bigger and more elaborate, in large part through the efforts of one man. Harry Yee was the head bartender for over thirty years at the Hawaiian Village Hotel, and was responsible for dozens of famous exotic cocktails, including the Blue Hawaii in 1957.

Harry's real genius, however, was the garnish. How's this for a hat trick:

In 1955, Harry was the first person to put an orchid in a drink. Yee said in a 1998 interview: "I was the first to use orchids. You know why? We used to use a sugarcane stick and people would chew on the stick, and then put it in the ashtray. When the ashes and cane stuck together it made a real mess, so I put the orchids in the drink to make the ashtrays easier to clean. I wasn't thinking about romance; I was being practical."

He created the Tropical Itch cocktail in 1957, and garnished it with a Chinese back scratcher, creating an instant icon, and no doubt providing a much needed boost to the struggling back scratcher industry.

Finally, in 1959, while serving a drink called the Tapa Punch, he decided to stick an umbrella into it. **And the world changed forever.**

Well, no not really, but it certainly cemented in the mind of the public the association of the cocktail umbrella and the exotic cocktail. I love the cocktail umbrella personally, but it's certainly for me a double-edged sword—as I'm trying to promote vintage recipes made with fresh ingredients and good spirits, the umbrella is closely associated with the kind of syrupy artificial drinks that the exotic cocktail devolved into in the '70s and '80s. So using them can have a kind of negative connotation and, in fact, Trader Vic couldn't stand umbrellas and never used them. But I like to think that I'm reclaiming the umbrella. And at the end of the day—guess what? People love 'em. They may not protect you from the elements, but they don't change the taste of your drink, either.

Below are some other fun and festive garnish ideas for your repertoire. The house style at Smuggler's Cove is largely to layer simple garnishes for a fuller look, such as combining mint sprigs, flowers, pineapple fronds, swizzle sticks, etc., rather than creating more elaborate carved pieces. This is for speed of service, and we like the effect.

EDIBLE FLOWERS

Yee used Hawaiian Vanda orchids, which are available online (see Resources, page 335). Or look for a produce supplier that carries Dendrobium or Karma orchids, which we use at Smuggler's Cove. If there was ever a simple, dramatic garnish, it's these little guys. They're sturdy, and if designated as food-safe, completely edible. They store well, typically lasting a week in the fridge. Other edible flowers are possibilities, but tropical flowers best complement exotic cocktails. Before Yee used an orchid, Vic had used edible gardenias to great effect. Another fun option that we use in our Hibiscus Rum Punch (page 176) is wild hibiscus flowers in syrup—an all-natural product that gives you a tasty and beautiful addition to your drink (see Resources, page 335).

ICE GARNISH

Donn was a master when it came to using ice as a garnish, creating simple but visually striking molds that not only looked great, but had the added bonus of helping keep the drink chilled. As early as the 1930s, he was creating ice shells for drinks like the Beachcomber's Gold. The ice cone came later as the signature garnish for the famous cocktail he invented during World War II: the Navy Grog (page 271).

Both of these garnishes require a bit of advanced planning and some freezer space, but are sure to wow your guests. You will also need to have very fine "snow" ice on hand (see page 228).

The magic of the ice shell has been kept alive at the Mai Kai in Fort Lauderdale, which passed down the trick to Jeff "Beachbum" Berry and to Tim "Swanky" Glazner, who have shared it with us. To make an ice shell, place a pile of "snow" ice that has sat out a minute or two first to get slightly "wet" and more pliable, in the center of a chilled coupe with a rounded bottom. Using the back of a barspoon, coat the entire inside of the glass by pressing the ice against the bottom and sides until you have an even coating that is ¼ to ½ inch thick. Freeze the glass for several hours. Let the coupe rest at room temperature about five minutes so that the ice is easily loosened from the glass. Once it's loose, use the barspoon to gently shift the shell to one side, such that one end extends about two inches above the lip of the glass, creating a "hood" that covers about half of the drink. Press more crushed ice into the now-exposed part of the coupe and over the already frozen shell to hold the hood in place. Refreeze the glass overnight. Pour the drink carefully into the ice-lined coupe, being careful not to disturb the hood. Serve, and admire the impressed expression on your guest's face.

The easiest way to form an ice cone is with the official Navy Grog Ice Cone kit, designed by Jeff "Beachbum" Berry (see Resources, page 335). If you're waiting for your kit to arrive in the mail and are craving a Navy Grog (page 271), here is how they used to make ice cones at Don the Beachcomber, as relayed to Jeff by tiki bartender Tony Ramos. Take your "snow" ice and pack it tightly into a pilsner glass about three-quarters of the way full. Push a chopstick or sturdy straw through the middle of the ice pack to make your straw hole, then gently remove the ice from the glass and freeze the ice cone overnight in a pan or baking sheet lined with waxed paper. Make your cocktail (a Navy Grog or other tropical drink served in a double old-fashioned glass would be appropriate here), and when you're ready to serve, remove your frozen ice cone from the freezer (if necessary, you can douse it with a little water to thaw the base, then remove it from the waxed paper), insert the cone into cocktail, insert straw into cone, and insert Navy Grog into mouth.

PINEAPPLE WEDGES, SLICES, AND FRONDS

To create pineapple wedges, you can use a corer or peel and cut a pineapple manually (see page 234). Once you have large spirals or whole pineapple quarters, cut down into wedges or cubes, cut a notch in the wedge, and hang on the side of the glass, or spear with a cocktail pick and rest across the top of the drink. A lot of places leave the peel on the wedge—easier to make, and the peel offers a pretty yellow-green contrast. But remember the words of Harry Yee—you will be cleaning up sticky partially chewed wedges.

An attractive, more delicate garnish is the thin pineapple slice. Lay a pineapple on its side and slice very, very thin, round slices. Line the inside of a Collins or highball glass by curving the pineapple slice against the inside wall of the glass.

Pineapple fronds make great quick and easy (but not edible) garnishes: insert one or fan several attractive, long leaves across the back of a drink.

CITRUS TWISTS, PEELS, WEDGES, AND WHEELS

A basic rule of thumb: use wedges and wide peels for additional flavor, and wheels and twists for the look.

In all four types of citrus garnish, choose fruit that is fresh, healthy, and firm—the better the fruit, the more peel oil it has. This fruit isn't for juicing, so pay close attention to the condition of the peel; select fruit with no blemishes, spots, or damage, which spread, especially once they are cut. And wash the fruit. It's going in a drink. It's easy to forget to do it. Finally, also from the obvious department: remove the little stickers.

SIDEWINDER'S FANG PEEL

As described earlier in the chapter, the garnish for the Sidewinder's Fang (page 62) is a great example of how a simple garnish takes on a more elaborate role when put in exotic cocktail context. To make the garnish for this dangerous concoction, grab an orange and, using a wide peeler, start at the top of the fruit and pull an approximately 1-inch-wide, shallow (no pith) continuous strip of peel, rotating the orange while gradually moving down and around the fruit, so as to remove the entire peel. As you work your way around the peel, you'll be able to use the already cut section as a guide, such that you are peeling below what has already been cut.

Our bartender Marcovaldo Dionysos upped the ante by creating a snake-like peel: After the peel is about ¾ inch long, alter the direction of the peeler slightly and finish peeling. The result is a rounded chunk of peel (the head) and a continuous length (the snake body). Use a straw to poke holes for eyes in the head. Then arrange the spiral along the inside of the snifter, with the head hanging over the edge of the glass. Fill the glass with crushed ice to hold the sidewinder peel against the side of the glass. Add Sidewinder's Fang cocktail. Drink up!

Saturn (see page 67)

FRESH MINT

Mint can be notoriously fussy to keep crisp and fresh, but it is essential to do so, as it is one of the most frequently called for and effective garnishes in exotic cocktails. Buy mint as close as possible to when you will use it, preferably the day of. Keep it in the refrigerator in a tightly sealed bag or herb storage container, as oxygen will affect its quality.

To prep mint, pick off any low-hanging leaves from the stem, leaving a full head of leaves at the top—I like clusters of about ten leaves. Or use a few clusters: make it lush!

Just before service, here are a few great tips I learned from bartender and consultant Peter Vestinos about how to keep your mint fresh on the bar while you're making drinks:

- Cut the stem of the mint at an angle, much the same way you would cut flower stems before placing in a vase, 4 to 5 inches from the top cluster of leaves. This step is essential because the base of the stalk was cauterized after being cut at the farm.

- Place the mint sprig, leaves-down, in ice cold water for 10 to 15 minutes in order to firm up the leaves and preserve the oils.

- Then place the mint stem down in very warm to hot water in a vessel (I like to use our barrel mug) on the bar top. The mint will remain bright, firm, and fresh for up to 5 hours.

One more vital step to take before putting mint in the cocktail: Slap it! Put the mint in the palm of one hand and give it a gentle slap with the other. This will bring the mint oils closer to the surface and release more of the aroma. Or slap the mint against the side of the serving glass—this not only releases aromatics but also brushes some of the oil onto the glass itself, leaving even more lingering aroma. After all, the mint is for your guests, not your hands.

MARASCHINO CHERRIES

In the nineteenth century, a maraschino cherry was a sour cherry that was packed in maraschino liqueur, but in the go-go twentieth century it became a mass-produced, chemical-laden little piece of neon-red plastic. However, you can and should find good quality cherries with no sulfites and no preservatives. Brands such as Luxardo, Fabbri, and Amifruit produce excellent real cherries. Note that some are preserved in spirits, so take care when adding them to nonalcoholic drinks.

ROCK CANDY STICKS

Used in Trader Vic's for a handful of grapefruit juice drinks (the Navy Grog [page 271], the Pogo Stick, and the Tutu Rum Punch), these can be fun to use in drier, tarter grogs or punches. They allow your guest to control additional sweetness that will be added to the drink as the sugar slowly dissolves (unless, of course, your guests eat them first. Sorry, Dr. Vicino, DDS).

SWIZZLE STICKS

Not to be confused with the swizzle stick tool (see page 234), the plastic, souvenir swizzle was invented in the 1930s. Lots of tiki bars had fantastic, ornate versions, and are much sought-after by collectors today. It can be a fun conversation starter for your guests or at a party to give everyone a different one.

PICKS AND FLAGS

A great way to include cherries, pineapple, or other garnishes is to use a small cocktail pick. There are lots of plastic versions available online, but if you want to be a bit greener, then the bamboo knot picks are also great. (Plus, bamboo is thematically appropriate!) See Resources, page 335. Or, use flag picks—a Trader Vic tradition that we've continued at the Cove. For example, we use a Norwegian flag for the Norwegian Paralysis (page 119), or a Jamaican flag in the Jamaican Planter's Punch.

SWIZZLE NAPKIN WRAP

This was the traditional way I learned to serve the Queen's Park Swizzle at Trader Vic's. It is basically giving the drinker something to hold on to so they don't have to hold a very cold frosted glass. I suggest using this for all swizzle cocktails. It's quick and easy and looks great! (See photo on page 117). To make one, you are essentially making the drink a little bandana: Take a cocktail napkin and unfold it into a square. Fold the opened square diagonally, creating a right triangle. Fold or roll the wide edge over a few times, and tie the two ends of the edge around your glass. For more fun, use colorful tropical-themed cocktail napkins when you wrap your swizzles.

Fire

What kind of tiki bar owner would I be if I didn't talk about fire for a minute? The beauty of fire is that it can be both a decorative garnish and a tool for adding aromatics to a drink. And, most of all, it's a crowd pleaser. Any time one of our flaming bowls is served to a small group, others in the bar point, wide-eyed, and ask, "What are THEY having?"

Our secret? We use a technique I learned from the mighty Bahooka, and have done my best to spread far and wide: Soak a plain bread crouton in pure lemon extract. Rest the crouton on a lime wheel floating on the surface of the drink, or put it in the center of your volcano bowl, and ignite.

For setting a drink on fire, we find 151 rum in a spent lime shell or the center of your volcano bowl yields a sad little blue flame. It can also be a little dangerous in bright conditions because you may not be able to tell that it's still lit.

Lemon extract, by comparison, is 164 proof, and fueled by the bread, it produces a quality and dramatic flame. We also shake a little cinnamon-nutmeg blend above the flame; the cinnamon creates dramatic sparks before the toasted spices fall on the surface of the drink.

A few very important notes about flame:

- Just as your mom told you—playing with fire is dangerous. Do not serve fire if you or your friends have already had a few—it should be done when you are sober and able to deal with fire carefully.

- When you serve a flaming drink, be sure and give an ample verbal heads-up to the guest, so they don't whip around and knock into it, etc. Also, it is a good idea to tell people to pull their hair, scarves, and body parts out of the way.

- Guests should blow out the burning crouton before they take their first sip. They or you can remove the burned crouton with metal tongs and extinguish it by dropping it into a glass of water.

THE FORMULA: CREATING YOUR OWN MODERN EXOTIC COCKTAIL

So what constitutes a modern exotic cocktail? For me, it's following the Donn template (see box opposite) of construction, adding some contemporary twists, but still incorporating a few recognizable flavors from the palettes discussed earlier. For example, you might play with the base spirit or use some unusual bitters or amaros in the drink, but by keeping the sour component and including some iconic ingredients like falernum or orgeat in the mix, you're paying homage to the structure and tradition while adding your own twist. Here are a few other suggestions to spur on your own creativity:

- **SOUR:** Use lemon, lime, and grapefruit rather than just lime. Make sure to pair orange with another, more sour citrus component.

- **SWEET:** Try a blend of maple syrup and honey, for example, or other sweeteners rather than sugar. Also, note that syrups and liqueurs each have differing degrees of perceived sweetness, so the same amount of one may not directly substitute for that same amount of another in a recipe (i.e. ¼ ounce of falernum, with its lime component, may be perceived as less sweet than, say, ¼ ounce of Benedictine, so, if substituting falernum for Benedictine in a recipe, you might need to add slightly more).

- **STRONG:** Blend your rums, or blend in other base spirits, or don't use rum at all. (Heathens!)

- **WEAK:** Add multiple fruit juices, seltzer, or even premium sodas. There's a lot of room in the "weak" category for experimentation. Why not beer?

- **SPICE:** Use single or blended spice syrups, hot spices, bitters, amaros, or roasted spices.

It's worth mentioning here that the temptation to elaborate the cocktail to sixteen, eighteen, or even twenty ingredients is great, but is also a waste. At some point, the ingredients will either start to clash, become muddied, or simply be unnoticeable. Some restraint, however silly that may sound within the context of exotic cocktails, is called for.

In the interest of service at the Cove, we batch a handful of the nonfresh, nonrum ingredients to make "mixes" like our Captain's Mix for the Captain's Grog (see page 65). But sometimes these mixes become inspiration for other drinks. It can be as simple as a daiquiri sweetened with the mix, or they can become the heart of a whole new exotic cocktail. Whenever possible, it's always better to find multiple uses for a versatile ingredient so that your bar is not filled with bottles that have only one application.

Additional Guidance

- **COCONUT CREAM:** Using seltzer with coconut cream is a great way to brighten what can be a heavy ingredient and it makes an attractive froth.

- **MOUTHFEEL:** A cocktail with a thin mouthfeel may have been flash blended or shaken too long. You can improve the texture with a small amount of demerara syrup (page 324)—even a dash improves viscosity while only adding minimal sweetness. If the mouthfeel is too syrupy, try serving an up drink long over ice or adding a splash of seltzer.

- **BALANCE:** Cocktail too sweet? Of course you can cut back on the sweetener or add more sour. But increasing the sour isn't always the best answer as too much acid can overwhelm other flavors. Note also that increasing the spirit can have a pleasant drying effect. A great exotic cocktail (or really any drink with a sour component) can be seen as an equilateral triangle, a perfect balance of sweet, tart, and spirit. No one side should be allowed to dominate to the detriment of the others. Of course, there's certainly room for flexibility here—one might make a superb isosceles or scalene cocktail. Just remember that trigonometry rarely makes for scintillating cocktail party banter.

- **UP DRINKS:** Don't be afraid to work with exotic cocktail flavors in up drinks. Enjoying fine rums, exotic flavors, and fresh ingredients on the stem is an elegant touch, and by now you've probably figured out that I think tiki is pretty fancy schmancy.

- **BASE SPIRIT:** It can be just as simple as changing one ingredient in an existing cocktail to create something dramatically different. Trader Vic found great success in simply playing with the base spirit in his greatest drinks: a Mai Tai with bourbon (Honi Honi) or tequila (Pinky Gonzalez) are excellent alternatives. At Smuggler's Cove, the switch from rum in a classic exotic cocktail (Polynesian Paralysis) to the somewhat improbable aquavit (Norwegian Paralysis, page 119) made something special and revealed that aquavit and orgeat make good drinkin' buddies in a cocktail.

- **COST CONSIDERATIONS:** Start your experiments with the less expensive ingredients. Build your sour, sweet, and spice in your mixing tin and straw test for sweet/tart balance before adding spendy spirits.

THE DONN TEMPLATE

An elaboration of the traditional planter's punch formula balancing the sour, sweet, spirit (rum), weak, and spice components and often including more than one of each component with the goal of producing a more complex and layered cocktail.

BOO LOO

ORIGIN *Circa 1965*

SOURCE Beachbum Berry Remixed, *adapted by Smuggler's Cove*

GLASSWARE *Hollowed-out pineapple with the core removed (see page 238)*

SERVES 2

6 (1-inch-square) chunks fresh pineapple

2½ ounces pineapple juice

1½ ounces fresh lime juice

1¼ ounces SC Honey Syrup (page 325)

1½ ounces blended aged rum ❸

1½ ounces column still aged rum ❹

¾ ounce black blended rum ❺

¾ ounce black blended overproof rum ❻

1½ ounces seltzer

GARNISH *Pineapple lid with two straw holes (see page 238)*

Add the pineapple chunks, pineapple juice, and lime juice to a drink mixer tin and muddle. Add the syrup, the four rums, and the seltzer with 12 ounces of crushed ice and 4 to 6 small "agitator" cubes. Flash blend and open pour with gated finish into a hollowed-out pineapple that has the core removed. Replace the lid and add two straws.

CARIBEÑO

Long, tall, and refreshing, with coconut water, lime, and your choice of rum or gin (both are traditional choices in the Caribbean).

ORIGIN: *Traditional Caribbean recipe*

GLASSWARE *Drained young coconut shell (see page 238)*

4 ounces coconut water

¼ ounce SC Demerara Syrup (page 324)

2 ounces column still lightly aged rum (see page 198) or London dry gin

GARNISH *None*

Add all the ingredients to a drink mixer tin. Fill with 12 ounces of crushed ice and 4 to 6 small "agitator cubes." Flash blend and strain into a coconut shell filled with cracked or cubed ice.

Monk's Respite

MONK'S RESPITE

ORIGIN *Created by Steven Liles*
GLASSWARE *Drained young coconut shell (see page 238)*

3 ounces fresh coconut water

½ ounce fresh lemon juice

¼ ounce SC Honey Syrup (page 325)

¼ ounce Yellow Chartreuse

1½ ounces Broker's gin

1 ounce seltzer

1 dash orange bitters

GARNISH *None*

Add all the ingredients to a drink mixer tin. Fill with 12 ounces of crushed ice and 4 to 6 small "agitator" cubes. Flash blend and open pour with gated finish into the empty coconut shell.

THE MASTADON

ORIGIN *Created by Alex Smith*
GLASSWARE *Hollowed-out pineapple (see page 238)*

3 ounces pineapple juice

½ ounce fresh lime juice

1 ounce passion fruit puree

½ ounce Licor 43

½ ounce Maraschino liqueur

1½ ounces blended aged rum ❸

1½ ounces bourbon

2 dashes Peychaud's bitters

GARNISH *Pineapple lid with a straw hole cut out (see page 238) or Mermaid Island (see page 252)*

Add all the ingredients to a drink mixer tin. Fill with 12 ounces of crushed ice and 4 to 6 small "agitator" cubes. Flash blend and open pour into a hollowed-out pineapple and add garnish.

PIÑATA

ORIGIN *Created by Marcovaldo Dionysos*
GLASSWARE *Hollowed-out pineapple (see page 238)*

- 3 ounces pineapple juice
- 1 ounce fresh lemon juice
- ¼ to ½ ounce SC Demerara Syrup (page 324)
- 1 ounce ginger liqueur
- ½ ounce St. Elizabeth Allspice Dram
- 1 ounce black blended rum ⑤
- 1 ounce blended lightly aged rum ②

GARNISH *Freshly grated nutmeg*

Add all the ingredients to a drink mixer tin. Fill with 12 ounces of crushed ice and 4 to 6 small "agitator" cubes. Flash blend and open pour into a hollowed-out pineapple. Garnish with freshly grated nutmeg.

NOTE The amount of SC Demerara Syrup varies depending on the sweetness of the ginger liqueur used. Adjust to taste.

BUMBOAT

ORIGIN *Created by Justin Oliver*
GLASSWARE *Hollowed-out pineapple (see page 238)*

- 2 ounces pineapple juice
- 1½ ounces fresh lemon juice
- ¾ ounce SC Cinnamon Syrup (page 327)
- 1 ounce rye
- 1 ounce blended lightly aged rum ②
- 3 drops almond extract
- 6 drops Bittermens 'Elemakule Tiki bitters
- ¾ ounce black blended overproof rum ⑥

GARNISH *A pineapple lid with a straw hole cut out (see page 238) or Mermaid Island (see below)*

Combine all the ingredients except the overproof rum in a drink mixer tin. Fill with 12 ounces of crushed ice and 4 to 6 small "agitator cubes." Flash blend and then open pour with gated finish into the hollowed-out pineapple. Float the overproof rum by gently pouring on top of the drink. Add garnish.

MERMAID ISLAND When coring your pineapple to use as a drink vessel (see page 238), rather than cutting out the core, an alternative is to leave the core in place to create a small "island" on which to place a mermaid and umbrella (see photo, opposite).

Bumboat

MAUNA KAI

KE LAU
Restaurant
Cocktail Lounge

KONA KAI

Navy Grog
A truly great blending of exotic rums and tropical fruit juices with an accent of Pimiento Dram.

Islander's Pearl
A delicate Ambrosia of West Indies Rum and the fragrant nectar of the Gods blended with the smoothness of the virgin pearl.

Cobras Fang
Demerara Rum, Limes, and Currast Syrup coiled with aromatic bitters.

Mount Kil
Specialty of the eruption of the rums fired u of the Tik

Coffee Grog
Fine rums and Kona Coffee blended with wild honey and delicate spices of the Far East.

"We take the pleasure of presenting the best group of rum concoctions prepared with the finest and oldest rum, together with all fresh fruit juices and exotic spices. Our master mixologist hopes to please your palate, quench your thirst, and win your deepest satisfaction. We believe all the emotions of man are contained in these tempting drinks and that by your participation they will add zest to your conversation, will stimulate your appetite, and give you the power to change the world."

—MENU AT THE LANAI

Eight Essential Exotic Elixirs

EXOTIC ISLAND DRINKS

ZOMBIE
The world famous
favorite . . . only
two to a customer
2.35

FOG CUTTER
A delectable drink
made with rum,
brandy and fresh
fruit juices.
A combination you
will long remember.
2.45

HEADHUNTER
A blend of juices
with fine white rum
and coconut milk
2.95

PLANTER'S PUNCH
A tropical tradition —
Jamaica formula
from Montego Bay
1.95

MAI TAI
Most exquisite!
Honolulu's favorite
with aged
Jamaican Rums
2.75

SCORPION BOWL
(For Two)
The Island's
favorite thirst
quencher
4.25

TIKI MUG
A dark, rich rare
rum makes this
a thirst quencher
2.45

PINEAPPLE PASSION
A blend of rare
aged Rums and
exotic nectars in
a fresh Hawaiian
Pineapple
3.00

**DOCTOR FUNK
OF TAHITI**
A truly tropical
drink originating
in Papeete and
redolent of French
rums and absinthe
2.45

NAVY GROG
A "twenty-one gun"
concoction of eight
ingredients.
2.75

From the menu of the Hu Ke Lau restaurant in Bloomfield, Connecticut

AS TIKI CONTINUED HIS GREAT MARCH ACROSS
AMERICA DURING THE GOLDEN ERA, THE BATTLEFRONT
WAS OFTEN FORMED BY THE MOST POPULAR DRINKS
OF THE DAY.

It's no accident that the cocktails making the most appearances under thatched roofs far and wide came from the minds of Donn and Vic. We celebrate these cocktails as the proud progenitors of many a menu. With the level of secrecy that many of these recipes were accorded, of course, many of these reinterpretations would be just that, like a giant rummy game of telephone, and the spread of altered recipes would ultimately hasten their demise. I am by no means suggesting that these are the only exotic cocktails you need to know, but I include these original recipes here with a place of honor because they are iconic drinks, and all have interesting histories. With these recipes in your repertoire, you can jump behind your (well-stocked) bar (or anyone else's) and have eight great drinks on hand—and some great stories to share while you mix them.

PLANTER'S PUNCH

This follows the classic rhyming formula, one of sour, two of sweet, three of strong, four of weak (weak being juices, or in our case, ice). We add two of the most popular ingredients in Jamaica (allspice, Angostura bitters) to round it out and give it depth.

ORIGIN *Traditional, adapted by Smuggler's Cove, 2009*
GLASSWARE *Collins or highball*

- 1 ounce fresh lime juice
- ¾ ounce SC Demerara syrup (page 324)
- ¼ ounce St. Elizabeth Allspice Dram
- 3 ounces blended aged rum (Jamaica) ❸
- 2 dashes Angostura bitters

GARNISH *Mint Sprig*

Combine all ingredients in a drink mixer tin with 12 ounces of crushed ice and 4 to 6 "agitator" cubes. Flash blend and then open pour with gated finish into a Collins or highball glass. Garnish with Jamaican sunshine (oh—and a mint sprig).

As punch made its journey across the world with the spice trade, it naturally wound up in the Caribbean. There was a reference to punch in Barbados as early as 1694, giving a recipe of two parts rum, one part water, sugar, lemon (or lime), cinnamon, clove, and nutmeg. Punch in the Caribbean began as something enjoyed by the plantation owners, or "planters" (hence the name). Over time, there were nearly as many recipes as there were planters to enjoy them, but they all followed the classic formula, complete with a catchy rhyme that can be remembered even after you've had a few. Many people tack on "And a touch of spice to make it nice" at the end, which can be bitters, nutmeg, or other Caribbean-grown spices. Travel anywhere in the Caribbean, and you will find a planter's punch on the menu, often reflective of the juices, spices, and rums of the island. In the 1920s, the planter's punch became linked strongly to Jamaica, and to Jamaican black rum, through much assistance by Myers's rum, which formulated and bottled a dark planter's punch Rum for use in the drink, and the fact that a planter's punch was served at the upscale Myrtle Bank and Tichfield Hotels in Kingston, Jamaica. It was likely here that Donn Beach sampled a planter's punch and would use it as the basis for many of his cocktails. To quote Jeff Berry, "To create his multi-ingredient, multi-layered Rhum Rhapsodies, he turned the simple planter's punch recipe lyric . . . into the libretto of a grand opera." There was no reason to limit the juice to just lime, the sweet to just sugar, or the strong to just one type of rum. And the exotic cocktail was born. What follows is the recipe you'll find at Smuggler's Cove, but we encourage you to play with the formula and come up with your own house planter's punch(es).

MAI TAI

Within the pantheon of exotic cocktails, one stands above the rest as the most iconic of the era. An elegant and simple concoction, really just a nutty rum margarita, it eschews the conventional structure established by Donn in favor of a more nuanced approach.

ORIGIN *Trader Vic, 1944, adapted by Smuggler's Cove*
GLASSWARE *Double old-fashioned glass*

- ¾ ounce fresh lime juice
- ¼ ounce SC Mai Tai Rich Simple Syrup (page 326)
- ¼ ounce SC orgeat syrup (page 330)
- ½ ounce Pierre Ferrand dry curaçao
- 2 ounces blended aged rum ❸ (see pages 262–64 for details)

GARNISH *Spent lime shell and mint sprig*

Combine all ingredients with 12 ounces of crushed ice and a few cubes in a cocktail shaker. Shake until a frost forms on the shaker and pour the entire contents into a double old-fashioned glass. Garnish with a spent lime shell and mint sprig.

A FEW NOTES ABOUT THE PREPARATION As I was taught as a bartender at Trader Vic's, the traditional lime juicer used for the Mai Tai was a Sunkist hand squeezer. You can still find vintage ones on eBay. The lime half is pinched (not turned inside out as with a modern hand juicer) to juice and you then rest the spent half on the bar while you finish the drink. The lime half should not be shaken with the drink as it makes the drink too bitter and doesn't leave you able to rest the shell on top to serve it. The spent shell should rest like a dome on top of the drink, with a mint garnish by its side—two aromatic components that are key to the taste of the drink. As the Trader said, it should look like a little tropical island with a palm tree on it. It's also interesting to note that at no point did the Trader ever add a float of rum to the Mai Tai. The float caught on as the Mai Tai traveled and (d)evolved. What I did learn while tending bar at Vic's was that years later, an old Trader Vic's regular in the Bay Area enjoyed his Mai Tai with a float of overproof Demerara rum. Preparing the Mai Tai this way became known as "Old Way." Not because it was the original recipe, but because the patron was old!

Just a handful of ingredients in small amounts act as the perfect foil to the full-bodied and complex Jamaican rum they were chosen to support. It became wildly popular, found its way to menus across the world, and ultimately became a kind of shorthand for exotic cocktails themselves.

If the Mai Tai had simply entered into the toolkit of classics that all bartenders know, and cemented its rightful place as one of America's greatest liquid achievements, the story would have a happy ending. But that's not what happened. What did happen is that the Mai Tai fell further and farther than any drink in cocktail history, becoming the most bastardized drink of all time. What most people think of as a Mai Tai today has in fact nothing to do with the original cocktail. While Mai Tai may translate to "the best" in Tahitian, in most bars around the world, it translates to "a bunch of rum, whatever juices are in the rail in front of you, more rum on top, and an umbrella." In a standard bar today, when you order a Manhattan, you will likely get some bourbon instead of rye, some old spoiled vermouth, and they will forget the bitters and shake the drink. But you will still be served something at least resembling a Manhattan. When you order a Mai Tai, you are likely to be served a drink with exactly zero of its original ingredients. In fact, the Alcohol and Tobacco Tax and Trade Bureau (TTB) has a class of "Recognized Cocktails," which they define as "Mixed drink that has gained trade and consumer recognition, containing one or more class(es) and/or type(s) of distilled spirits with flavoring and/or coloring materials." Within that class they have several types, including Manhattans, martinis, daiquiris, Tom Collinses, etc. The general definition of most of these is fairly accurate. For example, the margarita is defined as "Tequila, triple sec, and lime or lemon juice or oil or natural lime or lemon flavor." However, the Mai Tai is defined as "Rum and citrus juices, oils or natural citrus flavors." Vague enough to be meaningless.

Even within the craft cocktail community, where the original Mai Tai recipe is understood and respected, there is disagreement about the rums that should be used in place of the original J. Wray & Nephew 17-year (or, later, the 15-year—both are no longer made) that appeared in the original recipe. But to see how this cocktail has been so derailed by history, it's helpful to learn its full story.

The year was 1944. According to Trader Vic, he was at the service bar making drinks for two friends from Tahiti, Ham and Carrie Guild. According to Vic, "I took down a bottle of 17-year-old rum. It was J. Wray & Nephew from Jamaica; surprisingly golden in color, medium-bodied, but with the rich pungent flavor particular to the Jamaican blends." He combined this magical rum with orange curaçao, rock candy (sugar) syrup, orgeat (almond syrup), and the juice from one lime. When Carrie took a sip of Vic's concoction, she exclaimed "Maita'i Roe A'e" which translates from Tahitian as "Out of This World—The Best." The name stuck, and a legendary cocktail was born.

But the story doesn't quite end there. In the late 1940s, as Trader Vic's empire begins to expand, according to Vic, "The success of the Mai Tai and its acceptance soon caused the 17-year-old rum to become unavailable, so it was substituted with the same fine rum with 15 years aging which maintained the outstanding quality."

By the early 1950s, however, supplies of the 15-year also began to dwindle, and Vic did not want to be left unable to make his most popular and famous drink. "The supply of 15-year-old rum was becoming less than dependable so several other Caribbean products were tested for the same high qualities of flavor. Red Heart and Coruba were selected to be used in equal quantities along with the original 15-year-old to stretch the supply and maintain the character of the Mai Tai." The Mai Tai, in what Vic now referred to as the "First Adjusted

Formula" was then made with one ounce of 15-year and a one-ounce blend of Red Heart and Coruba rums, both black Jamaican rums—full-bodied, lightly aged if at all, and heavily colored.

Eventually even the 15-year-old J. Wray & Nephew supplies were no longer reliably available, so Vic decided to create his own rum to mimic the 17-year old J. Wray & Nephew. He began bottling a 15- and 8-year-old rum, both of consistent quality— and although they were excellent, they, in Vic's words, "didn't exactly match the end flavor of the original 17-year-old product. This desired nutty, and snappy flavor was added by the use of Martinique rum." In effect, he substituted Martinique rum for Red Heart or Coruba. This he called the "Second Adjusted Formula."

For those of you familiar with Martinique rum, this may seem like an unusual substitution. When we think of Martinique rum, we usually think of AOC rhum agricole—rum made from fresh pressed sugarcane juice and highly regulated in its production. As a result, most modern Mai Tais will call for a blend of Jamaican rum and AOC rhum agricole from Martinique. This makes a lovely Mai Tai, and experimenting with all kinds of rums in this drink can be rewarding. Vic built what is, perhaps, second only to the daiquiri, the perfect rum delivery system: a selection of ingredients that complement virtually all rums. But something about the grassy and herbaceous notes of rhum agricole did not make sense to me when being used as a black Jamaican substitute or being described as "nutty."

In order to understand why Vic would make such a substitution, you have to look at what Martinique rums were available in the United States in the 1950s. While a rhum agricole, Rhum St. James, was certainly available, it was too expensive to be a staple in the ever-popular Mai Tai. What was much more common, as reflected in the rum lists of Vic's books and menus,

was rhum traditionnel, rum made in the French islands from molasses, and not the fresh pressed cane juice of rhum agricole. Furthermore, these rums were in the style of black rum, blending the molasses distillate often with Jamaican rum, then heavily coloring it. There are, in fact, several recipes in Trader Vic's *Book of Food and Drink* where Vic calls for a "Dark Jamaica OR Martinique" rum. At other points in the book, he specifically calls out Rhum St. James, and does not refer to it as a Martinique rum—suggesting that when he wanted the grassy notes of an agricole, he would specify so.

If you look at the description of Martinique rum from Don the Beachcomber's 1934 rum list, Martinique rum was described as "heavy-bodied, medium pungency," and to taste "not as dry as the Cuban nor as rummy as the Jamaican." Again, not how one would typically describe rhum agricole. Vic's *Book of Food and Drink* (1946 and in the 1981 revision), his *Bartender's Guide* (1947 and in the revised 1972 version), and his 1940s-era menu include the following description of Martinique rum and available brands: "Martinique Rums: Commonly known as French rums, they are usually heavy in body, coffee-colored, very similar to Jamaica rums, but in many cases have the dry burned flavor of the Demeraras."

The sound you are hearing right now is the needle scraping across the record. THE COLOR OF COFFEE?! There is no Martinique rhum agricole that is the color of coffee. He is quite clearly referring to a black rhum traditionnel.

Vic's menu description goes on to list ten brands of Martinique rums, only one of which (Rhum St. James) I can confirm was a rhum agricole. So, even though, for posterity, Vic would ultimately brag that he used expensive Martinique rhum in his Mai Tai, such as the agricole-style St. James, this was unlikely. What he was probably using was Rhum Negrita, an affordable and available rhum traditionnel.

And what of the magical 17-year-old J. Wray & Nephew rum? Is it really gone, or were supplies just too difficult to serve the needs of the large Trader Vic's chain? It is among the rarest and most sought after rums in the world. The only known bottle in the world is currently owned by me, and I have not even tried it—it remains sealed in a climate controlled storage facility, but is photographed on page 260 for posterity.

In 2007, six bottles of barrel samples of the 17-year that had been in Wray & Nephew's lab were given to bartenders in the UK. Sadly, much of it went into rum and cokes, some into Mai Tais, as people didn't know what they had. Showing a hint at the value of this rum, however, one went to auction and fetched more than forty thousand dollars. Another ended up at the Merchant Hotel in Dublin in 2008 and gained huge notoriety as they made it available in the world's most expensive Mai Tai—costing thirteen hundred dollars. But even these lab samples are not an exact copy of the rum that would have been used by Trader Vic, however, as they are at a barrel strength of 75.2 percent ABV, and not the retail strength of 43 percent ABV.

And, nevertheless, all but one of these lab sample bottles are gone.

So, what's a poor bartender to do? Certainly, as mentioned above, I encourage you to experiment with rums in your Mai Tai. The margarita is the perfect vehicle for tequila, as it has two of its best friends in there—lime and orange. No one would ever tell you that there is only one tequila that can go in a margarita. In the same way, the Mai Tai is the perfect foil for a huge variety of rums. But the rum it was born with was 100 percent pot still rum with a tremendous amount of age on it. So ideally you're looking for a balance of full-bodied pot-still flavor tempered by quite a bit of oak, and given the products on the market today, you may find that your own blend will produce the most satisfying result. You might, for example, take a blended long aged rum and add just a half an ounce of a pot still unaged or pot still lightly aged rum to give it that pot-still boost. While, despite the occasional rumor, there may be no hope of seeing something like the original 17 year produced again, a few years ago I consulted with the people at Denizen Rum to help them create a rum that was faithful to Vic's Second Adjusted Formula, called Denizen Merchant's Reserve. It's a blend of 8-year-old Jamaican pot-still rum and molasses-based rhum grand arôme from Martinique. In other words . . . my theories put into practice. It remains the house Mai Tai rum at Smuggler's Cove.

The Trader in his element

DOCTOR FUNK

Well-known German doctor Bernard Funk was not only Robert Louis Stevenson's physician and friend, but was also the alleged inventor of an early version of this drink during his many years serving as a doctor to the people of Apia, Samoa.

ORIGIN *Trader Vic, 1946, adapted by Smuggler's Cove*
GLASSWARE *Double old-fashioned*

- ½ ounce fresh lemon juice
- ¼ ounce SC Grenadine (page 328)
- ½ ounce fresh lime juice
- ½ ounce SC Demerara Simple Syrup (page 324)
- ¼ ounce Herbsaint
- 2¼ ounce black pot still rum (see page 198)
- 1 ounce seltzer

GARNISH *Ti leaf or pineapple fronds*

Add all ingredients to drink mixer tin with 12 ounces of crushed ice and 4 to 6 "agitator" cubes. Flash blend and open pour with gated finish into a double old-fashioned. Garnish with a ti leaf or pineapple fronds.

NOTE Using a full flavored funky rum (no pun intended) is key to this cocktail as it stands up to and complements the Herbsaint. If Herbsaint is not to your taste, the Trader also made an alternate version called the Dr. Funk's Son, in which the Herbsaint is dropped, and a ½ ounce of the black pot still rum is substituted with ½ ounce of black blended overproof rum.

According to several 1920s accounts, the "Doctor Funk" concoction became known throughout the South Pacific, including Tahiti, and was comprised of absinthe, lime, and seltzer, with some variations, including grenadine. Claims about the drink's effects included that it "would restore self-respect and interest in one's surroundings when even Tahiti rum failed," and "an imparting of courage to live to men worn out by doing nothing." Furthermore, according to one account, "The doctor part of the drink's name made it seem almost like a prescription, and often, when amateurs sought to evade a second or third, the old timers laughed at their fears of ill results, and said, 'That old Dr. Funk knew what he was on about. Why he kept people alive on that mixture. It's like Mother's Milk.'"

Both Donn and Vic had Doctor Funk cocktails on their menus, much improving it with the wise addition of rum, making it the only exotic cocktail to have its origins in the South Pacific. Vic described it as a drink "which can be served any time of the day or evening, when something refreshing is in order. This drink and the sunrise in the morning are the only sure things they count on in Tahiti. I think it was invented to cure the cafard (the loss of one's mind from the heat)."

As the original Doctor Funk concoction had spread through the South Pacific, so did the tiki version spread through the diaspora, often getting renamed and, due to the usual secrecy around recipes, altered along the way. The Doctor Funk became the Doctor Funk of Tahiti with Trader Vic, the Mr. Funk, The Dr. Fong, The Dr. Wong. Some menus even acknowledged the change adding "(aka the Doctor Funk)" after their own drink name. However, there was one defining characteristic that made it through the various iterations and always tied it back to the original good doctor's concoction. There was no doubt, when you ordered your Dr. or Mr. Funk variant, you would taste absinthe (or Herbsaint) loud and clear.

ZOMBIE

Notorious would be an understatement. Donn's most famous and lethal concoction, it too has been abused beyond recognition in the past. Urban legends about its madness-inducing properties and menu warnings about a two-per-person limit ("for your own safety") cemented this drink in history.

ORIGIN *Donn Beach, 1934, adapted by Smuggler's Cove*
GLASSWARE *Zombie glass*

- ¾ ounce fresh lime juice
- ¼ ounce fresh grapefruit juice
- ¼ ounce SC Cinnamon Syrup (page 327)
- 1 teaspoon SC Grenadine (page 328)
- ½ ounce John D. Taylor's Velvet Falernum
- 1½ ounces blended aged rum ❸
- 1½ ounces column still aged rum ❹
- 1 ounce black blended overproof rum ❻
- 2 dashes Herbstura

GARNISH *Mint sprig*

Combine all ingredients in a drink mixer tin with 12 ounces of crushed ice and 4 to 6 "agitator" cubes. Flash blend and open pour with gated finish into a Zombie glass. Garnish with a mint sprig and healthy dose of trepidation.

At first glance, the recipe appears to be an unwieldy ratio of ingredients that don't seem like they should work. It is a testament to Donn's deft skills as a mixologist and his understanding of the interplay of ingredients that seemingly impossible recipes form complex and engaging masterpieces.

Complete with its own namesake glass, the Zombie may be the only exotic cocktail to rival the Mai Tai in stardom. Invented by Donn in 1934, there are several origin stories. Was it in fact, as claimed on the 1941 menu, a carefully crafted concoction that took Donn months of research and dozens of bottles of rum to perfect—the drink he called his "mender of broken dreams?" The more fun but likely untrue story is that it was the result of throwing something together for a traveling businessman who asked for help with his hangover and to get him through a tough meeting. Allegedly, the customer later reported back to Donn that he "felt like the living dead—it made a zombie out of me!" Who knows? Whatever the truth, we do know that it became a drink whose reputation preceded it—have a Zombie, and you were going to end up on the floor. The drink became more and more famous, and soon knock-off Zombies appeared on menus across the country but, thanks to Donn's ingenious system of maintaining ingredient secrecy, there was only one place to get a real Zombie in the day. However, thanks to the tireless work of tiki revivalist Jeff "Beachbum" Berry, who ultimately unearthed the original 1934 recipe and the final mysterious ingredient in the puzzle, "Spices #4," (cinnamon syrup), you, too, can now mix up your own Zombie in the comfort (and safety) of your own home.

NAVY GROG

In the tiki heyday, there were a lot of drinks called grogs that departed considerably from a historic grog. They appropriated the name and imagery of something hearty and robust in order to appeal to the men at the bar, who would not be seen ordering something dainty like a Blushing Orchid.

ORIGIN *Trader Vic's version, 1940s, adapted by Smuggler's Cove*

GLASSWARE *Double old-fashioned*

¾ ounce fresh lime juice

¾ ounce fresh grapefruit juice

¼ ounce SC Demerara syrup (page 324)

¼ ounce St. Elizabeth Allspice Dram

1 ounce pot still lightly aged (overproof) rum ❶

1 ounce blended lightly aged rum ❷

1 ounce column still aged rum ❹

GARNISH *Mint sprig or Rock Candy Stick or Ice Cone*

Flash blend and open pour with gated finish into a double old-fashioned glass. Garnish with a mint sprig or rock candy stick and a toast to sailors of yore.

DARE TO COMPARE For the Don the Beachcomber version, substitute the simple syrup and allspice dram with 1 ounce of SC honey syrup (page 325) and ¾ ounce of seltzer. The Don the Beachcomber version was traditionally served with an ice cone (see page 241). If serving with an ice cone, after flash blending, strain over the ice cone.

While it's true that Donn was conscious of creating smaller and more "delicate" drinks to appeal to his female guests, and that drinks like the Navy Grog were meant as the masculine counterpoint, today, well, you should drink whatever the hell you like and not worry about it.

Made strong, with three types of rum, it was described on the Don the Beachcomber menu as "A robust rum punch dedicated to the gallant men of the American navy." Though invented by Donn Beach, it is the Trader Vic's Navy Grog that has garnered notoriety through its infamous imbibers.

Probably the most famous Navy Grog enthusiast was President Richard Nixon, a former navy lieutenant who had served in the South Pacific. Legend has it that he would slip away to the D.C. Trader Vic's, Sixteenth and K, housed within the Capitol Hilton Hotel. Often, according to Henry Kissinger, Nixon would insist on having cabinet members in tow. Later, during the Watergate hearings, story has it that after everyone had gone home, Vic's would keep the bar open with just one bartender, and Nixon would sneak in a back entrance at three in the morning, have a few Navy Grogs, and pour his heart out to the bartender. And, true to bartender code, that bartender has never shared what Nixon told him over forty years ago.

And then there was record producer Phil Spector. The night he killed Lana Clarkson, he went on a bit of a bender. One of the stops on his booze tour was his regular haunt, Trader Vic's Beverly Hills, where he ordered not one, but two Navy Grogs. Trader Vic's bartender Ming Fong Chu would later be called to testify at the murder trial as to the potency of the drink. He confirmed that yes, each Navy Grog contains three shots of rum, and was one of the strongest drinks Vic's served.

SCORPION

Steve Crane's riff on Trader Vic's iconic drink brings better balance and complexity to this famous recipe. Vic invented the idea of the shared bowl with long straws in the 1940s by reviving the dormant punch tradition and marrying it to the traditions of the kava bowl ceremony, which he witnessed in Micronesia.

ORIGIN *The Luau, 1958, adapted by Smuggler's Cove*

GLASSWARE *Large (32-48 ounce) scorpion bowl and long 20" luau straws (see Resources) or other punch bowl or decorative bowl with a ladle and cups.*

SERVES *4*

- **2 ounces fresh lime juice**
- **4 ounces fresh orange juice**
- **1½ ounces SC Demerara syrup (page 324)**
- **2 ounces SC Orgeat (page 330)**
- **2 ounces brandy**
- **4 ounces London Dry Gin**
- **4 ounces blended lightly aged rum** ❷

GARNISH *None*

Combine all ingredients in a mixing tin without ice and roll (pour back and forth) with another mixing tin to combine ingredients evenly and split in half. Add ice to each cup and flash blend with a drink mixer for 3 seconds. Pour contents of both cups into a 4-person ceramic Scorpion Bowl. Serve with 20-inch luau straws for easier sharing. Add fire to taste.

When groups come into Smuggler's Cove, they rarely resist the siren song of the communal bowl drink. The original Scorpion was a Trader Vic drink of orange, lemon, orgeat, white Puerto Rican rum, and brandy. It initially appeared in his *Bartender's Guide* and *Book of Food and Drink* proportioned as a punch recipe, with a small bit of gin, and lengthened with half a bottle of white wine. To quote Vic, "I'll never forget a very beautiful form of gentle anesthesia served one night at a luau up in Manoa Valley in Honolulu. . . .The object of greatest interest was a tremendous Chinese earthen crock which easily held twenty gallons of punch. In it our host had prepared Honolulu's famous Scorpion, a drink which does not shilly-shally or mess around in getting you under way." By the time this magical drink emerged on the menu at Steve Crane's Luau in Beverly Hills, it had transformed to include lime instead of lemon, and the gin had reappeared, though this time in equal proportion to the rum. It is this version we find more complex and interesting and chose to serve at the Cove. And, of course, we throw in a bit of fire.

FOG CUTTER

Another of Vic's most famous drinks, the Fog Cutter is still served today at his restaurants around the world. Our version incorporates the pisco preferred by the Don the Beachcomber chain at later locations in their Fog Cutter to give it a brighter, more vegetal character. (We're trying to make them friends in heaven by fusing their recipes.)

ORIGIN *Trader Vic, 1940s, adapted by Smuggler's Cove*
GLASSWARE *Zombie glass or Fog Cutter mug*

- 1 ½ ounce fresh lemon juice
- 1 ½ ounce fresh orange juice
- ½ ounce SC Orgeat (page 330)
- 1 ounce pisco
- ½ ounce gin
- 2 ounces blended lightly aged rum ❷
- ½ ounce oloroso sherry

GARNISH *Swizzle stick and mint sprig*

Combine all ingredients except the sherry in a drink mixer tin with 12 ounces of crushed ice and 4 to 6 "agitator" cubes. Flash blend and open pour with gated finish into a Zombie glass or Fog Cutter mug. Float sherry by gently pouring on top of the surface of the drink and then garnish.

The Fog Cutter is from a family of similar style drinks from Vic (lemon, orange, orgeat, rum)—that includes the Scorpion. Over time, the recipe was tweaked, and by the 1950s had become the Samoan Fog Cutter, with less brandy, and less rum. The Fog Cutter was one of Vic's most clever integrations of multiple base spirits in a drink, and the overall effect is uniquely bright and refreshing while the rich oxidized flavor of the oloroso becomes an unexpected foil. While it certainly changed, and usually not for the better, as it traveled to other menus, it was one of the most often duplicated drinks of the golden era.

SINGAPORE SLING

Though its roots lie in Southeast Asia, it became one of the greatest tiki bar staples, and a rare departure from rum.

ORIGIN *Classic, adapted by Smuggler's Cove*
GLASSWARE *Collins or highball*

> 2 ounces seltzer
>
> ¾ ounce fresh lemon juice
>
> ¼ ounce SC Demerara Syrup (page 324)
>
> ½ ounce Cherry Heering liqueur
>
> ¼ ounce Benedictine
>
> 1½ ounce London Dry Gin
>
> 1 dash Angostura bitters
>
> 1 dash orange bitters

GARNISH *Lemon wedge speared with a cocktail umbrella*

Add the seltzer to the bottom of a Collins or highball glass. Add the rest of ingredients to a cocktail shaker with cubed or cracked ice. Shake and strain into the glass. Gently add cubed or cracked ice to glass and add garnish.

While not an exotic cocktail by definition, the Singapore Sling is a perfect example of the kind of drinks that came from outside the world of tiki establishments and took up residence on tiki menus everywhere. Vic's first menu included a section titled "Drinks I Have Gathered from the Four Corners of the Globe" and included the Singapore Sling.

Rarely, if ever, however, has there been as much confusion and controversy about such a famous drink, reflected in the fact that several versions are in Trader Vic's *Bartender's Guide* from 1947, including a Raffles Hotel Sling, a Singapore Sling #1, and a Singapore Sling #2. There seems to be at least unanimous agreement about *who* invented it and *where*, but the rest, including the drink ingredients themselves, and even what to call the darn thing (some early recipes refer to a Straits Sling) remains a bit of a mystery. Ngiam Tong Boon was a Chinese-born bartender who moved first to Vietnam, where he trained, and then moved to Singapore, where he worked first at the Adelphi Hotel, and then ended up at what became Singapore's finest hotel, Raffles. He started at Raffles sometime around the beginning of the twentieth century and died in 1915, putting the invention of the Singapore Sling somewhere in between. There is reference to a "pink sling" in a Singapore newspaper in 1903, suggesting the invention was before then. Likely a riff on the popular gin sling, it is distinguished by a reddish color, which would have, in theory, stemmed from the inclusion of cherry. Here, too, there is controversy, as to the type of cherry—varying from a drier kirsch style, to Heering cherry liqueur, to cherry brandy, depending on accounts. The Raffles bar itself was revamped in the 1970s, and it was at that time that they claimed that the original recipe was invented in 1915, and had been sourced from a visitor to the bar who, in the 1930s, had written down how the drink was made. Their recipe includes the controversial addition of pineapple and grenadine, and some think this was an attempt to make the drink more appealing to the 1970s crowd, at a time when fruitier drinks were more popular. At Smuggler's Cove, we decided to try several versions and combinations of the many proposed recipes, and settled on the one we liked best.

PART FIVE

CREATING PARADISE

"Discover the mystery and enchantment of an imaginary distant island—a world of perpetual dusk, potent libations . . . and tiny umbrellas."

—FROM THE MENU AT SMUGGLER'S COVE

the Tiki Look and Feel

Bob Van Oosting and Leroy Schmaltz of Oceanic Arts

EVERYONE HAS THEIR OWN VISION OF PARADISE—AND
IT DOESN'T ALWAYS INCLUDE ISLANDS. "PARADISE"
CAN BE A HIKE THROUGH A QUIET FOREST AFTER A
RAINSTORM, A LONELY DESERT FILLED WITH DRAMATIC
VISTAS, OR A WIND-SWEPT MOUNTAIN COVERED WITH
FRESH POWDER.

But for many American people in the middle of the twentieth century, there seemed to be a shared ideal. A space that was at once inviting yet dangerous, cozy yet mysterious. The tiki bar. But what makes a great tiki space? From décor to drinks to music and more, some factors are quantifiable, others hard to exactly put your finger on. You'll just know by the third round of drinks. A great tiki bar can provide an intoxicating (literally) sense of escape, shelter, adventure, camaraderie, mystery, danger—all at the same time. Let's start with a few of the broader themes that I think make for a great tiki bar, whether it's in a commercial space, or inside what used to be your guest bedroom.

THE CONTRAST

The more dramatic the contrast is from your surroundings, the more effective the sense of escape. Contrast can take many forms. Sometimes, as is the case with Smuggler's Cove, the exterior is kept deliberately anonymous to heighten the dramatic shift after you enter. The classic Trader Vic's locations within Hilton hotels provided a dramatic shift from the rest of the austere hotel space. It can contrast with a busy urban center filled with modern architecture. Even the Mai Kai in Fort Lauderdale with its tropical gardens and palm trees wouldn't seem much of a contrast in sunny South Florida, but its position on North Federal Highway nestled among endless faceless furniture stores, car dealers, and strip malls makes the contrast especially pronounced. The space may even just stand out against the weather. Some of the greatest and most storied tiki bars of old, like the late, lamented Kahiki Supper Club in Columbus, Ohio, were made all the more special by providing a warm respite from the January chill. Your own garage Polynesia creates a secret contrast to the neat and tidy row of suburban sprawl lining your street. Whether it's your backyard oasis, your basement, or your spare room, imagine the neighbor's surprise and confusion upon entering for the first time, or perhaps catching just a glimpse one day as the garage door comes down. To paraphrase Hunter S. Thompson, "With a bit of luck, his life will be ruined forever. Always thinking that just behind some garage door in any suburban tract, men in Hawaiian shirts are getting incredible kicks from things he'll never know."

THE DARKNESS

A great tiki bar should be enveloped in perpetual twilight. Like being on a torch-lit lanai at dusk, the warm soft colors of a good tiki bar fill you with a

The discreet exterior of Smuggler's Cove

sense of relaxation. Lots of amber lights, accented by a colorful variety of illuminated glass floats and fish traps provide all you need. And the best way to achieve perpetual twilight is to avoid windows altogether. With escape being such a vital component of a memorable tiki experience, the last thing you want on your voyage to the South Seas is to look out the window at roaring traffic, busy humanity, or ugly architecture. It's important to remember that tiki bars came of age in America at a time when drinking in a bar was something most people didn't advertise themselves doing. The combination of puritanical morals and a Protestant work ethic meant that society frowned upon drinkers. As a result, most bars of the era were built without windows, often with entrances built around corners so even opening the door didn't immediately reveal who might be bending elbows indoors. All the better for the design of a good tiki bar. Even some of Donn's and Vic's places that were located in Hawaii didn't have windows, an incredible illustration of the power of the Poynesian Pop illusion: Even when you've actually arrived in paradise, the paradise created within was so much more powerful. Even those with home tiki bars located outside in backyards will admit that their lovingly crafted spaces reach their zenith as twilight arrives and the torches are lit.

THE WATER

There is something truly enchanting about the sound of running water in a tiki bar. A stream, fountain, aquarium, or waterfall can add so much to the atmosphere, as most find the effect calming. Water is integral to the experience and during the heyday, the venues that were the most forceful proponents of High Tiki design had elaborate networks of streams and pools surrounded by rock walls and connected by bridges. The now-closed Kona Kai in Chicago was built almost entirely over water, while the sadly now-gutted Islands restaurant in San Diego featured water pouring from giant clam shells embedded in rock walls and flowing under bridges throughout the dining room. Even the smallest of home bars can be enhanced by a small desktop fountain or even recorded water sounds.

THE TIKIGEMÜTLICHKEIT

Gemütlichkeit **most closely translates** to English as coziness, but in German it additionally means tranquility, comfort, or a lack of stress. I love this word because nothing sounds less cozy than the word gemütlichkeit, but it also goes some ways toward defining the somewhat nebulous sensation of safety I feel in a tiki bar. What I call tikigemütlichkeit is very important to a good tiki bar, and this can be created in a number of ways, including the dim lighting, sounds of water, and quiet music. But it's also important to keep it intimate—low ceilings, booths or huts that ensconce and further "shelter" you from the "elements." Lots of twists and turns, or a maze-like interior can add to this—as was the case at the sadly gone Bahooka in Rosemead, California. That's not to say that dramatic interiors aren't striking as well—but they work best when least expected. Frank Lloyd Wright was fond of having dark narrow entrances in his homes so that when you reached the main area— often with a much higher ceiling—you were more struck by the dramatic reveal. Like entering the main room of the Mai Kai after coming through the low entryway—the sight of the peaked roof with its dozens of lights is breathtaking. But the rest of its enormous interior is a series of smaller rooms designed to make the dining experience more personal.

THE ESCAPE

To escape. From the world outside, your job, the demands on your life—whatever causes you stress. In mid-century America, it was expectations, morality, conformity. The tiki bar was where you could loosen the tie and let the rum wash the worries away. Today, less of an escape from morality perhaps, but certainly a need to escape from a barrage of communication and information—emails, texts, social media. The outside world can find you anywhere now, and it wants answers right away. Smuggler's Cove has terrible mobile phone reception, and we don't offer Wi-Fi. There are few chances in life to simply put down the phone and connect instead with your friends, your partner, or your Mai Tai. The gods want you to relax.

Escape is a dying art. Most Americans scarcely even take vacation anymore and, when they do, they more often than not still bring at least a little work with them. Even what should be the pleasures of the modern world never let you forget where you are. Modern dining wants you to worship the food, but is less interested in transporting you somewhere else to enjoy it. Open spaces with large windows bring the world inside, and austere furnishings keep you from getting too comfortable. Close seating and hard surfaces mean reduced privacy and elevated noise levels. It may seem hard to imagine, but there once was a time before dining out became an Instagrammable, full-contact sport. Constant reminders about the local sourcing of food and the reclaimed wood on the walls assuage feelings of guilt, but also subtly reinforce that everything outside the door of the restaurant is falling apart—that the forests are disappearing, that the American food system is in crisis. Tiki bars just want you to have a couple of hours to unwind.

It's hard for many of us in the twenty-first century to stop looking through our postmodern glasses, and it's easy to dismiss the tiki bar with a seen-it-all-before sneer (or worse, find it indistinguishable from a modern family restaurant chain). Family-friendly jungle-themed restaurants never let you forget you are in a cartoon with chatty animatronic animals guiding you to the gift shop. A good tiki bar didn't have to explicitly tell you to HAVE A GOOD TIME. The space itself implied it. And the tiki bar and restaurant was a resolutely adult experience in its prime. But as those adults had children, and took them to the dwindling number of places that remained, the few who were not dismissive or horrified had indelibly strong and positive memories of the experience. That it seemed to them very real and very grown up and very escapist. And the seeds of the revival were planted.

BUILDING YOUR OWN POLYNESIAN POP PARADISE

For many, the call is simply too powerful to ignore. Whether it's the conversion of your own garage or the bar down the street into your vision of paradise, the very best examples share many of the same tenets. When your wish is to create a fully immersive experience for you and your guests, no detail is too small to overlook, and the smallest visual error can pull you out of the moment.

One thing that I've found in the finest spaces, both private and commercial, is that for those of us who are Polynesian Pop's most ardent followers . . . *it is not kitsch.* It is not ironic. I see beauty and artistry in paintings, carvings, ceramics, and fabrics. Whether the design comes from authentic Polynesian tradition or from the mainland artists they inspired, the best bars are the ones whose designers really believe that it's a tasteful and stylish design aesthetic. Approach your décor with sincerity, go all in, and you'll create a more honest experience. If your guests think it's kitschy or cute, that's fine. As long as it puts a smile on their faces. We are here to delight and entertain.

I will always maintain that an exotic cocktail tastes better served under a thatch roof with some exotica playing in the background. Exotic cocktails can't exist in a vacuum. Atmosphere is part of the experience. Conversely, I can make the best Vieux Carré in the world, with the highest quality ingredients, the perfect temperature and dilution, and in gorgeous vintage glassware and serve it to you at Smuggler's Cove and it will never, ever taste as good as having one where it was invented, at the Carousel Bar in New Orleans.

Tiki: The God of Doomed Relationships

A brief, but important word before we continue: As I hope I've made clear by now, embracing tiki and its lifestyle fully can be an all-encompassing proposition. It's far more than just a cocktail fad. And while it has an undeniable magic, it can also have tremendous aesthetic, time, and financial demands. And quite frankly, the ancient gods can really torpedo a relationship if there's one partner who just really is not into it at all. Over the last two decades, I have witnessed several relationships and marriages implode over one partner's passion for the exotic. Needless to say, it's a good idea to have a talk about tiki before you drink too deeply of its rum-filled waters. Ask your doctor if tiki is right for you.

How Will Your Paradise Look?

As highlighted in the style boxes (pages 26, 28, 35 and 55), Polynesian Pop draws from many influences and evolved over the years. Just as each subsequent style added a new layer of depth to the one that came before it, so too do the best tiki bars have layers and layers of décor for you to enjoy as your eyes gaze across the space. Each visit should reveal previously unnoticed pieces that will enchant your guests. It's an oft-repeated adage that a good tiki bar is never finished, and it's the truth. But if you feel intimidated, I have excellent news: Almost everything you need to make your place look amazing can be found in one store. And they ship!

The Magic of Oceanic Arts

Since opening in 1956, Oceanic Arts, in Whittier, California, has been responsible for decorating virtually every top tiki bar in the United States, and many overseas as well. Founded by Robert Van Oosting and LeRoy Schmaltz, two college friends who carved Polynesian masks and weapons for a little extra income, it is a warehouse filled with treasures of the islands and a feast for the eyes. In 1960, the pair traveled extensively through the South Pacific for over three months to learn more about the peoples and arts that had inspired them and to establish export contacts. They set up shop in Whittier upon their return, and their original art and imports have been the backbone of projects from Trader Vic's, Don the Beachcomber, the Kona-Kai chain, Disney's Polynesian Village Resort, apartment complexes, and much more. Oceanic Arts exists today both as resource and museum, and a visit to their hallowed halls is a must-do for any serious enthusiast. Bring a sense of wonder and a lot of room on the ol' credit cards. There, you can purchase virtually all of the elements fundamental to a tiki bar.

NATURAL MATERIALS OF THE TROPICS

These materials are typically sourced from plants in the South Pacific.

- Bamboo poles, fencing, blinds, and door curtains
- Monkeypod (raintree wood)
- Bindings (sisal rope, sea grass braid, bac bac braid)
- Matting (lauhala, bac bac, bamboo board, sea grass rugs)—traditional woven mats to be used on floor, walls, or ceiling
- Thatch (raincape, nipa, abaca)
- Driftwood, both decorative and sometimes even cosmetically structural

POLYNESIAN ARTS

Both Polynesian sourced and Poynesian Pop inspired:

- TIKIS!
- Carved posts, molding, and trim—with tikis or inspired patterns
- Masks
- Weapons
- Shields
- Oars and paddles
- Outrigger canoes
- Drums
- Tapa—patterned barkcloth made in many South Pacific islands. (This beautiful handmade material varies by country, but is superb as a striking and traditional wall or ceiling covering)
- Tropical lamps from bamboo, tapa, shell, various mattings and bindings

BEACHCOMBER FLOTSAM AND JETSAM

- Driftwood
- Fish traps
- Bottles
- Shells
- Used fish netting
- Glass fishnet floats—intact or as lamps
- Shark jaws or teeth

NAUTICAL DÉCOR

- Block and tackle
- Cleats
- Rigging
- Marine rope
- Anchors
- Portholes
- Cannons
- Harpoons
- Dock pilings with rope wrap
- Buoys
- Ship's wheels
- Rope boat bumpers
- Cork and rope
- Figurehead
- Ship lanterns
- Port and starboard lights
- Elements of merchant life including architectural/garden jade tiles, sake barrels, barrels, crates, cargo nets filled with assorted goods

PAINTINGS

- Evocative island scenes
- Island images on black velvet by artists such as Edgar Leeteg
- Dozens of contemporary artists

EARTH

- Lava and sandstone rock
- Water features (ponds, waterfalls, streams, bridges)
- Vines
- Tropical plants
- Coconuts
- Fake (or real if you have seventy years to spare) tropical birds
- Flowers and leis
- Puffer fish and puffer fish lamps
- Tiki torches—electrical indoors, gas or oil outside

VINTAGE POLYNESIAN POP EPHEMERA, FOR CONTEXT

- Mugs
- Menus
- Album covers
- Matchbooks
- Ashtrays
- Swizzle sticks

A FEW THINGS TO REMEMBER

- Don't forget the music! Exotica music by performers both legendary and contemporary adds the right mysterious and evocative feeling. A little Caribbean, hapa haole, and more can make it more up-tempo.

- The A-frame entrance over the door can be a subtle but welcoming signal, and an A-frame interior when possible evokes the longhouses of Polynesian cultures that became such a key architectural feature during the heyday.

- A small footbridge, whether leading to your space or even inside your space and ideally over water, symbolizes a transition from one world to the next, and a passage toward escape. Even on a small scale, they have a powerful effect.

- Don't forget the tikis! A sign that reads "tiki bar" does not make it a tiki bar. Also, and with apologies to my friends with "tiki bar" signs, a great tiki bar should be pretty self-explanatory.

A FEW THINGS TO AVOID

- White walls! White ceilings! Cover it all up and escape!

- Windows or passages to the real world.

- Televisions—the electronic passage to the real world.

- Other elements of mid-century design or culture. Drive-ins and tail-finned Cadillacs have their place, but they are representative of the busy, forward- thinking American era of progress that tiki was in sharp contrast to.

Returning to a "simpler" time did not mean chrome and steel.

- Surfboards . . . are a matter of some debate. It may seem counterintuitive to not include surfboards, as they would seem so closely related. The Mai Kai in Fort Lauderdale did, for many years, have a "surfboard bar," in which they used a beautiful wooden surfboard as the bartop. However, historic tiki bars do not typically have surfboards on the wall or in their murals. That's because at the time, tiki bars were about fine dining and suburban backyard culture—and what the surfers' parents were likely doing while their kids were hitting the waves. But tiki and surfing were not strangers. Established in Hawaii and long a part of Hawaiian culture, surfing was also part of Hawaiian mythology, including surfing gods. As surf culture took a hold in California, tikis became a symbol of that connection, and tiki pendants were considered good luck. However, this was about an homage to Hawaii, and not a connection to the "uncool" tiki palaces that the surfers themselves were unlikely to be going to, unless dragged by their parents for a family dinner.

A note about Florida tiki bars and why they are different. You will note when traveling in South Florida and the Keys that there seems to be a tiki bar every mile. A paradise for the tiki lover. Well, not quite. For over a century, Seminoles in Florida made huts with palmetto thatch built over a cypress log frame called chickee huts. Their durability proved to be tough enough to handle Florida weather. During the post–World War II development boom along Florida's Gold Coast, chickee huts were used all over as kiosks in front of new housing developments, as outbuildings in new homes, or as gazebos and poolside bars. With the arrival of the Mai Kai and the Polynesian Pop boom, they gradually became called tiki huts, and to this day palmetto-topped cypress structures are called tiki bars . . . even if there are no tikis to be found.

A FEW THINGS TO PLAN FOR

I'm not a contractor, so I can only offer some helpful hints here, but just a few things that I've learned through doing this several times—and making some mistakes along the way. With a few pro tips from some of my favorite tiki designers as well.

- When starting out, give some thought to the ultimate goal, layout, and some of your design ideas.

- Think about wiring, plumbing needs, fire retardant coatings on some of the natural materials as needed, and permits as needed. If you want to have effects down the road, prewire the space with CAT5—it can't hurt.

- Coffee makes a great natural stain for lauhala and bamboo.

- Put a layer of oriented strand board (OSB, also known as sterling board) over all the walls and ceiling as your first layer. You'll never have to go hunting for studs. And you will be hanging a lot of stuff.

- When hanging natural materials as wall coverings, line things up by eye—most mats and tapas don't have perfect right angles, and bamboo isn't perfectly straight. Too many perfect right angles makes the place look too manufactured.

Flotsam and jetsam

"To hell with the conventional, the right fork, the right goblet, the fashionable flower arrangement. You can have more real fun with a flower behind your ear, a sparerib in one hand, and a drink in the other than you ever will all swaddled in damask, sterling, and cut crystal. Just one thing is needed to complete the scene—good companionship."

—TRADER VIC

the Tiki Party

Revelling Revivalists

TRADER VIC ONCE SAID, "SPEND TIME WITH YOUR GUESTS—NOT MAKING MIXED DRINKS."

This is the most important secret you need to know about throwing a successful tiki party—and the keyword is "punch." When I first got heavily into tiki in the late 1990s, I know I was as guilty as the next person of throwing parties where I didn't spend enough time with my guests. I was so excited to try out a new tiki cocktail I'd discovered in one of Beachbum Berry's books or invented myself, that I stood the entire night, trapped behind my home tiki bar making drinks to order. I couldn't really talk to anyone because I was concentrating on making them a great drink. And, soon, there was a long line of thirsty people. As guests left at the end of the night, they all said to us, "Great party. Sorry we didn't get to hang out with you, Martin." After a few parties like this, I ran across Vic's words of wisdom. I then began putting my energy toward choosing recipes for two or three fantastic punches, and doing all the prep the day of the party, timing it so the juice was squeezed in the late afternoon/early evening, and the punch had time to chill for an hour or so before the party. The doorbell rang, and I was finished with my bartending duties and could enjoy my guests.

Later in this chapter, I'll share some tricks of the trade to making a great party punch, but first, let's learn a little more about how punch entered the world of tiki.

PUNCH AND POLYNESIAN POP

As the eighteenth century marched on, the glory days of punch seen in colonial times faded—and seemed likely to be gone for good. With the Industrial Revolution, we all became busy, busy, busy. If you had time to sit around a punch bowl, you were admitting you had nothing else to do. Among the wealthy, cocktails were becoming increasingly popular, but the working class began to favor beer. It is worth noting that while Jerry Thomas's 1862 guide had fifty-nine punch recipes, most were from old recipes and not from him, and by his 1887 guide, even these had moved to the back of the book. There was probably also, on some level, the sense that, in a society that celebrates democracy and individual freedom, people didn't want to be told what to drink, or to share their drink—we each wanted a choice. And, let us not forget, distillation methods continued to improve from the nineteenth century on, so the very raison d'être for punch (to cover up the harsh and rough booze being drunk), was no longer an issue. And, with a global economy, there was also a greater choice of those spirits from which to choose. So, while punch lived on as a single serving drink, such as the Pisco Punch, the communal punch faded away. To quote journalist, author, and rum historian Wayne Curtis, punch became a ceremonial drink "consigned to live out its retirement at regimental reunions and college dances."

However, there was one place where communal drinking was going to shine once again: the tiki bar. During his early travels to the South Pacific, Trader Vic recognized the importance of communal drinking to a good party. He watched Tahitians have three-day-long parties where they just kept replenishing a large punch with whatever was lying around. He also observed the shared hands-on experience of the kava bowl throughout the islands. A plant native to the South Pacific sometimes referred to by its scientific name, Piper methysticum, as well as *kavakava, keu, awa, ava,* and *yogana,* kava produces a slightly bitter, slightly frothy, aromatic, resinous brew capable of inducing tranquility and an ultimate sense of well-being. The roots and lower stems of the plant are chewed (often by children) and the extraction is spit into a wooden bowl then mixed with water and strained into coconut bowls from which it is drunk.

Vic knew punch was due for a revival and that the hands-on experience of communal drinking would be a unique feature at his restaurants. He commissioned the manufacture of large ceramic bowls for people to share, and served them with long (18 to 20-inch) straws. In true Polynesian Pop style, however, Vic brought back the look and communal aspects, without any of the real cultural authenticity of the ritual (for example, chewing of roots, and so on). But he knew that it would make good menu copy. His menu read: "In ancient Polynesia ceremonial luau drinks were served in festive communal bowls. I offer my interpretation of the time-honored custom."

Put everything together—the history of punch, the flavor of the Caribbean, the communal drinking of punch, the hands-on rituals of the South Seas, and the scorpion bowl tradition was born. It took years for other tiki establishments to join the scorpion bowl craze, but it began to spread. The Mai Kai in Fort Lauderdale added its own twist with the introduction of the Mystery Drink and Mystery Girl ritual (see Mai Kai—the Mothership, page 319).

I can say that the popularity of the bowl drink is alive and well. At Smuggler's Cove, especially on a Thursday, Friday, or Saturday night, we sell tons of these bowls. It becomes a group bonding experience—something to be shared, photographed, and enjoyed together. What's better than a birthday cake on your birthday? A bowl that all of your friends are enjoying together. Add a mystery girl, or the magic ingredient, fire, and it's theater, too.

MAKING YOUR OWN GREAT PUNCH

Choosing Your Recipes

The three communal drinks we included elsewhere in this book (Top Notch Volcano, page 134; Arrack Punch, page 163; and Scorpion, page 272) can certainly be multiplied easily to serve more people. We have also provided a few fun recipes for exotic punches that are tried and true in this chapter.

I also encourage you to take a favorite tiki recipe for an individual drink, and multiply it by ten or twenty for a fun punch. HOWEVER, there are some rules to follow when doing this:

Start with a base recipe that contains at least four ounces of mixer (juice and syrups) and at least a 2:1 ratio of mixer to rum. Generally, drinks that are served long (in a Collins or Zombie glass over ice) work well. In other words, as wonderful as a Mai Tai is, it does not multiply to a wonderful punch. While you don't want to be accused of being cheap with the hooch in your punch, you also don't want people wasted in the first fifteen minutes of your party.

Be careful with bitters/tinctures/absinthe because of the size of dashes and potency of flavor. Notice how the size of the dashes changes depending on how full the bottle is. A single dash in an individual cocktail can vary in size, and likely won't ruin the drink, but multiply by eight or more, and those variations can have disastrous effects. I suggest you start by halving the amount of bitters and then adding any additional dashes to taste.

Be sure to include at least one nonalcoholic punch for your guests (CLEARLY LABELED!). When making a nonalcoholic punch, it is not quite as simple as skipping the booze. You want to make sure the other ingredients are still tasty without the hooch, and it is balanced drink that doesn't just taste like a glass of juice. Recipes need to be heavy on the juice component, and those with more unusual juices (guava, peach, etc.) and using more flavorful syrups instead of just simple syrup (e.g., cinnamon, molasses, maple) will work well. Ginger beer is a great choice because it gives the drinks complexity and spice notes, which will keep things interesting. Remember that most bitters are technically alcoholic, so they should be left out of nonalcoholic drinks.

Grapefruit is a fairly common exotic cocktail ingredient. However, when choosing which punches to serve, it is a good idea to make sure at least one of your punches does not include grapefruit. This is because grapefruit contains compounds that block an enzyme that allows your body to break down certain medications, making it dangerous for many people to consume. The number of prescription drugs that make grapefruit a no-no is on the rise (currently numbered at over eighty), so many of your guests likely can't drink it.

Mixing Your Punch

You've chosen a winning recipe—now it's time to prepare the punch! You will want to assemble your punch about one or two hours ahead of time so that it can be chilled in advance.

Start by combining the juices, sweeteners, and spices in a large sealable container such as a Rubbermaid MixerMate or Arrow Slimline Beverage Dispenser.

Juice the fruit as close to service as possible, but with enough time to chill it down with the rest of the punch ingredients. Also, it takes longer than you think when you're juicing enough fruit for, say, sixty servings of punch. I would suggest starting your juicing three hours before your party. See page 233 for more tips on juicing.

Taste this initial sour-sweet-spice mixture, make adjustments as needed, and retest—but only do small

> *"It's time we dragged the punch bowl down from the attic where it has been collecting cobwebs since the repeal of prohibition. Just why people fight shy of punches has always puzzled me. A party seems to take on a warmer note and a friendlier spirit when guests can dip themselves a little libation, clustered around a punch bowl like bees around a honey pot."*
>
> —TRADER VIC

tweaks at a time. (For example, depending on the size of your punch, add 2 ounces more lime juice for more tartness, 2 ounces more syrup for sweetness, 1 or 2 extra dashes of bitters). Take your time: Making incremental adjustments rather than one large one helps prevent ruining a large and expensive punch.

Add your spirits and any other ingredients to the sealable container EXCEPT carbonated ingredients like sparkling wine, soda water, and the like. Those should be chilled separately, unopened, until right before service.

Chill sealed containers for 1 to 2 hours.

Assemble all of your now-chilled ingredients (both carbonated and noncarbonated) in your serving vessel (see Serving the Punch, following) and mix well. Do some additional taste testing by serving a small amount in a glass with ice, and make any minor tweaks as needed.

Chilling the Punch

Watery punch is your enemy. You're putting out a big batch of punch and you want it to last the length of your party. Here's how.

As mentioned, chill your ingredients in advance of serving to preserve the punch for the duration of your party.

Don't pour your punch over cubed or cracked ice in the serving vessel. Use block ice. This is where you can have some fun. Make the block ice yourself by freezing water in silicone cake molds, Tupperware containers, etc. Line the bottom of the molds or container(s) with sliced citrus, berries, edible flowers, and herbs before freezing. Serve with the bottom side up for a beautiful floating centerpiece.

Block ice will give you staying power, but the downside is that you might not actually have enough dilution. For this reason, we provide guests with a cooler full of ice and a scoop and suggest that they serve themselves punch over ice. However, if you prefer to serve your punch without ice, as is more traditional, then you should mix in a bit of cold water to your assembled punch before you serve it. A good rule of thumb is about ¼ ounce of water per serving.

Serving the Punch

So, what to serve your beautiful punch in? Don't sweat it if you don't have a crystal bowl—let's face it, that's not very tiki anyway. Instead, be creative: Use anything food-safe and dress up the outside. According to Trader Vic, you can use a plastic tub, koi pond, hollowed-out log, five-gallon oil drum, or a baby's bath (Note: Don't actually use an oil drum. Vic was of hearty stock.) Wooden bowls can be sealed with a food-safe oil used for salads bowls. But, there's no resin that I've been able to uncover in the United States that's truly food-safe.

> *"The very amplitude of the bowl itself suggests hospitality, and an invitation to quench thirst, which no service of single small glasses can ever effect."*
>
> —CHARLES H. BAKER JR., *THE GENTLEMAN'S COMPANION*

Having an outside party? I have just the thing, thanks to this handy tip from spirits writer David Wondrich: A few days before the party, make a cylindrical ice block in a large pasta pot. Put the block into a five gallon cylindrical cooler, fill the cooler with your chilled punch, seal the lid, and the punch will survive during a hot day. Have some fun decorating the cooler (see opposite). No one wants to look at a big plastic cylinder!

For garnishing your punch, use thinly sliced fruit that is an ingredient in the punch (limes, oranges, lemons, etc.), and float a few edible orchids on top.

As for glassware for your guests, a mix of punch cups, small tiki mugs, ceramic coconuts, or whatever you have a few of will work great. There are plenty of inexpensive glass and ceramic solutions—avoid using plastic. Thrift stores are chock full of mix-and-match opportunities. Another fun party idea is to ask your guests to bring their favorite drinking vessel (but always have a few extra on hand for those who don't). Another great option, especially if you entertain a lot, is to get custom glassware made, perhaps with a tiki print or the name of your home bar (see Resources, page 335).

NON-PUNCH COCKTAIL IDEAS

Obviously, I'm a proponent of punch at a party. If, however, you want to do your own bartending, here are a few tips.

Pick three or four recipes and create a drink menu for your guests. Offer a variety of drinks, and make sure to have a nonalcoholic and nongrapefruit option (see Choosing Your Recipes, page 300). As much as possible, treat each cocktail on the menu like a punch and prebatch it before the party—this saves enormous time, but still allows you to make individual drinks for your guests. If your individual drinks are being elaborately garnished, do so with the nonalcoholic drinks as well so those guests still feel a part of the fun.

- Estimate how many of that particular drink you think you'll serve (1½ times the number of guests is usually a good estimate).

- Multiply the ingredients for that cocktail by that estimated number of serves.

- In a large pitcher or beverage container, combine the cocktail ingredients (without ice) ahead of time. Do not include in your prebatch any carbonated elements, eggs or egg whites, milk or cream components, or bitters—these should be added at serving time.

- For all of the ingredients you included in your prebatch, calculate how many ounces go into a single cocktail—this tells you how much of your prebatch you need per serving.

- Keep your prebatch chilled until the start of the party.

Once your party starts, all you need to do is stir, shake, or blend and then strain your prebatch along with any of the excluded components. Make two or three of a particular drink—most times, people are happy to grab what's ready rather than wait.

If you still really, really want to bartend from scratch, be sure to prejuice, bottle, and label your citrus, and put your syrups in easy to use squeeze bottles or glass bottles with speed pourers. Pull out just the spirits and liqueurs you need for the cocktails on your menu in front of you. And, I'd still recommend you have a punch in a different part of the room for guests to have while they wait or instead of waiting.

Also, use small glasses and pour or serve smaller drinks than you would normally—split a large individual drink into four old-fashioned–size glasses—people will get to try more things, and you can make fewer drinks.

Another fun idea is to put out recipe cards and the necessary ingredients and let people mix their own. Same rules apply as when you're doing the bartending. Presqueeze the juices, label everything, and make it as easy for your guests as possible. Put out a few jiggers, spoons, shakers, etc. It's a good way to get folks to mingle and chat about what they made. It's a good idea to have different drink "stations" at the party, so everyone isn't crowded into your kitchen or around one small table in the yard.

A FEW OTHER THINGS TO REMEMBER

Spread your punches and food out in different areas, if possible, to keep the flow going.

Have plenty of glassware at the ready, and some kind of marker so people can reuse their glasses. If your party is large, you might want to consider renting glassware from a party supply place—as an added bonus, you can usually return them dirty. No dishes! I don't love drinking out of plastic, but if you choose this route, leave out lots of markers so that people can mark their cups and you can reduce waste.

Have plenty of water around—a few pitchers in a few different rooms with glasses or cups out, or bottled water with markers so people can refill their

bottle. When people see water, they'll drink water, and this is a good thing.

Have a few clean rags and bar towels easily accessible for spills.

Have easily accessible trash and recycling containers scattered about to ease your cleanup.

SHOPPING FOR YOUR PARTY

You can't have too much ice. A good rule of thumb for general built or shaken cocktails or when serving a punch is 1 to 1½ pounds per guest, but if you are making exotic cocktails, especially grogs or swizzles, you should count on 2 to 2½ pounds per guest. Also, remember that all of these estimates are just for the guests' actual drinking needs. If you need ice to chill down beer, punch, soda, water, then you need to add those bags to your calculations, and factor in extra if the drinks will be outside in the sun, or in a hot room.

You should always buy more citrus than you think you'll need. Use the following as a guide, but then throw some extras in for garnish, and to have on hand for guests who want to go rogue, or when, toward the end of the party, you're out of punch and someone wants to start experimenting. If possible, try to find a Mexican or Chinese market, as usually the limes, lemons, and oranges are much more affordable than at a chain grocery store.

Some helpful information on yields/conversions (although note that yields may vary depending on seasonality):

1 lime = 1 ounce juice

1 lemon = 1½ ounces juice

1 orange = 3 ounces juice

1 grapefruit = 8 ounces juice

1 pineapple = 16 ounces juice

1 (750 ml) bottle = 25 ounces juice

1 (Liter) bottle = 33 ounces juice

DRESSING THE PART

A variety of vintage attire is illustrated on pages 306–7 to inspire your inner tiki fashionista.

Aloha Shirt

Anyone who knows me, knows I am rarely seen without a vintage aloha shirt (aka Hawaiian shirt) on. Even when dressing up, I will often wear an aloha shirt with my suit. In fact, people I know well have often walked right past me on those rare occasions that I choose to wear "street attire," not recognizing me in a sweater.

Starting out as custom-made printed shirts for the 1920s cruise boat tourists by small local tailors, the first mass-produced printed aloha shirt came about in the early 1930s. With such widespread tourism to Hawaii in the tiki heyday, a flood of souvenir shirts and dresses returned with sun-drenched travelers. These were trotted out for the occasional backyard luau, but mainly sat unworn in the back of the closet. This is why when you find them at estate sales and in thrift stores, they are often still in nearly mint condition. Sometimes a husband and wife today are lucky enough to find a matching set from back from the golden era—and even luckier if the stars align, and the sizes worn by today's couple match those of the happy 50s couple.

The Hawaiian shirt has gotten a bad rap over the years, and has come to symbolize a loud, garish American on vacation, or the fraternity party equivalent of the toga. As with many things, aloha shirts have also become more cheaply made with polyester fabric, plastic buttons, and nontraditional patterns. For these reasons, to me it is important to seek out vintage shirts from the 1940s to 1960s. These are often made from rayon or, even more desirable to me, bark cloth. Patterns are traditional floral or tapa prints, and typically have double stitching on the

seams. Metal buttons, often in the form of Chinese coins, are another tip-off that it's an older shirt.

It is fun to see the evolution of the patterns follow the evolution of the craze, and fashion in general, with some of the later 1960s patterns and colors becoming more psychedelic.

While some may see it as morbid or depressing that many of the people who originally bought these may no longer be with us, to me wearing these vintage clothes is a wonderful way to carry on their memory. You are wearing an outfit worn for happy times—vacations, parties, and, of course, tiki bars.

Lei

It can be pretty expensive to get fresh leis for all of your guests (though if you want to, see Resources, page 335), but try to get the better quality fake leis—not the nightmare scratchy plastic ones that don't even resemble a flower. A true sign of tiki's decline in

the 1970s are those relics from the past. Party supply stores usually now have a range of quality. It is a fun souvenir for people to take home, and helps "tiki up" people who didn't dress in tropical attire.

Another ice breaker is to have guests make their own lei. You need about fifty fresh orchids per lei, a spool of monofilament thread or waxed dental floss, and large needles. Each person should cut about seven feet of thread. Fold the thread in half, and thread the needle so the needle sits at the halfway point. Tie a large knot with the ends of the thread, but be sure to leave about five inches of thread past the knot (this will be the thread you will need to tie the lei around your neck). Loose Dendrobium orchids are available in bulk online, usually in batches of one hundred (see Resources, page 335), or if you have orchids on the stem, remove them from the main stem.

To make the lei: Take the loose orchid and remove the remaining stem. Push your needle gently through the base of the flower and up through its center. Gently slide the threaded flower down to the knotted end. Repeat and gently stack the orchids one inside the other along the string until you have about five inches of thread remaining without flowers. Cut the thread next to the needle, and knot off the ends next to the last flower, leaving loose threads beyond the knot. Tie the loose ends together, place the lei around your neck, and go get yourself an exotic cocktail—I'd say you've earned it.

And don't forget the finishing touches: There are plenty of contemporary artists and vendors offering amazing hair flowers, shell necklaces, bracelets, and tiki pendants to fully accessorize your tiki experience (see Resources, page 335).

Other Fun Touches

FOOD

Fabulous drinks are only one part of an unforgettable home tiki party. Great pupu platters piled high with tasty tidbits complete the experience. There is a wondrous symbiotic relationship between exotic cocktails and fried foods. Where you might initially find yourself wary of a platter of deep-fried goodies, watch what happens to your steely resolve after the first Mai Tai—it will be impossible to pull you away from the egg rolls. Remember that Donn gave us rumaki and Vic brought us Crab Rangoon, and I think they had a pretty good idea of what they were doing. Make your tiki food look festive. Garnish it like a drink with flowers, tropical leaves, and more. Look for vintage serving platters for a period feel. But don't feel like the food has to be exclusively vintage—mix in modern bites with the luau classics. There's great contemporary cuisine that draws inspiration from the same sources as the "Polynesian" food of yore, where Hawaiian, Southeast Asian, Caribbean, and Cantonese flavors mingle in exciting new ways. Just don't look for recipes here because I can't cook.

DÉCOR

If you're not up for building a home tiki bar (YET!), there is a lot of fun you can have with inexpensive tiki décor for your party. But—you have to choose carefully and wisely. There is a lot of plastic junk out there.

Decorate your party with a few of the inexpensive elements from page 289—netting, rope, shells, flowers, real or fake plants, driftwood—anything from placing it on the tables on which you're serving your punch, to hanging some of the décor around your backyard or home. A quick, easy, and fun idea is to fill a fishing net with seashells, starfish, glass bottles, driftwood, and other flotsam and jetsam and hang it.

We've already discussed the pineapple's merits as an ingredient, garnish, and a vessel, but its magic doesn't stop there—why not use it for décor as well? For centuries, the pineapple has been a symbol of hospitality and welcome, harkening back to the Caribs, the indigenous people of the Lesser Antilles, who used it as a sign of welcome to their village. Some early seventeenth-century sea captains who had made tropical travels put a pineapple outside their home as a signal that they were home safe and welcoming visitors. As the pineapple made its way to Colonial America and Europe, it began as a rare and much sought-after treat, and thus also was a symbol of honor to guests when it was served—so much so that it was not uncommon for hosts in Colonial America to rent a pineapple and use it as table decoration, only to return it uneaten for someone else to use for the fruit. The pineapple was often carved into entryways of hotels, homes, and bedposts, and used in napkins, tablecloths, and other items that greeted a guest, and to this day remains a powerful symbol in the hospitality industry. What better way to bring tiki and hospitality together than to use the symbol of the pineapple? A few whole pineapples scattered about your party is a wonderful addition—they make a natural centerpiece to your food or punch table or bar, especially when surrounded by its tiki brothers and sisters—limes, lemons, oranges, and grapefruits. Suddenly you have a splash of color—and a handy backup of fruit for drinks late in the evening.

Flowers, like gardenias, floating in fishbowls, add an aromatic and attractive element to the party.

Candles are always a natural, especially to set the mood for an indoor party. Outdoors, go for their tiki big brother—the tiki torch. These can often be found at large hardware stores or in party supply places and are a cheap and effective way to set the mood. Early summer is a great time to stock up on these, as well as plants and other party décor, because many stores big and small have "Hawaiian" and "tropical" displays and sales.

Ti leaves or banana leaves are a tropical way to decorate your serving platters. Banana leaves are usually available at Asian or Mexican markets in the freezer and can be defrosted prior to service. Ti leaves can often be found at florists, as they are used in flower arrangements.

MUSIC

Along with exotica and other lounge music, the tiki sound incorporates hapa haole (traditional Hawaiian music with lyrics sung in English that was especially popular from 1915 through the early 1960s) as well as, emerging later in the tiki craze, sounds of surf music in the early 1960s that paralleled the increased interest in the sport. Many talented and dedicated new bands have formed in the last two decades to cover old favorites and to produce new music in these styles, and many of the golden era sounds have been remastered and reissued (see Resources, page 335, for a few suggestions). A combination of some traditional exotica, other lounge, or hapa haole alongside some modern tiki-inspired acts sets a nice tropical mood for a cocktail party.

HONDO HATTIE'S JUNGLE PUNCH!

Created for a Tiki Oasis preparty at the Walt Disney Family Museum, this is a rare instance where I will use blue curaçao—and only to simulate the green water of the Jungle Cruise attraction.

ORIGIN *Created by Martin Cate*
GLASSWARE *Punch glassware (see page 303 for ideas)*

- 1 ounce fresh lemon juice
- ½ ounce SC Honey Syrup (page 325)
- ¼ ounce blue curaçao
- ¼ ounce tawny port
- ½ ounce John D. Taylor's Velvet Falernum
- ¼ ounce natural pear liqueur (such as Mathilde Poire)
- 2 ounces blended aged rum ❸
- 1 dash Angostura bitters

GARNISH *None*

Multiply the ingredient quantities by the number of guests. Combine all the ingredients except the ice in a beverage dispenser or other sealable container and whisk together. Chill for 1 to 2 hours prior to serving. Add large blocks of ice to the dispenser or serve over a large block or smaller blocks of ice in a punch bowl. See pages 300 to 303 for tips on preparing, chilling, and serving your punch.

KAHIKO PUNCH

ORIGIN *Created by Martin Cate*
GLASSWARE *Punch glassware (see page 303 for ideas)*

- 1 ounce fresh lemon juice
- 1½ ounces SC Passion Fruit Honey (page 325)
- ½ ounce SC Cinnamon Syrup (page 327)
- ½ ounce SC Hibiscus Liqueur (page 331)
- 2 ounces pot still unaged rum (see page 197)
- 6 drops Bittermans 'Elemakule Tiki bitters

GARNISH *Edible orchid*

Multiply the ingredient quantities by the number of guests. Combine all the ingredients except the ice in a beverage dispenser or other sealable container and whisk together. Chill for 1 to 2 hours prior to serving. Add large blocks of ice to the dispenser or serve over a large block or smaller blocks of ice in a punch bowl. Garnish individual servings with an edible orchid. See pages 300 to 303 for tips on preparing, chilling, and serving your punch.

TRIUMVIRATE PUNCH

In honor of the three Masters of the Cove who grace the label of our Triumvirate rum: Ron Roumas, Mark Holt, and John Boatwright.

ORIGIN *Created by Martin Cate*
GLASSWARE *Punch glassware (see page 303 for ideas)*

- ¾ ounce fresh lime juice
- 1 ounce SC Passion Fruit Honey (page 325)
- ¼ ounce St. Elizabeth Allspice Dram
- 1½ ounces pot still unaged rum (see page 197)
- 2 dashes Angostura bitters
- Pinch of freshly grated nutmeg

GARNISH *Mint and a smile*

Multiply the ingredient quantities by the number of guests. Combine all the ingredients in a beverage dispenser or other sealable container and whisk together. Chill for 1 to 2 hours prior to serving. Add large blocks of ice to dispenser or serve over a large block or smaller blocks of ice in a punch bowl. Garnish individual servings with mint and a smile. See pages 300 to 303 for tips on preparing, chilling, and serving your punch.

EUREKA PUNCH

Created originally for National Lemonade Day (really), the drink was turned into a bowl drink for four and served on the menu at San Francisco's Tonga Room in 2013.

ORIGIN *Created by Martin Cate*
GLASSWARE *Punch glassware (see page 303 for ideas)*

- 1½ ounces fresh lemon juice
- 1 ounce SC Honey Syrup (page 325)
- ½ ounce Yellow Chartreuse
- 1½ ounces column still aged rum ❹
- 1 dash Angostura bitters
- 2 ounces real ginger ale

GARNISH *Lemon wedge or twist and mint sprig*

Multiply the ingredient quantities by the number of guests. Combine all the ingredients except the ginger ale in a beverage dispenser or other sealable container and whisk together. Chill for 1 to 2 hours prior to serving. Add large blocks of ice to the dispenser or serve over a large block or smaller blocks of ice in a punch bowl. Top with ginger ale and stir. Garnish individual servings with a lemon wedge or twist and a mint sprig. See pages 300 to 303 for tips on preparing, chilling, and serving your punch.

YULETIDAL WAVE

Bringing a little tiki to your next holiday party.

ORIGIN *Created by Martin Cate*
GLASSWARE *Punch glassware (see page 303 for ideas)*

- 2 ounces pineapple juice
- 1 ounce fresh lemon juice
- ½ ounce natural pear liqueur (such as Mathilde Poire)
- ½ ounce Licor 43
- ¼ ounce St. Elizabeth Allspice Dram
- ½ ounce brandy
- 1 ounce bourbon
- 1 ounce column still aged rum ❹

GARNISH *None*

Multiply the ingredient quantities by the number of guests. Combine all the ingredients except the ice in a beverage dispenser or other sealable container and whisk together. Chill for 1 to 2 hours prior to serving. Add large blocks of ice to the dispenser or serve over a large block or smaller blocks of ice in a punch bowl. See pages 300 to 303 for tips on preparing, chilling, and serving your punch.

RUMBUSTION PUNCH

Named in honor of our rum club, we often serve this at our quarterly Convocations and other Rumbustion Society events.

ORIGIN *Created by Martin Cate*
GLASSWARE *Punch glassware (see page 303 for ideas)*

- 1 ounce fresh lime juice
- ½ ounce SC Demerara Syrup (page 324)
- ¼ ounce SC Cinnamon Syrup (page 327)
- 1 ounce blended aged rum ❸
- 1 ounce blended lightly aged rum ❷
- 2 dashes Herbstura (page 228)

GARNISH *None*

Multiply the ingredient quantities by the number of guests. Combine all the ingredient except the ice in a beverage dispenser or other sealable container and whisk together. Chill for 1 to 2 hours prior to serving. Add large blocks of ice to dispenser or serve over a large block or smaller blocks of ice in a punch bowl. See pages 300 to 303 for tips on preparing, chilling, and serving your punch.

EPILOGUE: THE HERITAGE OF TIKI

With each passing day, the lure of the tiki grows stronger. Every year more people erect temples of leisure in cities across the United States, both commercial and private. Whether it's a new bar in a "tiki-underserved" community, or your own vision of a backyard paradise, the very best draw upon the iconography and imagery of those that have come before, and add their own unique touches. We study the pictures, talk to the artists, mixologists, and musicians, and blend their work in concert to create a complete experience. Oftentimes, our inspirations come from the dusty ephemera of lost sanctuaries that delight us with their stunningly realized spaces and make us yearn for a world when they were a common sight. But sometimes—we get lucky, and discover that a handful of gems from the golden age do survive, and continue to stir our passions. Smuggler's Cove is guided by a compass rose that points west to east across the United States toward the two brightest beacons of historic tiki: the Tiki-Ti and the Mai Kai. These essential living pieces of tiki history provide an unbroken link to the past that helps us to understand how these places operated, thrived, and survived through the glorious ups and perilous downs of the tiki era.

TIKI-TI—THE LEGACY

Ray Buhen spent twenty-six years in the trenches of tropical drink warfare, most notably as one of the early bartenders of Don the Beachcomber from 1933 to 1937. He would go on to ply his trade at many of Southern California's most famous exotic watering holes: The Luau, China Trader, and the Seven Seas. By the time he purchased his father-in-law's violin shop on Sunset Boulevard in Los Angeles in 1961, he arrived armed with an arsenal of exotic cocktail recipes, trade secrets, and rum blends that few understood. And he put them all to work in the way he knew best: an array of unmarked bottles holding mysterious syrups, spices, and juices that remain closely guarded secrets to this day.

The first to be privy to the drinks was his own son, Mike, followed by Mike's own sons, Mike Jr. and Mark. And it would stay that way for more than half a century. In fact, the first actual nonfamily employee of the Tiki-Ti would not be hired until their fifty-fourth year of business. The recipes evolved with time as the neighborhood did, adding tequila to drinks, for example, to please a changing clientele. But while the Tiki-Ti may have bent somewhat, it did more to change the drinking habits of its clientele than the reverse. The menu today consists of over eighty exotic cocktails—period. Nary a drop of beer or wine is to be found, nor any other classic cocktails. The premium rums on the back bar number about four. For fifty-five years, the Tiki-Ti has remained singular in its focus to serve you exotic cocktails the way Ray Buhen imagined.

Ray's original vision for the Tiki-Ti lives on today. The bamboo and tapa that he hung himself is still there, preserved in amber by decades of smoke; the shelves and walls burst with years of collected tiki ephemera. But there's another kind of tiki ephemera that collects there as well, and you'll find them on the barstools. The Tiki-Ti is home to a remarkable community of passionate regulars who belly up to the bar, usually a few times a week. And where in many bars you might find this crowd ordering a beer and a shot, you'll see them all happily asking for a Sumatra Kula, Shark's Tooth, or Puka Puka. This isn't a bar to visit only for special occasions; this is a proper neighborhood bar, albeit one where the chosen tipple is likely to be served in a giant goblet with thirteen ingredients. This is a place where organic traditions like the passionate chant of "Toro! Toro!" rise with each order of a Blood and Sand, and where each Wednesday, those assembled turn to face the portrait of the late Ray Buhen, raise their glasses, and offer a toast to Ray, the Master Ninja.

From left: Mark Buhen, Mike Buhen, and Mike Buhen Jr.

PUKA PUNCH

ORIGIN *Tiki-Ti, 1961*

SOURCE Beachbum Berry Remixed, *adapted by Smuggler's Cove*

GLASSWARE *Large (22-ounce) brandy snifter*

- 1 ounce fresh lime juice
- ¾ ounce fresh orange juice
- ¾ ounce pineapple juice
- 1 ounce SC Honey Syrup (page 325)
- ¾ ounce SC Passion Fruit Syrup (page 325)
- ½ ounce John D. Taylor's Velvet Falernum
- 1 ounce blended aged rum ❸
- 1 ounce blended lightly aged rum ❷
- ¾ ounce black blended rum ❺
- 1 dash Angostura bitters
- ¾ ounce black blended overproof rum ❻

GARNISH *Mint sprig*

Add all the ingredients except the black blended overproof rum to a drink mixer tin. Fill with 18 ounces of crushed ice and 4 to 6 small "agitator" cubes. Flash blend and open pour into a large brandy snifter and add crushed ice if needed to fill. Float the overproof rum by gently pouring on the surface of the drink, then add garnish.

MAI KAI—THE MOTHERSHIP

The Mai Kai opened in 1956 on a then-dusty stretch of Fort Lauderdale's North Federal Highway. Built directly upon the shifting sands of sunny South Florida, it was one of the largest tiki palaces of the era, and fortunately for all of us, it remains steadfastly in place—a beautifully preserved time capsule of the absolute pinnacle of High Tiki design. Founded by two brothers from Chicago, Bob and Jack Thornton, the Mai Kai was born of their vision to bring some of the grandeur of their hometown's tiki bars to a then largely desolate part of Fort Lauderdale. Anxious to capitalize on the "snowbird" trade, the boys rounded up a then-staggering $300,000 and poached some of the top staff from the Chicago location of Don the Beachcomber. Their vision brought together the best of what the Polynesian Pop restaurant experience had to offer: Donn's famous cocktails and hospitality, the Chinese ovens of Trader Vic's, the intricate and layered décor of The Luau, literal (and proudly advertised) "tons" of authentic Polynesian artifacts, and a nightly floor show that took guests on a tour of the islands. The Thorntons didn't just dream big, they dreamed in Cinerama. Eight dining rooms, each one large enough to swallow the Tiki-Ti whole, can seat nearly five hundred people, with room for another hundred fifty in the adjacent Molokai Bar. A lush tropical garden connects hidden outdoor seating areas via a waterfall-strewn meandering path.

As you approach along the busy thoroughfare of today's North Federal Highway, past miles of nameless big box retailers before arriving at the anomaly of the Mai Kai, it initially hides many of its treasures from view. What you do see is a wonderland of waterfalls, rock, bridges, and lush tropical vegetation, beckoning you inside. But even with the teaser outside, you will be unprepared for the delights that lie within. As you turn off the street and drive over a series of wooden slats, they rumble under your wheel like a rickety bridge, immediately signaling that you're about to be transported. Entering the front doors, you turn left into the Molokai Bar, a beautifully appointed dark and woody space with miles of ships rigging, simulated rainstorms against the windows, and nautical décor that begins to reveal itself as your eyes adjust. The stunning long wooden bar is inviting, but you may soon notice a few unusual features: namely, the lack of bottles or bartenders. Like the great tiki bars of old, the Mai Kai still produces its secret elixirs out of sight of the guest, with only a small hatch occasionally revealing a mysterious arm pushing a drink through the opening. The Thorntons lured bar manager Mariano Licudine out of the cold of Chicago's Don the Beachcomber with the promise of his own program and bar setup. He was, in the words of Jeff Berry, a "human Rosetta

Molokai Bar (above) and the Gardens at Mai Kai (right)

Stone—a living key to the tropical kingdom." Armed with Donn's secret recipes, the Mai Kai's drinks became justifiably famous.

While you're likely to fall into a pleasant trance while relaxing in the Molokai, soon your dinner reservation will draw you toward the main dining room and the towering A-frame ceiling will reveal itself. Disappearing almost completely into darkness with only a few points of dim light from gnarled tropical lamps above, the space is dramatic but warm. And as dinner is served, the stage explodes into the Polynesian Dance Revue, a fury of color and motion and the longest-running show of its kind in the continental United States begins. The show is still choreographed by Mireille Thornton, a dancer from Tahiti who started performing at the Mai Kai in 1961, married Bob Thornton in 1971, and is one of the partners today. Her efforts, along with the many dancers who have performed at the Mai Kai for more than half a century, provide the guest with a glimpse into the authentic performing arts of many South Pacific cultures, and adds a rich layer to the experience. As an operator, to see the Mai Kai running at full throttle on a Saturday night, with multiple dinner seatings, three exhausting performances of the revue, hundreds of diners, and food and exotic cocktails firing at breakneck speed is to witness amazing restaurant logistics in action. But as a guest, you're not likely to ever know the controlled chaos in back, because just as Steve Crane would have wanted it, your experience will always be one of enjoyment and relaxation.

You may choose to take your nightcap with a pleasant stroll through the gardens before returning to the valet stand. And you will drive off knowing that you have been part of an experience that has delighted people from South Florida and indeed the whole world for sixty years. The Mai Kai remains a beacon for celebrating life's milestones; people will fondly recall birthdays, weddings, reunions, and more where memories are highlighted by the exotic cocktails and soft lighting. You may also drive off and reflect that experiences like the Mai Kai once dotted the American landscape, because we needed to get out of the world, even if only for a few hours. And we still do today.

The Mai Kai will take you back to dining as event, experience, and escape. Today, you can still stand at the entrance, or during the show, and look at the faces of first-time visitors as their eyes widen, mouths agape at the spectacle. I see the same sense of surprise and wonder on the faces of first-time guests at Smuggler's Cove. It could be the drama of the Cove's interior, the surprising contrast with our plain exterior, or the simple truth that people just aren't accustomed anymore to visiting a space that takes you away. It will come as no surprise that the Mai Kai's Molokai Bar, with its heavy emphasis on the

Molokai Bar

nautical while remaining true to tiki tradition was an inspiration cornerstone
for me.

So I ask each of you to look for that sense of wonder again. It's unquestionably hard to remove the layers of cynicism, irony, and detachment that build
like a protective shell over modern people. Constant exposure to information
and technology almost from birth has produced a generation that has never
known a life without the world's knowledge at its fingertips. So how do we
find charm in a charmless world? I won't pretend to know how, but I certainly
suggest we try. We have long since left Eden, and can no longer claim igno-
rance of the world beyond our borders. But the urge to escape is inside all of us,
and does not diminish as the planet grows ever smaller and more connected.
In fact, the urge may be more powerful than ever. In the words of the Kon-Tiki
Ports menu, "The simple life does have its excitements." And they remind us
why we fell in love with tiki bars in the first place: To gaze into the dimly lit
ephemera-strewn crevices. To listen to the sound of the running water and
soft music. To sip a potent rum-laced libation under the protective stare of an
imagined idol. And to remain *captivated*.

HOUSE-MADE INGREDIENTS

2:1 SIMPLE SYRUP

MAKES *4 cups (32 ounces)*

- **2 cups water**
- **4 cups granulated sugar**

Bring the water to a boil in a saucepan over high heat. Add the sugar and stir with a whisk until the sugar is dissolved, about 1 minute (the water should become clear such that you can see the bottom of the pot). Immediately remove from the heat. Store in a lidded bottle or other sealed container in the refrigerator. The syrup will keep, if refrigerated, for several weeks.

NOTE This recipe easily scales up to make more. One helpful tip: when you're making a 2:1 simple syrup, the liquid yield is equivalent to the amount of sugar. So, to create 40 ounces of simple syrup you would use 40 ounces (5 cups) of sugar to 20 ounces of water.

SC DEMERARA SYRUP

MAKES *4 cups (32 ounces)*

- **2 cups water**
- **1 cup demerara sugar**
- **3 cups granulated sugar**

Bring the water to a boil in a saucepan over high heat. Add the demerara sugar and stir vigorously with a whisk (or use an immersion blender) until the sugar is dissolved, about 1 minute (the water should become clear such that you can see the bottom of the pot). Add the granulated sugar and stir vigorously until dissolved, about 1 minute. Immediately remove from the heat and let cool. Store in a lidded bottle or other sealed container in the refrigerator. The syrup will keep, refrigerated, for several weeks.

NOTE The recipe easily scales up to make more. One helpful tip: when you're making this syrup, the liquid yield is equivalent to the amount of total sugar used. So, to create 8 cups (64 ounces) of syrup you would use 8 cups (64 ounces) of sugar (6 cups white sugar, 2 cups demerara) to 4 cups (32 ounces) of water.

SC HONEY SYRUP

MAKES *3 cups (24 ounces)*

- 1½ cups honey
- 1½ cups water

Heat the honey in a saucepan over medium heat until runny and not viscous—nearly to a boil but not quite. Add the water to the hot honey and whisk together. Immediately remove from the heat. Let cool. Store in a lidded bottle or other sealable container in the refrigerator. The syrup will keep, refrigerated, for several weeks.

NOTE 1 This is an equal parts honey-to-water recipe. One handy tip: After you pour the honey from its container into the saucepan and start to heat it, add water to the empty honey container until one-quarter full. Seal the container and shake vigorously to remove all of the honey clinging to the sides of the container. Then fill the rest of the container with water, and add the liquid to the saucepan when the honey is ready.

NOTE 2 For a richer honey flavor in your cocktails, you may wish to try 2 parts honey to 1 part water (3 cups of honey to 1½ cups of water) and experiment with different varieties of honey to find your favorite.

SC PASSION FRUIT SYRUP

MAKES *3 cups (24 ounces)*

- 1½ cups Funkin passion fruit puree (see Resources, page 335)
- 1½ cups 2:1 Simple Syrup, cooled (see page 324)

In a bowl, whisk together the fruit puree and the syrup. Pour into a lidded bottle or other sealable container and store in the refrigerator. The syrup will keep, refrigerated, for up to 10 days.

NOTE Increase the amount of puree for a tarter syrup.

SC PASSION FRUIT HONEY

MAKES *3 cups (24 ounces)*

- 1½ cups honey
- 1½ cups Funkin passion fruit puree

Heat the honey in a saucepan over medium heat until runny and not viscous—nearly to a boil but not quite. Remove from the heat and whisk in the passion fruit puree. Let cool. Pour into a lidded bottle or other sealable container and store in the refrigerator. The syrup will keep, refrigerated, for up to 10 days.

SC MAI TAI RICH SIMPLE SYRUP

MAKES *4 cups (32 ounces)*

- 2 cups water
- 4 cups demerara sugar
- ½ teaspoon vanilla extract
- ¼ teaspoon salt

Bring the water to a boil in a saucepan over high heat. Add the demerara sugar and stir vigorously with a whisk (or use an immersion blender) until the sugar is dissolved, about 1 minute (the water should become clear such that you can see the bottom of the pot). Immediately remove from heat and let cool. Add the vanilla extract and salt and stir to combine. Pour into a lidded bottle or other sealable container and store in the refrigerator. The syrup will keep, refrigerated, for several weeks.

SC VANILLA SYRUP

MAKES *4 cups (32 ounces)*

- 2 cups water
- 4 cups granulated sugar
- 2 (8-inch) vanilla beans

Bring the water to a boil in a saucepan over high heat. Add the sugar and stir with a whisk until dissolved, about 1 minute (the water should become clear such that you can see the bottom of the pot). Immediately remove from the heat. Halve the vanilla bean pods lengthwise and scrape the seeds into the syrup. Cut the scraped pods into thirds and add to the syrup. Stir well. Cover and let sit at room temperature for 12 hours. Strain through cheesecloth into a bowl and then pour through a funnel into a lidded bottle or other sealable container. The syrup will keep, refrigerated, for several weeks.

SC CINNAMON SYRUP

MAKES *4 cups (32 ounces)*

   2 cups water

   3 (6-inch) cinnamon sticks, halved

   4 cups granulated sugar

Put the water in a saucepan. Add the pieces of cin-namon stick to the water and bring to a boil over high heat. Add the sugar and stir with a whisk (or an immersion blender) until dissolved, about 1 minute (the liquid should become clear such that you can see the bottom of the pot). Immediately remove from the heat. Cover and let sit at room temperature for 12 hours. Strain through cheesecloth into a bowl and then use a funnel to pour into a lidded bottle or other sealable container. The syrup will keep, refrigerated, for several weeks.

NOTE We use cassia in our cinnamon syrup, but you can try the milder, sweeter ceylon cinnamon to add a different note.

SC MOLASSES SYRUP

MAKES *4½ cups (36 ounces)*

   2 cups water

   4 cups granulated sugar

   4 ounces Brer Rabbit Mild molasses

Bring the water to a boil in a large saucepan. Add the sugar and stir with a whisk (or use an immersion blender) until dissolved, about 1 minute (the water should become clear such that you can see the bottom of the pot). Stir in the molasses. Immediately remove from heat and let cool. Pour into a lidded bottle or other sealable container and store in the refrigerator. The syrup will keep, refrigerated, for several weeks.

NOTE For a richer molasses flavor, increase the molasses-to-sugar ratio.

SC GRENADINE

MAKES *3 cups (24 ounces)*

2 cups POM Wonderful
100 Percent Pomegranate juice

2 cups granulated sugar

Add the pomegranate juice to a nonreactive saucepan. Bring the juice to a boil over high heat. Add the sugar and stir with a wooden spoon (or use an immersion blender) until dissolved, about 1 minute. Remove from heat and let cool. Pour into a lidded bottle or other sealable container and store in the refrigerator. The syrup will keep, refrigerated, for several weeks.

SC COCONUT CREAM

MAKES *about 3½ cups (27 ounces)*

1 (13½-ounce) can Thai Kitchen
or other unsweetened coconut milk

¼ teaspoon salt

13½ ounces 2:1 Simple Syrup (page 324)

In the can, the coconut milk will be partly solidified, with some liquid at the bottom. Use a spatula to gently scrape the contents of the can into a mixing bowl. Add the salt. Use an immersion blender or an electric hand mixer to combine the solids and liquid. Add the simple syrup to the mixing bowl (equal parts—use the empty coconut milk can to measure the simple syrup). Blend the ingredients with an immersion blender or electric hand mixer until well combined. Pour into a lidded bottle or other sealable container and store in the refrigerator. The coconut cream will keep, refrigerated, for 2 weeks.

SC JERK SYRUP

MAKES *2 cups (16 ounces)*

1 cup water

2 cups granulated sugar

2 teaspoons SC Jerk Seasoning (recipe follows)

Bring the water to a boil in a saucepan over high heat. Add the sugar and seasoning and stir with a wooden spoon (or immersion blender) until dissolved, about 1 minute (the water should become clear such that you can see the bottom of the pot). Immediately remove from the heat. Let cool. Strain through cheesecloth into a bowl. Use a funnel to pour into a lidded bottle or other sealable container and store in the refrigerator. The syrup will keep, refrigerated, for several weeks.

SC JERK SEASONING

MAKES *about 2 tablespoons*

1¾ teaspoons ground dried thyme

1 teaspoon freshly ground allspice berries

1 teaspoon freshly ground black pepper

½ teaspoon freshly ground cinnamon

¼ teaspoon freshly ground nutmeg

1 teaspoon cayenne pepper

¼ teaspoon salt

Add all the ingredients to a bowl, and mix together until well combined. Store any extra in a ziplock bag or other sealable container for future use.

SC ORGEAT

MAKES *5 to 6 cups (40 to 48 ounces)*

- 1 pound blanched almonds (3½ to 4 cups)
- 4 cups water
- 5 cups white granulated sugar (depends on yield of almonds; see method)
- ¼ teaspoon rose water
- ¼ teaspoon orange flower water
- 2 teaspoons column still lightly aged rum (adds shelf life)

Add the almonds and water to a large pot and bring to a boil over high heat. Strain almonds and set aside in a large bowl, while also reserving the remaining "almond water" in a separate bowl.

In a food processor fitted with the steel blade, grind 2 cups of the boiled almonds into small, rice-size pieces, about 10 seconds. Slowly add about 11 ounces of the "almond water" to the food processor and blend until the water and almonds combine to an "almond paste," about 10 seconds. This "paste" will be the consistency of Cream of Wheat or watery oatmeal. Pour contents into a gallon pitcher. Repeat with the remaining almonds and "almond water," and add this second batch of "almond paste" to the first batch.

Let the almond paste cool for about 1 hour. Set a fine-mesh wire strainer lined with cheesecloth over a 4-quart pot. In batches, ladle some of the "almond paste" into a square of cheesecloth in your hand and

squeeze out the liquid ("almond milk") from the paste over the cheesecloth-lined strainer and into the pot. Discard the dry almond remains. Repeat until all paste has been strained. At the end, you may want to also squeeze the cheesecloth that lined the strainer to get the last of any remaining liquid.

Then set the fine-mesh wire strainer lined with new cheesecloth over a 4-cup glass measuring cup. Pour the almond milk through the cheesecloth-lined strainer into the measuring cup and make note of the yield (you should have about 2½ cups of almond milk). Set a fine-mesh strainer lined with cheesecloth over a clean 4-quart pot and pour the almond milk through the cheesecloth-lined strainer into the pot.

Measure twice as much sugar as the almond milk yield (about 5 cups) and add to the pot of almond milk. Stir with a whisk over low heat until the sugar is fully incorporated into the milk, creating a thick syrup, about 15 minutes. Taste it—it is ready when there is no grittiness. Remove the pot from the heat. When the syrup begins to cool add the rose and orange flower waters and the rum. Stir periodically as it cools. It may separate so a thick skin forms on the surface. Stir vigorously to reincorporate the skin as best as possible into the rest of syrup. Once completely cool, stir vigorously and then strain through a metal-screened or cheesecloth-lined funnel (to remove any residual undissolved matter) into a sealable storage container. The orgeat will keep, refrigerated, for several weeks.

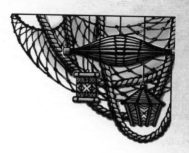

SC HIBISCUS LIQUEUR

MAKES *4 cups (32 ounces)*

½ cup honey

2½ cups SC Spiced Hibiscus Infusion (recipe follows)

1 cup 2:1 Simple Syrup (page 324)

In a microwave, heat the honey in a microwave-safe bowl until runny, about 40 seconds (or, heat in a saucepan on the stovetop for approximately 3 minutes over medium heat). Add the infusion and syrup and stir to thoroughly blend. Transfer to bottles and seal well. The liqueur will keep refrigerated for several weeks.

SC SPICED HIBISCUS INFUSION

MAKES *about 4 cups (32 ounces)*

3 quarter-size discs of unpeeled fresh ginger

10 whole cloves

1 liter blended lightly aged rum ❷

¾ cup dried hibiscus flowers (see Resources, page 335)

In a large glass jar with a lid, combine the ginger, cloves, and rum and let sit, covered at room temperature, for 24 hours. Strain out the cloves and ginger from the rum and discard. Add the dried hibiscus flowers to the rum. Let sit, covered at room temperature, for 48 hours. Strain the dried flowers from the rum and discard. Transfer the infused rum to glass bottles and seal well. The infusion will keep at room temperature on your shelf for at least 6 months.

SC HELLFIRE TINCTURE

MAKES *about 2 cups (16 ounces)*

   4 cups mixed fresh hot chiles (such as
   habanero, Fresno, red jalapeño, and so on),
   coarsely chopped, stems and seeds included

   1 cup dry white wine

   2 cups brandy

In a large saucepan over medium heat, cook the
chopped peppers with the wine until the peppers are
soft and the wine has been absorbed or evaporated.
Remove from the heat. Let the peppers cool. Put
them in a sealable glass jar with the brandy, seal well,
and let sit at room temperature for two weeks. Strain
through cheesecloth into a large container, then
transfer to sealable bottles. The tincture will keep at
room temperature for at least a year.

NOTE WARNING! When you are making this, you
are essentially creating pepper spray in the air. Wear
a dust mask and open the windows to your kitchen.

LI HING MUI SYRUP

MAKES *about 2 cups (16 ounces)*

   2 teaspoons li hing mui powder
   (see Resources, page 335)

   2 cups granulated sugar

   1 cup water

Stir the li hing mui powder into the sugar in a bowl.
Bring the water to a boil in a saucepan over high
heat. Add the li hing mui–sugar mixture and stir until
dissolved, about 1 minute (the liquid should become
clear such that you can see the bottom of the pot).
Remove from the heat and let cool. Store in a lidded
bottle or sealable container in the refrigerator for
several weeks.

CROUTONS FOR FLAMING BOWLS

MAKES *about 150 (¾-inch-square) croutons*

1 loaf thin-crusted white bread, crusts trimmed and bread cut into ¾-inch cubes

Preheat the oven to 200°F. Put the cubes in a single layer on a baking sheet. Heat until they are dry and crisp, 45 minutes to 1 hour. Let cool completely on the baking sheet, then store in an airtight plastic container. They will keep for several weeks.

RESOURCES

Here are a few suppliers for ingredients, décor, artifacts, and information for the enthusiast to get started on tiki. This is only the beginning! Once you are hooked, you will find much more! A great way to dive into the deep end is to attend one of the big annual tiki events where there are vendors, music, and more.

ANNUAL UNITED STATES TIKI GATHERINGS

Chicago Area Tiki Tour (Chicago, Illinois)
fraternalorderofmoai.org/events/catt

Mojave Oasis (Mojave Desert, California)
mojaveoasis.com

Ohana: Luau at the Lake (Lake George, New York),
an event thrown by a cult within a cult, the Fraternal Order of Moai.
fraternalorderofmoai.org/ohana

The Hukilau (Fort Lauderdale, Florida)
thehukilau.com

Tiki Caliente (Palm Springs, California)
tiki-caliente.com

Tiki Kon (Portland, Oregon)
tikikon.com

Tiki Oasis (San Diego, CA)
tikioasis.com

CLOTHING, FABRIC, JEWELRY, SHOES, AND ACCESSORIES

Black Pearl Designs
blackpearldesigns.com

De Tiki
facebook.com/DeTikiCustomCarvings

Eric October
spoonflower.com/profiles/
eric_october

Mahalo Tiki
mahalotiki.com

Michael Uhlenkott Design
spoonflower.com/profiles/muhlenkott

Tiki King
tikiking.com

Tiki Val's Closet
tikivalscloset.com

Viva Dulce Marina
vivadulcemarina.com

VINTAGE

Dave Wolfe/Wolfe Den Vintage
facebook.com/Wolfe-
Den-Vintage-160402520682580

Laurel Canyon 1969
etsy.com/shop/laurelcanyon1969

Trader Trixie
etsy.com/shop/tradertrixie

COCKTAIL INGREDIENTS

BITTERS

Bittermens
bittermens.com

EDIBLE HIBISCUS FLOWERS

Wild Hibiscus
wildhibiscus.com

LI HING MUI POWDER

Widely used in Hawaii, li hing mui powder is made from dried Chinese plum, and tastes sweet, sour, and salty all at the same time. When buying li hing mui powder, look for the rare brands that do not contain the artificial sweetener aspartame. We can only recommend Grandpa Mui's All Natural Li Hing Mui Powder. It is available online in white or colored with carmine—a natural red dye that is made from crushed beetles (not vegetarian).

OnoPops
onopops.com/shop_li_hing_mui.php

MARTINIQUE SUGARCANE SYRUP

Kegworks
kegworks.com/bar-tools

ORGEAT AND OTHER SYRUPS

BG Reynolds Syrups
bgreynolds.com

Orgeat Works
Latitude 29 Formula Orgeat
orgeatworks.com

Small Hand Foods
smallhandfoods.com

PASSION FRUIT CONCENTRATE (FROZEN)

Perfect Puree
perfectpuree.com

PASSION FRUIT PUREE

Funkin
funkinusa.com

PASSION FRUIT SYRUP

Aunty Lilikoi
auntylilikoi.com

SPICES AND DRIED HIBISCUS FLOWERS

San Francisco Herb Company
sfherb.com

SPRUCE BEER SODA EXTRACT

The Cellar Homebrew
cellar-homebrew.com

COCKTAIL EQUIPMENT AND OTHER SUPPLIES

20-INCH GIANT LUAU STRAWS

Restockit
restockit.com

BAMBOO KNOT COCKTAIL PICKS, COCKTAIL UMBRELLAS

Amazon
amazon.com

CENTRIFUGAL JUICER FOR PINEAPPLE

Breville
breville.com

COCO JACK (FOR OPENING YOUNG COCONUTS)

coco-jack.com

COCKTAIL EQUIPMENT (INCLUDING MARTINIQUE SWIZZLE STICK, AKA BOIS LÉLÉ)

Kegworks
kegworks.com/bar-tools

COCKTAIL EQUIPMENT (INCLUDING DASHER BOTTLES, ICE CONE MAKER, PEARL DIVER GLASS, SWIZZLE CUP, AND BLUE BLAZER MUGS)

Cocktail Kingdom
cocktailkingdom.com

DRINK MIXERS

Light Duty: Hamilton Beach 760C Classic DrinkMaster Drink Mixer

Medium Duty: Waring PDM series Drink Mixer

Weapons Grade: Hamilton Beach Single-Spindle Drink Mixer HMD200 Series

Amazon
amazon.com

ICE CRUSHER

Waring Pro IC70 Professional Stainless Steel Large-Capacity Ice Crusher
Amazon
amazon.com

MUDDLERS

Mister Mojito
mistermojito.com

PARTY SUPPLIES

ARTIFICIAL LEIS AND LANTERNS

Oriental Trading Company
orientaltrading.com

CUSTOM GLASSWARE

South Pacific Promotions
southpacificpromotions.com

FLOWERS FOR DRINK GARNISH, DÉCOR, AND LEIS

Wholesale Tropical Flowers
wholesale-tropical-flowers.com

MUSIC (EXOTICA, TRADITIONAL HAWAIIAN, AND HAPA HAOLE)

APE
tikimania.com/docs/ APE_simians.html

Clouseaux
clouseaux.com

Digital Podcast
digitiki.com/radio/index.html

Ding Dong Devils
facebook.com/dingdongdevils

Dionysus Records
dionysusrecords.com/home

Don Tiki
dontiki.com

Ìxtahuele
Ixtahuele.com

Kitty Chow and Fisherman Trio
exotikshow.wordpress.com

Mele.com Online Retailer
mele.com

Mr. Ho's Orchestrotica
orchestrotica.com

Sven A. Kirsten Presents the Sound of Tiki
A curated exotica compilation.
amazon.com

The Crazed Mugs
crazedmugs.com

The Waitiki 7
facebook.com/TheWAITIKI7

Tiki Joe's Ocean
tikijoesocean.com

Tikiyaki Orchestra
tikiyakiorchestra.com

**FOOD AND DRINK RECIPES
(ALSO SEE BIBLIOGRAPHY)**

Mid-Century Menu
www.midcenturymenu.com

Total Tiki App
beachbumberry.com/
publication-total-tiki.html

TIKI MUGS

**LARGE-SCALE MUGS
FOR COMMERCIAL USE**

Munktiki
munktiki.com

Tiki Farm
tikifarm.com

SMALL-SCALE RUNS AND COLLECTABLE MUGS

Crazy Al
tikimania.com

Eekum Bookum
etsy.com/shop/EekumBookum

Gecko
southseaarts.com

Johnny Velour
johnnievelour.com

Munktiki
munktiki.com

Squid
squidart.com

Tiki Kaimuki
tikikaimuki.com

Tiki Objects by Bosko
tikibosko.com

Tiki Tony
tikitony.com

ONLINE TIKI MUG GUIDE

Ooga Mooga
ooga-mooga.com

TIKI BAR BUILD-OUT AND DESIGN

Bamboo Ben
facebook.com/
BambooBenCustomTropicalDecor

Bosko
tikibosko.com

Notch
facebook.com/TopNotchKustoms

Tiki Diablo
tikidiablo.com

TIKI CARVINGS AND OTHER DÉCOR

Bosko
tikibosko.com

Brad Parker
tikishark.com

Crazy Al
tikimania.com

Dave Hansen/Lake Tiki
facebook.com/laketikiwoodcrafts

Doug Horne
etsy.com/shop/DougHorneArt

Lamps by Kahaka
flickr.com/photos/rocknrollwoody/
albums/72157600546621178

Oceanic Arts
oceanicarts.net

Shag
shagstore.bigcartel.com/products

Smokin Tikis
smokin-tikis.myshopify.com

Sophista-tiki
etsy.com/shop/sophistatiki

Taboo Island
tabooisland.com

TIKI COMMUNITY AND REVIVAL

Critiki News
news.critiki.com

Tiki Central
tikiroom.com

Tiki Magazine
tikimagazine.com

Clockwise, from top left: artists and designers Tiki Diablo, Bamboo Ben, Bosko, and Crazy Al

BIBLIOGRAPHY AND ADDITIONAL READING

RUM AND RUM HISTORY

Barty-King, Hugh, and Anton Massel. *Rum: Yesterday and Today*. London: Heinemann, 1983.

Broom, Dave. *Rum*. South San Francisco: The Wine Appreciation Guild, 2003.

Coulumbe, Charles A. *Rum: The Epic Story of the Drink that Conquered the World*. New York: Citadel Press Books, 2004.

Curtis, Wayne. *And a Bottle of Rum: A History of the New World in Ten Cocktails*. New York: Crown Publishers, 2006.

Foss, Richard. *Rum: A Global History*. London: Reaktion Books Limited, 2012.

Gjelten, Tom. *Bacardi and the Long Fight for Cuba*. New York: Penguin, 2008.

Ministry of Rum: www.ministryofrum.com

Pack, A. J. *Nelson's Blood: The Story of Naval Rum*. Emsworth: Kenneth Mason, 1982.

Smiley, Ian, Eric Watson, and Michael Delevante. *The Distiller's Guide to Rum*. Hayward: White Mule Press, 2013.

Smith, Frederick. *Caribbean Rum: A Social and Economic History*. Gainesville, FL: University Press of Florida, 2005.

Williams, Ian. *Rum: A Social and Sociable History*. New York: Nation Books, 2005.

COCKTAIL TECHNIQUE

Abou-Ganim, Tony, with Mary Elizabeth Faulkner. *The Modern Mixologist: Contemporary Classic Cocktails*. Chicago: Surrey Books, 2010.

Hamilton, Edward. *The Complete Guide to Rum: An Authoritative Guide to Rums of the World*. Chicago: Triumph Books, 1997.

Hollinger, Jeff, and Rob Schwartz. *The Art of the Bar: Cocktails Inspired by the Classics*. San Francisco: Chronicle Books, 2006.

Kaplan, David, Nick Fauchald, and Alex Day. *Death & Company: Modern Classic Cocktails*. Berkeley, CA: Ten Speed Press, 2014.

Morganthaller, Jeffrey, and Martha Holmberg. *The Bar Book: Elements of Cocktail Technique*. San Francisco: Chronicle Books, 2014.

Verhoog, Jeroen. *Walking on Gold. The History of Trading Company E&A Scheer: A Journey Through Four Centuries*. Noordwijkerhout: Druno & Dekker.

COCKTAIL HISTORY AND HISTORIC RECIPES (NON-TIKI)

Baker, Charles H. *The Gentleman's Companion*. New York: Crown Publishers, 1946 (first published in 1939).

Bolton, Ross. *Bar La Florida Cocktails 1935 Reprint*. Createspace, 2008.

Craddock, Harry. *The Savoy Cocktail Book*. London: Pavillion Books, 2007 (first published in 1930).

Diffords Guide: www.diffordsguide.com

Haigh, Ted. *Vintage Spirits and Forgotten Cocktails*, Deluxe Edition. Beverly: Quarry Books, 2009.

McDonnell, Duggan. *Drinking the Devil's Acre: A Love Letter from San Francisco and Her Cocktails*. San Francisco: Chronicle Books, 2015.

Thomas, Jerry. *The Bartenders Guide: How to Mix Drinks, or the Bon-Vivant's Companion.* New York: Mud Puddle Books, 2008 (first published in 1862).

Wondrich, David. *Imbibe!* Updated and Revised Edition. New York: The Penguin Group, 2015.

Wondrich, David. *Punch: The Delights (and Dangers) of the Flowing Bowl.* New York: The Penguin Group, 2010.

SCIENCE OF COCKTAILS

Arnold, David. *Liquid Intelligence: The Art and Science of the Perfect Cocktail.* New York: W. W. Norton & Company, 2014.

TIKI HISTORY AND EXOTIC COCKTAIL RECIPES

Beachbum Berry's Total Tiki App: www.beachbumberry.com/publication-total-tiki.html

Bergeron, Vic. *Frankly Speaking: Trader Vic's Own Story.* Garden City: Doubleday & Company, 1973.

Bergeron, Vic. *Trader Vic's Bartender's Guide.* Garden City, NY: Doubleday & Company, 1947.

Bergeron, Vic. *Trader Vic's Bartender's Guide,* Revised. Garden City, NY: Doubleday & Company, 1972.

Bergeron, Vic. *Trader Vic's Book of Food and Drink.* New York: Doubleday & Company, 1946.

Bergeron, Vic. *Trader Vic's Rum Cookery & Drinkery.* Garden City, NY: Doubleday & Company, 1974.

Berry, Jeff. *Beachbum Berry's Intoxica!* San Jose, CA: SLG Publishing, 2002.

Berry, Jeff. *Beachbum Berry's Potions of the Caribbean: 500 Years of Tropical Drinks and the People Behind Them.* New York: Cocktail Kingdom, 2014.

Berry, Jeff. *Beachbum Berry Remixed: A Gallery of Tiki Drinks.* San Jose, CA: SLG Publishing, 2010.

Berry, Jeff. *Beachbum Berry's Sippin' Safari: In Search of the Great 'Lost' Tropical Drink Recipes . . . and the People Behind Them.* San Jose, CA: SLG Publishing, 2007.

Berry, Jeff. *Beachbum Berry's Taboo Table: Tiki Cuisine from Polynesian Restaurants of Yore.* San Jose, CA: SLG Publishing, 2005.

Berry, Jeff, and Annene Kaye. *Beachbum Berry's Grog Log.* San Jose, CA: SLG Publishing, 1998.

Bitner, Arnold. *Scrounging the Islands with the Legendary Don the Beachcomber.* Lincoln: iUniverse, 2007.

Bitner, Arnold, and Phoebe Beach. *Hawaii: Tropical Rum Drinks & Cuisine by Don the Beachcomber.* Honolulu: Mutual Publishing, 2001.

Carter, Duke. *Tiki Quest: Collecting the Exotic Past.* Chicago: Pegboard Press, 2003.

Crane, Cheryl. *Detour: A Hollywood Story.* New York: Avon Books, 1988.

Kirsten, Sven A. *The Book of Tiki.* Cologne, Germany: Taschen, 2000.

Kirsten, Sven A. *Tiki Modern . . . and the Wild World of Witco.* Koln, Germany: Taschen, 2007.

Kirsten, Sven A. *Tiki Pop: America Imagines Its Own Polynesian Paradise.* Koln, Germany: Taschen, 2014.

Siegelman, Steve. *Trader Vic's Tiki Party! Cocktails & Food to Share with Friends.* Berkeley, CA: Ten Speed Press, 2005.

Teitelbaum, James. *Tiki Road Trip: A Guide to Tiki Culture in North America.* Solana Beach, CA: Santa Monica Press, 2007.

Von Stroheim, Otto, and Justin Giarla. *Tiki Art Two: The Second Coming of a New Art God.* San Francisco: 9mm Books and The Shooting Gallery, 2005.

A FEW OF MY FAVORITE TIKI SPOTS

I'm proud and honored today by the loyal regulars who join us at Smuggler's Cove several nights a week to bend elbows, talk rum and tiki, and share a laugh with our staff and old friends. Having been able to take many of them to distilleries around the world has been an incredible reward. Great bars build great communities, no matter what the theme, and I love being around people who love tiki bars. We will likely never see tiki rise to the ubiquitous levels of the golden era, but as more and more tiki temples are erected in America and around the world, it's comforting to know that a vacation in a glass and a welcome smile dressed in an aloha shirt from the next barstool over is an alternative to the ordinary in cities far and wide.

Below are a few bars that I enjoy in the United States that fully embrace the tiki aesthetic in look, or offer a full menu of exotic cocktails, or (ideally) both! There are, no doubt, others I have yet to venture into, and countless wonderful tiki bars around the world, many of which I've had the pleasure to imbibe in. To find additional spots both old and new around the globe, check out the website Critiki (www.critiki.com).

Hale Pele, Portland, Oregon

PART OF THE TIKI REVIVAL

Bamboo Hut
(San Francisco, California)

Beachbum Berry's Latitude 29
(New Orleans, Louisiana)

Clifton's Pacific Seas
(Los Angeles, California)

Don the Beachcomber
(old place rebranded,
Huntington Beach, California)

False Idol
(San Diego, CA)

Forbidden Island
(Alameda, California)

Foundation
(Milwaukee, Wisconsin)

Frankie's Tiki Room
(Las Vegas, Nevada)

Golden Tiki
(Las Vegas, Nevada)

Grass Skirt
(Columbus, Ohio)

Hale Pele
(Portland, Oregon)

Kona Club
(Oakland, California)

Lei Low
(Houston, Texas)

Longitude
(Oakland, California)

Lost Lake
(Chicago, Illinois)

Otto's Shrunken Head
(New York, New York)

Porco Lounge and Tiki Room
(Cleveland, Ohio)

Psycho Suzi's Motor Lodge
(Minneapolis, Minnesota)

Purple Orchid
(El Segundo, California)

Saturn Room
(Tulsa, Oklahoma)

Tacoma Cabana
(Tacoma, Washington)

Three Dots and a Dash
(Chicago, Illinois)

Tiki Iniki
(Princeville, Hawaii)

Tonga Hut
(Palm Springs, California)

Trader Sam's Enchanted Tiki Bar
(Anaheim, California)

Trader Sam's Grog Grotto
(Orlando, Florida)

Trader Vic's
(Portland, Oregon)

UnderTow
(Phoenix, Arizona)

REMAINING FROM THE GOLDEN ERA

Chef Shangri-La
(Chicago, Illinois)

Hala Kahiki
(Chicago, Illinois)

Mai Kai
(Fort Lauderdale, Florida)

Tiki-Ti
(Los Angeles, California)

Tonga Hut
(Hollywood, California)

Tonga Room
(San Francisco, California)

Trader Vic's
(Atlanta, Georgia; Emeryville,
California)

Trad'r Sams
(San Francisco, California)

RUM BARS

In addition to the tiki bars listed previously, many of which carry several sipping rums to enjoy, there are several other rum-focused spots you should know about:

Caña (Los Angeles, California)

Cienfuegos (New York, New York)

Cubaocho (Miami, Florida)

Eva's Caribbean Kitchen
(Laguna Beach, California)

Hobson's Choice
(San Francisco, California)

Kill Devil Club
(Kansas City, Missouri)

La Descarga
(Los Angeles, California)

Rum Bar at the Speakeasy Inn
(Key West, Florida)

Rum Club
(Portland, Oregon)

Rum House
(New York, New York)

Rumba
(Seattle, Washington)

The Rum Line
(Miami Beach, Florida)

ABOUT THE AUTHORS

Martin Cate is a rum and exotic cocktail expert and the owner of Smuggler's Cove in San Francisco. Smuggler's Cove opened in 2009 and has been named one of the World's 50 Best Bars (*Drinks International*, 2011, 2012, 2013, 2014, and 2015), 50 Best Bars on Earth (*The Sunday Times*, London), Top Ten Food and Beverage Concepts of the Last 25 Years (*Cheers Magazine*), 13 Most Influential Bars of the 21st Century (Liquor.com), and America's Best Bars (*Playboy*, 2012 and *Esquire*, 2013).

Martin has been actively involved in the tiki and cocktail community since the late 1990s, and made his passion his profession in 2004 when he started bartending at Trader Vic's San Francisco before opening Forbidden Island in 2006 and Smuggler's Cove in 2009.

A member of the United States Bartenders Guild (USBG), Martin is also a passionate rum collector, and has visited dozens of rum distilleries around the world. He conducts educational seminars and adjudicates rum and cocktail competitions across the United States, Europe, and the Caribbean.

In 2015, along with partners Alex Smith and John Park, Martin opened Whitechapel in San Francisco to bring the same passion for history and craft to the world of gin. He is also the co-owner of Hale Pele in Portland and a partner in Lost Lake in Chicago and False Idol in San Diego.

In 1999, **Rebecca Cate** inadvertently fueled Martin's madness by famously uttering words (which she thought were a joke) about making a spare bedroom a home tiki bar. Since then, however, she too has been swept up in the tiki fantasia, first as an enthusiast, then helping Martin open and run Smuggler's Cove, while juggling a full-time career as a research psychologist "on the side." Rebecca earned her PhD in personality and social psychology from The University of California at Berkeley in 2006, and has spent over a decade leading large-scale studies of behavioral health interventions as well as topics related to retirement and longevity. The opportunity to coauthor this book has allowed what had been just a weekend and vacation escape to turn into a full-time journey.

INDEX

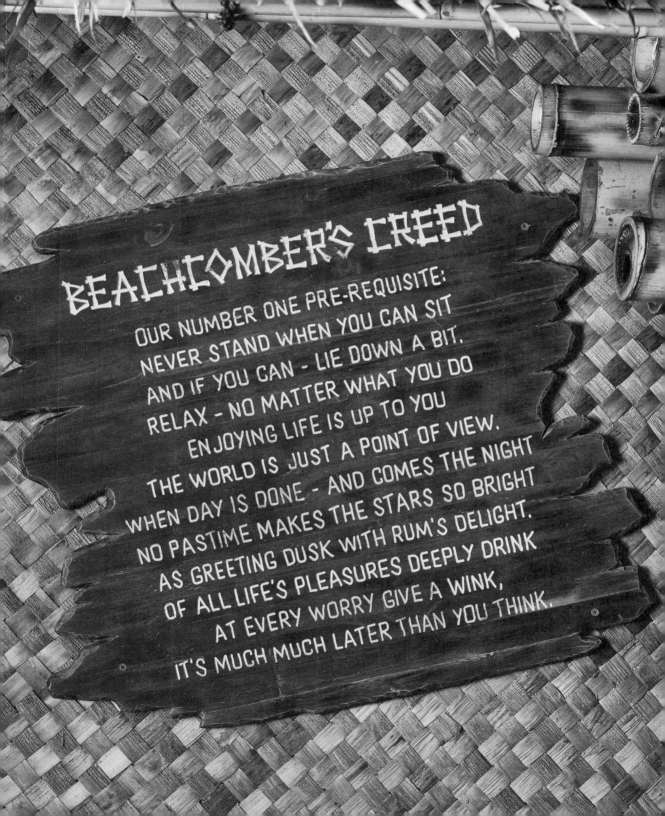